"The worlds of wonder that Nichola: ing memoir include rural Dutch-America, a Kuyperian mind-set, analytical philosophy, humane pedagogy, art understood as craftsmanship, the deep realities (joy and sorrow alike) of family, and more. This book is as deeply moving as it is beautifully understated."

— Mark A. Noll
University of Notre Dame

"This marvelous memoir embodies everything I admire about Nick Wolterstorff. It is wise, humane, and beautiful, infused with love and a passion for justice. It is also wonderfully witty in a way befitting someone who taught us that God's shalom is a world bursting with delight. I was absorbed by it, and when I put it down, I was grateful and inspired."

— James K. A. Smith
Calvin College

"I never took a course from Nick Wolterstorff, but he has been my teacher for the past half-century. The range of his contributions to the Christian life of the mind is amazing. But now, in this fine memoir, we get an even richer picture—a portrait of what it means to journey through life as an integrated person who exhibits in a very personal way a profound commitment to truth, beauty, and justice."

— Richard Mouw
Fuller Theological
Seminary

"Nicholas Wolterstorff's memoir is a treasure. I literally could not stop reading it. Readers will find deep insights into such diverse worlds as small-town life, philosophy, the academic world, and the world of family and friends that we all inhabit. Wolterstorff provides a rich account of a life of Christian faith lived with integrity, an attractive picture of a version of Christianity that is open-minded and warm-hearted, rooted in gratitude and love for God's creation and redemption."

— C. Stephen Evans
Baylor University

"This colorful, revealing memoir defies stereotypes of analytic philosophers and modest Calvinists alike. It may not surprise those familiar with the life and work of Nicholas Wolterstorff, the leading light of a remarkable renaissance of Christian learning, that he could write such a moving book. But what a feast awaits readers old and new, religious and secular, academic or not. Opinionated but not grumpy, personal but not egocentric, Wolterstorff weaves his many loves—intellectual perplexity, politics, art, music, architecture, education, nature, and even the intricacies of Japanese ceramics and Danish furniture—into a compelling narrative of philosophical wonder and divine grace. Vintage Wolterstorff, *In This World of Wonders* bears witness to a generous Christian humanism sorely needed today."

— Eric Gregory
Princeton University

"Nicholas Wolterstorff is best known as one of the leading figures in the revival of Christian philosophy. But to those who have had the good fortune to meet him, he is even more remarkable for his open-minded readiness to engage with anyone, to learn from anything, and to bring his keen critical intelligence to bear on the most unlikely subjects. This memoir reflects that open-minded spirit, as it brings out the many communities, events, and relationships that have shaped him. Warmly recommended."

— Jean Porter
University of Notre Dame

"Wolterstorff's memoir is a window into the recent history of modern philosophy, a light on the tangled engagement of Christianity with the late modern world, and—above all—a lens into a life and calling lived within and out of community. *In This World of Wonders* is a joy to read— illuminating, wise, and gracious as the man himself."

— James Davison Hunter
University of Virginia

"How should one live? The question sounds abstract, as if a treatise were the expected answer. But the life for which you actually bear responsibility is your response, as the particular person you are, to the wonders and horrors in your midst, in a world that will not let you wait until all the evidence is in. This memoir by Nicholas Wolterstorff invites us to listen in while he reflects on what he has experienced and done. Here are the births, deaths, relatives, loves, associates, schools, churches, injustices, homes, struggles, projects, ideals, and patches of sedge that have mattered to him. If you have found any of his other books rewarding, you should certainly read this one."

— Jeffrey Stout
Princeton University

"Nicholas Wolterstorff has contributed so much over the course of his life, and this memoir, told with incredible grace, humility, and charm, gives us a fascinating look at how his faith, theology, and commitment to justice have been shaped and put to use. Nick's emphasis on learning and listening has blessed him with an incredible wealth of knowledge, from which we can all learn something that will in turn deepen our own faith, understanding, and love for the world in which we live. His is a life worth reading about, and he is someone I deeply admire."

— Jim Wallis
Sojourners

"If you ever thought philosophy dull, read this book and think again. Nick Wolterstorff describes the rich landscape of his life—art, music, love, grief, the academy, houses, travel, family, furniture, and much more—in a vivid, fast-paced, and deeply moving account. From these foothills there rise up the mighty peaks of his life's work: justice, liturgy, peace, divine discourse, lament, politics, Reason, Being, Knowing. Seeing these in the context of Wolterstorff's remarkable life, we see in new ways why they matter for all of us."

— N. T. Wright
University of St. Andrews

"Nicholas Wolterstorff's fingerprints are all over the better sort of American evangelicalism, from the revival of Christian philosophy to a reawakening of passion for social justice to the renewal of interest in liturgy and the arts. If you lived through these things, as I did, this book is for you."

— David Neff
Christianity Today

"No one in recent times has contributed more to more areas of Christian philosophy than has Nick Wolterstorff. He is a sort of Thomas Jefferson in the range of his interests and mastery. In his memoir he puts his thinking and activities in personal contexts. The story of the modest circumstances of his early years is particularly fascinating, especially in light of the richness of the experiences that follow."

— George Marsden
University of Notre Dame

"Nick Wolterstorff's memoir demolishes common stereotypes of academics. The role of the ivory tower pales in significance in comparison to his Dutch immigrant community in Minnesota. This would be a compelling story even if it were not a first-person eyewitness account of the extraordinary twentieth-century renaissance of Christian philosophy. Beyond that, it is a moving reflection on a life marked by grace, grief, and gratitude."

— Kevin J. Vanhoozer
Trinity Evangelical
Divinity School

"Always poignant, evocative, and honest, Wolterstorff leads us through one remarkable vignette after another with the deftness of a master. When you have finished reading, you will feel pain that it's time to leave his world of wonders."

— Cornelius Plantinga Jr.
Calvin Institute
of Christian Worship

In This World of Wonders

Memoir of a Life in Learning

Nicholas Wolterstorff

WILLIAM B. EERDMANS PUBLISHING COMPANY

GRAND RAPIDS, MICHIGAN

Wm. B. Eerdmans Publishing Co.
4035 Park East Court SE, Grand Rapids, Michigan 49546
www.eerdmans.com

25 24 23 22 21 20 19   1 2 3 4 5 6 7

ISBN 978-0-8028-7679-9

Library of Congress Cataloging-in-Publication Data

A catalog record for this book is available from the Library of Congress

To Claire,

to our children and their spouses:

Amy, T.J., Eric, Robert, Mari, Klaas, Tracey, Christopher,

and to our grandchildren:

Nick, Maria, Ian, Nina, Phoebe, India, Kees

Contents

Contents

Preface

I have written this memoir—reluctantly—at the urging of several friends. I grew up in a Dutch immigrant community in southwest Minnesota, a community whose members retained the self-deprecating ethos of the Reformed Church in the Netherlands, in which they had been reared. That ethos conspired with Minnesota culture, also self-deprecating, to drill into us that we were never to call attention to ourselves. The idea was not that we were to think poorly of ourselves. Nothing wrong with taking quiet pride in one's accomplishments; and if someone pays you a compliment for what you have done, graciously accept their praise. But don't let it go to your head. And never toot your own horn. It was not a soil that nourishes autobiography. Add to this the fact that I have never kept a journal, and that my memory is no better than average. My memoir, if I were to write one, would be fact-starved compared with most memoirs.

Even if I had kept a journal, and even if my memory were better than it is, why would anyone want to read about my life? Most of my days as an adult have consisted of reading philosophical books and articles, taking notes on my reading, thinking hard, writing philosophical books and articles, preparing notes for classes and public lectures, teaching classes and delivering public lectures, listening to talks and lectures, leading discussions, participating in discussions, talking with students and colleagues, reading student papers, and so on—year after year. Mine has been a life in learning: a life spent learning, and a life spent sharing learning. There have been no affairs, no embezzling, no shootings, no addictions, no divorces, no serious accidents or illnesses, no gambling away of anybody's life savings. How dull! Why would anyone want to read about such a life? Boring!

Maybe not. It has been my great privilege to have participated in an extraordinary renaissance of Christian philosophy—and of Christian learning more generally. Perhaps an insider's perspective on how this most unlikely development came about would be of interest to some people. Moreover, my life has not only been a life in learning, it's been a life of engagements with God, with family and friends, with institutions, with art, gardens, and buildings, with births, deaths, and suffering—engagements often surprising and unanticipated. Many of those engagements, in addition to being interesting in their own right, have shaped how I think. Readers might be interested in the awakenings, the affections, the opportunities, the sorrows, that have led me to think what I have thought, to write what I have written, to love what I have loved, to support the causes I have supported.

And something else might prove of interest to readers. Mine has not been the life of a solitary individual in an alien world discovering his true self. Mine has been a life in community—in many communities: the communities of two small Minnesota villages, the community of an extended family, the community of Christian philosophers, the community of philosophers in general, of local religious communities, and of various academic communities. I have been shaped by those communities, by movements and developments within them, by their traditions. I have, in turn, contributed to shaping them. In the telling of my life, I would be telling about those communities, telling about them from the vantage point of my participation.

Overall, my life-in-community has been an expansive opening-out from the community of the small village in which I was reared. But, though I long ago left that community for other larger communities, I have not left behind the ways in which I was shaped by that community. In particular, I have not left behind the religious tradition of Reformed Protestantism into which I was inducted. Running throughout the expansion of my life-in-community is the thread of religious continuity.

The challenge I faced in describing this dimension of my life was to do so in such a way that those who are not religious, and those whose religion is quite different from mine, would not be put off: that is, the challenge of being particular without being parochial. The reader will discover that my way of being religious is very different from the aggressive, aggrieved, and adversarial way that is presently so prominent on the American scene.

I decided to cope with the paucity of facts by not even attempting to write the story of my life; instead, I would offer a series of vignettes, more or less following the order of my life. I would recall events and situations that were formative for me, projects and actions that contributed prominently to the shape my life has taken. Now and then I would recall an episode that was quirky or touching, memorable even if not formative.

A number of the vignettes tell of my life as a philosopher. The challenge I faced in telling about that part of my life was to compose the vignettes in such a way that philosophers would not find what I say too simplistic, and nonphilosophers would not find it too complicated.

I think of the succession of vignettes as scenes on a journey through the landscape of memory. As a scene catches my eye, I stop to look. I move on, and another scene catches my eye. There are benches here and there where I can sit and reflect on the significance of what I am seeing. Now and then, I glance ahead.

A consequence of this memoir's being a series of vignettes and not the story of my life is that there is no dropping of names of famous people I have met. Nothing lost there. A related consequence, however, is that many longtime friends also never get mentioned. I very much regret that. Their absence from these pages certainly does not mean that I do not treasure their friendship.

I am grateful to Kelly Clark, Ivy George, and Jon Pott for urging me to write this memoir, for wearing down my reluctance, and for reading successive drafts of the manuscript and offering sage advice for improvement. I also thank Terence Cuneo for reading and offering helpful comments on a draft.

The title was suggested to me by Jon Pott. It's a line from J. M. Coetzee's novel of 1990, *Age of Iron*, which I quote in the final section of the memoir. A good friend, René van Woudenberg, called my attention to the fact that "World of Wonders" is also the title song of the 1986 album by the Canadian singer and songwriter Bruce Cockburn.

May 2018

ONE

My People

Bigelow, my birthplace, tiny village on the prairies of southwest Minnesota, population around two hundred. The streets had no names, the houses no numbers. Everybody knew where everybody lived, no need for names and numbers. If a visitor came to town and asked directions to someone's house we said, "Head west; at the second intersection, turn south; it's the third house on the east side of the street." We used the compass points—not left and right—to give directions. Every street ran either due north and south or due east and west.

The houses, for the most part, were frame, two stories with front porches, painted white, set on large lots with no fences, giving children lots of space to play and roam. Adults minded each other's children. We children quickly learned who was "bossy" and who was "nice."

The center of the village was called "downtown": a grocery store, where my father was employed, a hardware store, a farm implement shop, a blacksmith, the post office, where people picked up their mail (there was no home delivery), the village library, and, across the railroad tracks, the grain elevator. Downtown was the center of everyday village life. When people shopped or picked up their mail they would chat, or as they put it, "spend some time visiting." Everybody walked to where they were going—downtown, to church, to school, to friends. When you met people on the sidewalk, you looked them in the eye and greeted them, you did not look down or away.

Understatement was the rule. If someone asked how you felt and you felt great, you said, "Been worse." If you felt wretched, you said, "Been better." School was a three-block walk from our house. One winter day, when the temperature was thirty degrees below zero, our mother said, "Bundle up tight; it's a bit nippy this morning."

Everybody went to church, so far as I knew, with the exception of the Yeskes, our landlords across the street. Families were intact, or perhaps the breakdowns of relationships were concealed from us children: I don't recall hearing of any divorces, of any single mothers other than widows, of any abused spouses or children. J. D. Vance, in *Hillbilly Elegy: A Memoir of a Family and Culture in Crisis*, a book that has received a good deal of attention in recent years, describes growing up not long ago in small villages in northern Kentucky and southern Ohio. Alcoholism was rife, as was abuse of children and spouses; people went through serial marriages and divorces; girls got pregnant in their mid-teens and dropped out of school; a number of men in the village preferred living on welfare to working for a living; the language people used when speaking to each other was foul and abusive. The Bigelow of my youth was another world altogether. Bigelow was Norman Rockwell's America.

It was because of the railroad that the village was named "Bigelow." The railroad company that originally laid the tracks was the St. Paul and Sioux City Railway. When the company determined the path of the tracks between St. Paul and Sioux City, it also decided to establish a few villages along the way, and one of those was the future Bigelow. The directors of the company decided to honor one of their fellow directors, Charles Henry Bigelow, by naming the village-to-be after him. The tracks reached the location of our village in September 1872; the site was platted, and a dedication was made a year later. There is no record of Mr. Bigelow's ever having set foot in the village.

There was no depot in Bigelow. Trains stopped to load grain from the elevator and to unload coal; otherwise, they went straight through, blowing their whistle. I remember only one exception: in 1940, the campaign train of Wendell Wilkie, the Republican candidate for President that year, stopped in Bigelow, and Wilkie gave a brief campaign speech from the platform at the rear of the caboose. We schoolchildren were dismissed from classes to attend the big event.

On the Fourth of July, everybody gathered in the village park. A so-called canteen had been constructed where you could buy soft drinks (we called them "pop"), chewing gum, Cracker Jacks, hot dogs, candy, and ice cream. There were races, ball games, and other contests; but mostly, people stood around visiting. At around two o'clock in

4

the afternoon, everybody stopped talking and listened to a speech delivered by a minister or public official who lauded the freedom we enjoyed as Americans. For most Americans today, the Fourth of July is no more than a welcome midsummer day off, an opportunity to get together with relatives and friends and to watch fireworks. In Bigelow, in the 1930s, it was the day on which the entire village assembled to celebrate America as a land of freedom and opportunity.

The adults must have followed the progress of World War II; news would have come over the radio. But I don't recall their talking much about the war, and I didn't pay much attention to it. I was more aware of the "war effort," as it was called, than of the war itself. I was well aware of the rationing of sugar and gas. My twin sister, Henrietta, and I went through the village with our coaster wagon collecting small pieces of scrap metal, which we then sold at the grain elevator for pocket money. None of our classmates did that. People must have thought, "Those poor Wolterstorff twins." We were all taught how to identify German planes, and, periodically, village air-raid drills were held. Father was an air-raid warden, assigned to walk through the village during an air-raid drill to see to it that no light was coming from any windows. When I asked why the Germans would want to bomb Bigelow, the answer I got was, "You never know."

The prairie here is gently rolling hills. One can see for miles and miles, with nothing to break one's line of sight. The terrain is divided into sections, each section a square mile, with roads running north and south and east and west between the sections. The resolute march of the grid is halted only when it comes to a swamp or a lake, of which there are many in Minnesota, but not many in the southwest corner. This was farm country. Most farms were quarter-sections—160 acres. The main crops were corn and oats, some soybeans, some barley, some flax, clover and alfalfa for hay. Every farm had animals: cows, horses, pigs, chickens. The chickens were free to range around the farmyard; cows and horses grazed in the pastures, kept in by sturdy fences.

Every farmyard had a house and barn, a pig house, a chicken coop, a granary, and a windmill. The barns, some of them truly majestic, were almost all painted barn-red. Bordering every farmyard on the northwest was a grove of trees that had been planted to protect against the prevailing northwest wind. Things that were no longer of use were tossed or hauled into the grove, making it a child's heaven: here, a discarded washing machine made of wooden staves, there, an automobile allowed to rust, over there, a broken-down wooden wheelbarrow.

To my eye, there is nothing more beautiful than this gently rolling countryside in late July and early August, when the sky is bright blue with a few scattered clouds; when the corn, marching in rows up and down the hills, is six feet tall; when the oats have ripened and turned golden brown; when cows and horses are grazing in the pastures. It's a quiet serene beauty, the only movement that of clouds and their shadows and of animals grazing. Those who live in the mountains or at the seashore are likely to overlook this beauty. The beauty they are familiar with is assertive—jagged peaks or surging tides. Instead of discerning the alternative beauty of the landscape of my childhood, they find it lacking in beauty, perhaps boring. Nothing calls for attention, other than the big red barns and the windmills punctuating the landscape. Pastor Ames, in Marilynne Robinson's novel *Gilead*, speaks for me: "Here on the prairie there is nothing to distract attention from the evening and the morning, nothing on the horizon to abbreviate or to delay. Mountains would seem an impertinence from that point of view."[1]

But change has come. Horses are gone—their power replaced by the horsepower of diesel engines. Where individual farmers once farmed 160 acres, they now farm many hundreds, sometimes thousands, with gigantic pieces of machinery. Farmhouses stand deserted,

---

1. Marilynne Robinson, *Gilead* (New York: Farrar, Straus and Giroux, 2004), 246.

barns are falling down, windmills have been sold for scrap. The pastures have been plowed under and sown to cash crops—corn and soybeans—and the fences pulled up. There are no cows and horses grazing, no chickens running free around the farmyard. Cows, pigs, and chickens are cooped up in big low sheds. What remains is only the quiet beauty of crops on the rolling hills and clouds casting their shadows.

In the village, the stores and shops of downtown are gone, replaced by empty lots and ugly metal sheds, or "pole barns"—containing what, I do not know. The village is bleak, deserted, shorn of welcome, and everything lovable is gone. Where once there was a buzz of human activity, now there is nothing: no small groups of people spending time visiting with those from the other side of town or with farmers who have driven in to shop. People now drive to Worthington, the county seat ten miles to the north, to do their shopping.

Our little church is boarded up. The stately and spacious brick building on the north edge of town where my siblings and I went to elementary school is also boarded up, and weeds have taken over the driveway. Nobody walks to go somewhere—there's nowhere to go. The highway that ran through the village alongside the railroad tracks has been diverted a few miles east, leaving the village stranded. The streets now have names and the houses have numbers, for the benefit, I was told, of medical-emergency vehicles from Worthington. The street names are pompous: the main street in the village is now Broadway, the street that goes through the village park is Park Avenue. I trust that those who assigned these pompous names to the streets of our little village had a good laugh while doing so.

Our house in Bigelow did not have central heating. The kitchen was warm in the winter from the heat thrown off by the cooking stove, fueled by corncobs and coal. In winter, most family activity took place in the kitchen. There was a heater in the living room, but it was ignited only on special occasions. The bedrooms were unheated, and when we children were ready for bed, we heated flat stones on the kitchen stove, wrapped them in paper and cloth, and placed them in the bed at our feet. By morning, beautiful designs in frost had formed on the windows from the moisture of our breath.

Our house also did not have running water. Rainwater was collected in a cistern adjacent to the house; we pumped it out with a small pump in the kitchen. Adjacent to our lot was a barnyard, where Mr. Yeske kept a few cows for milking. The well in the middle of his barnyard was where we got drinking water. Once, when I went to pump water in the winter, the pump was covered with gorgeous white hoarfrost, and I stuck out my tongue to lick it. My warm tongue melted the frost and stuck to the pump. When I pulled it away, skin from my tongue remained attached to the pump.

We did not have plumbing in our house; instead, we used an outhouse that was some distance from the house. In the winter, we used chamber pots. Ours was the finest outhouse I knew of, built by my father, sturdy and attractive, as was everything he built. A favorite Halloween prank of teenagers in the village was to tip over outhouses. The outhouse lore in the village was that once a cranky elderly widow, whom nobody liked, was in her outhouse when it was tipped. Ours was never tipped, probably because it was not only built to last but was also large—as outhouses go.

We had no telephone. In recent years, Henrietta and I have often wondered how arrangements were made for visits with relatives and friends on farms and in neighboring villages. Neither of us has any idea. We did not get a newspaper, nor did anybody else that I knew of; our news about the outside world came by radio.

We did have a car, and our house had electricity. For the first eight years of my life, however, we did not have a refrigerator, so we stored food that had to be kept cool in the cellar. Some neighbors had ice chests. In summer, a man would come through the village with a horse and wagon selling big chunks of ice that had been cut in winter from one of the nearby lakes and stored in a shed under straw. Wearing a leather apron on his shoulders, he would grab a chunk of ice with an iron claw, hoist it onto his shoulders, and carry it into the houses of neighbors who had ice chests.

I knew about the conveniences of modern life—running water, indoor plumbing, central heating, telephones, refrigerators—but I did not regret not having them. I did not think, "If only we had indoor plumbing," or "I wish we had running water." Most of our neighbors and relatives did not have these conveniences either. It was a hard life, especially for women. But we were taught to be content with what we had, thankful for what was good in our lives, and not to dwell on what we lacked that others had. From an early age, I learned to be grateful.

Henrietta and I were born on January 21, 1932, delivered on the dining-room table, so we were told. I was named after our paternal grandfather, my sister, after our maternal grandmother.

Our mother, Agnes (née Feenstra), died when we were three and a half years old, ten days after giving birth, six weeks prematurely, to another set of twins, Cornelius John and Cornelia Joanne, this time in the clinic in Worthington. I have only one memory of her alive: sitting in a rocking chair, holding me on her lap after I had stumbled on a boardwalk outside and gotten dozens of slivers in my forearms. She was ill for much of her second pregnancy, but the doctors in Worthington were unable to diagnose the problem. After the younger twins were born, her condition worsened rapidly, so our father drove her to the Mayo Clinic in Rochester, where she was diagnosed with colon cancer and told that she had only a short time to live. She begged to see "the kids" one last time; so two of her brothers and her sister immediately drove Henrietta and me to Rochester. We arrived in the middle of the night, whereupon our uncles and aunt were told, I learned later, that we could not see her until the day shift came on. When we did get to see her, she had already died. I have a clear memory of riding through the night, but none, strangely, of seeing my mother in her hospital bed. She died on July 5, 1935, at the age of twenty-nine. Henrietta recently wrote to the Mayo Clinic, asking whether they still had the medical report of our mother's illness in their files. They did, and they sent us a copy.

Her body was brought back to Bigelow for the funeral and for burial in the village cemetery. I can see the open casket standing in our living room before it was brought to the church. An older cousin told me some years ago that, just before the casket was closed in the church, my father lifted up Henrietta and me to kiss our mother for the last time—but I don't remember that. Strangely, I do have the vivid memory of eating strawberries when the relatives gathered at our house after the burial.

Whenever I get back to Bigelow, I go to visit our mother's grave in the village cemetery, out in the rolling hills, the only visible farm buildings off in the distance. The last time was in the company of my wife, Claire, my sister, Henrietta, and our youngest son, Christopher, who had come along on the trip from Michigan to Minnesota to see some of my childhood haunts and to make the acquaintance of relatives. A cold rain was blowing across the prairie. Suddenly, standing before her tombstone, I was overcome with grief—and gratitude. I broke down. Never before, when standing there in the cemetery, had this happened. Why now? "Mother Agnes, you ushered me into this world, set me on my feet, and then were snatched away, much too soon. I scarcely knew you."

A few years ago I gave some talks at the Mayo Clinic to their medical-ethics group, which was headed up by a former student of mine, Jon Tilburt. During the course of my visit, someone asked me whether this was my first visit to Mayo. I said it was—but then corrected myself. I had been to the Mayo Clinic once before.

My People

I do not recall finding our mother's death traumatic, but it's possible that I have repressed the memory. Our family was part of an extended family of grandparents, aunts, uncles, and cousins living in the area; Henrietta and I had seen them often and knew them well. Now they cared for us. We lived with our maternal grandparents on their farm for a year or so, then, for a few years, with the newly married younger sister of our mother and her husband on their farm. We often saw and played with cousins. We were enveloped in a circle of love and care. Henrietta and I were constant companions, never separated: we played together, did assigned chores together, went to school together, did everything together. I was never the only child; there were always two of us.

But after losing our mother, we were now also losing our father. Every now and then, the relatives that Henrietta and I were staying with would take us home to Bigelow to see him, and now and then, he would come to see us. On a few occasions, he hired a housekeeper for a few months, and all four of us children (the two sets of twins) were together at home; but then it was back to relatives. I was becoming more attached to the relatives we stayed with than to Dad.

In October 1939, when Henrietta and I were seven, our father married Jennie Hanenburg, from Edgerton, Minnesota, a village forty-five miles to the northwest. Their acquaintance came about in a most unusual way. In a meeting of pastors of area churches of the denomination we were members of, our pastor from Bigelow mentioned our recently widowed father to the pastor from Edgerton, and asked him whether there were any women in his church who might be suitable for our father to marry. Jennie Hanenburg came immediately to mind. So the two pastors arranged, on the spot, a date and a time for my father to drive to Edgerton to meet her—which he did. The story in the Hanenburg family was that Jennie insisted that no man could possibly be coming to meet her—she was already in her mid-thirties—but had to be coming to meet her much younger sister, Clara. So when Dad drove up, she was quite disheveled.

After the wedding, all four of us children—Henrietta and I, Cornie and Joanne—returned from living with relatives to live with Dad and Mother Jen in Bigelow. But I no longer felt close to Dad, nor did I ever again feel close. The bonds of childhood affection had been ruptured by having had relatively little contact with him between the time Mother Agnes died and the time he remarried. Mother Jen was a wonderfully inventive and creative homemaker, and was un-failingly generous to all. She was loved by all who knew her. But I never acquired for her the affection of a child for a parent. I became devoted, but not close.

I think our father was more affected by the death of our natural mother than I was. He never talked about it, and I never asked him. His second marriage was happy. But there was a certain melancholy about him; he did not readily laugh. His melancholy had a number of sources, as we shall see, but surely one of them was the death of his young wife, leaving him with four children, two aged three and a half and two, newborn.

We were poor. Father's salary at Horstman's Grocery was obvi-ously meager. But we had a large vegetable garden, a sizable strawberry patch, and an apple orchard. We grew many more vegeta-bles than we could eat in the summer; what we did not eat fresh was canned, and those canned supplies lasted until fresh vegetables from the garden were again available in late spring. We stored potatoes and carrots in the cellar. We canned apples from the orchard, and those lasted us through the winter. When one of our uncles on the farm butchered a cow or hog, he would bring us some of the meat, and we would then have fresh meat for a week or two. What we did not eat fresh was canned. The only things we bought from the grocery store were staples: flour, sugar, and so forth. Mother Jen baked all the bread, and it was superb. She also did a great deal of sewing, especially for herself and the girls.

Christmas gifts were useful things, mostly items of clothing—socks, scarves, mittens. We had very few toys. The Christmas catalogues from Sears, Roebuck and Montgomery Ward opened up before us a never-never land that we imagined and dreamed about but could not enter. I did not think of us as poor—rather, as *having enough*. Enough was sometimes not much: supper might consist of nothing more than bread over which hot bacon fat and syrup were poured, along with canned green beans. We ate what was set before us, and no meal was ever skipped.

The living conditions of most people in the village were much like ours. Our landlords, the Yeskes, were better off than we were, and there were a few people in the village who had enough money to buy fresh fruit and vegetables from the grocery store in the winter. I watched them when my father occasionally took me along with him to the store. But it didn't matter; we had enough. Nothing in my environment made me envy those who had more. The advertisements on the radio were mostly, as I recall, for soap and cold cereal.

Perhaps our poverty weighed on our parents; they had to see to it that we had food and clothing and that the rent was paid. They could not ease up on their frugality, but poverty did not grind them down. Unlike the hillbilly poverty that J. D. Vance describes in *Hillbilly Elegy*, ours was not a poverty that crushed the spirit and destroyed families. There was laughter. We played games together as a family—checkers, Chinese checkers, chess, carroms, and many more.

Our father worked downtown in Horstman's Grocery. Early in World War II, he announced that he was leaving to find work elsewhere, and that we would stay behind. He found employment at the Samsonite factory in Denver, which, we were told, was manu-facturing wartime materiel of some kind. I assumed that his leaving home to work in Denver was part of the "war effort." Uncle Hank Feenstra and his family had moved to Denver a few years earlier, and Dad stayed with them.

Not until many years later, after his death, did I learn from one of my uncles the real reason Dad left town: Mr. Horstman had fired him on the charge of embezzlement. The charge would have seared his soul: he had a well-deserved reputation for rock-solid rectitude. Now rumors and whispers would have raced through the village, peo-ple wondering, "Was Matt not who we thought he was?" My father would have known what people were thinking and whispering. He had been shamed, deeply shamed. I now realize that he left Bigelow not only to find work but to get away from the shame. After a few years, it came to light that the embezzler was Mr. Horstman's own son. Mr. Horstman apologized and offered my father his old job back, but Dad declined.

Was it a mistake for Dad and Mother to protect us children from the shame by not telling us what had happened? I don't know.

There was always much work to be done, and, from an early age, we children were conscripted to join in: dusting, mopping, wash-ing dishes, drying dishes, peeling potatoes, hauling water, bringing in coal, shoveling snow, mowing the grass, planting the garden, weed-ing the garden, picking peas and beans, peeling apples, washing win-dows, hanging out the wash, taking in the wash, making soap. Each of us had assigned tasks. From an early age, we acquired the habits of responsible work.

Still, there remained time to play outdoors with the other chil-dren in the neighborhood. We did lots of pretending: pretend school, pretend church, pretend housekeeping. We played softball, of course, and "hide and go seek," "kick the can," "ring around a rosey," and other traditional children's games that were taught us by the older children. Many of them had nonsensical names that I have only heard, never seen written down: *pum pum pullaway, ollie ollie oxen all in free, anti aye over.* These games are unfamiliar to my children and grandchildren.

I remember very little of elementary school, which is strange, since I was good at it and liked it. Several of the school districts around Bigelow had been consolidated. The single-room schoolhouses out in the country had been boarded up, and a sizable building constructed in the village. Children were bused in from the surrounding farms. Each grade had, as I recall, about fifteen students, two grades to a room.

My only clear memory of Bigelow Elementary School is of singing from *The Golden Book of Favorite Songs* in the all-school assemblies that were held in the school gym. I have a worn copy in my possession. Leafing through it now, I see that it was astoundingly eclectic: patriotic songs ("America, the Beautiful"), Civil War songs ("Tenting Tonight on the Old Camp Ground"), Stephen Foster songs ("My Old Kentucky Home"), Negro spirituals ("Swing Low, Sweet Chariot"), evangelical hymns ("Jesus, Lover of My Soul"), Christmas songs ("The First Noel"), children's songs ("Baa! Baa! Black Sheep"), even a Dutch round, *De Bezem, de Bezem* ("The Broom, the Broom").

After school, when I wasn't doing assigned chores or playing with neighborhood children, I read anything I could get my hands on, mostly adventure stories: the Hardy Boys series, the Bobbsey Twins series, novels by Jack London, Zane Grey, Booth Tarkington, Grace Livingston Hill. No literary classics there! During the school year, I took out books from the small school library; in the summer, I read whatever I found around the house, including Longfellow's *Hiawatha*, which I loved. Our parents never read to us, other than, after meals, from the Bible and from Egermeier's *Children's Bible Story Book*. There were no children's books in our house in Bigelow, other than the children's Bible story book.

Each year, on the first day of May, Henrietta and I made small decorated baskets, put a bit of candy in them, and delivered these so-called May baskets to our classmates in the village. I have no idea where this tradition came from or what it meant.

For a couple of years, when I was nine and ten, I stayed, for most of the summer, on the farm of my paternal grandmother and her eldest son, my unmarried uncle, Case. I picked up household Dutch from them. My grandmother, whose maiden family name was van Arkel, I came to know well—or thought I did (it turned out that I knew her less well than I thought). Both of my parents were immigrants from the Netherlands. They came to America along with their parents and siblings—my birth mother when she was six, my father when he was twelve. I know a bit about the circumstances of the immigration of my father's family, but almost nothing about the immigration of my mother's family, the Feenstras.

My father's family lived in the Dutch city of Utrecht, where my grandfather was a cabinetmaker. I have inherited a few of the hand tools he took with him to the new country; burned into some of them are the initials NW. The family left Utrecht for America in early December 1915, embarking at Rotterdam on the ship *Rotterdam* and disembarking at Ellis Island on the 22nd of that month. Most of those who emigrated from the Netherlands to this country in the latter part of the nineteenth century and the early part of the twentieth did so for religious or economic reasons. Not so my father's family, according to the story I was told: the story was that my grandmother did not want her sons to be drafted into the Dutch army.

Why would a family from the Dutch city of Utrecht settle in the farm country of southwest Minnesota? To my chagrin, it never occurred to me to ask this question until those who could answer it had died. Presumably, there was someone in the area who sponsored them. But was there no option other than Bigelow? My uncles all became farmers. My father did not, nor did my grandfather; the latter eked out a meager living as a carpenter and died in 1931, the year before I was born, at the age of sixty-one, sixteen years after the family had immigrated to Minnesota. Nobody ever talked about him and, to my regret, I never asked about him, so I have no idea what he was like as a person.

One day in the late 1980s, when I was teaching at the Free University of Amsterdam, someone identifying himself as Bert van Arkel phoned me, said that he was a relative of mine on my paternal grandmother's side, and said that he and his wife would like to have lunch with me. Bert, a retired minister, proved to be a genealogy buff. He knew all about the extended van Arkel family and how I fitted into the family tree. At the end of our lunch he remarked that, since he had some time on his hands, he was going to go into the records in Dutch churches to trace my Wolterstorff ancestry.

Within a month or two he had traced my Wolterstorff ancestry back to a Juriaan Wolterstorff, who was married in 1727 in the small Dutch village of Hazerswoude, near Leiden—and the trail ended there. His profession was given as surgeon. A year or two later, when I was again teaching in Amsterdam, another person called me up and said he would like to meet and talk about my Wolterstorff ancestry. When we met, he brought with him the pages outlining the Wolterstorff family tree from the large set of volumes, published shortly before World War II, tracing the genealogies of Germans. The family was traced back to an Anton Woltersdorf (Latin: Antonius Wolterstorpius), who was born in 1430 in the small German village of Neuruppin in northern Germany. Over the centuries, a good many Wolterstorffs had been either pastors or educators.

In the German genealogy, one line of the Wolterstorff family tree ended with a Georg Wolterstorff, born on May 17, 1699; no date was given for his death. It turned out that the birthdate of Georg in the German records was the same as the birthdate of Juriaan in the

Dutch records that Bert van Arkel had explored. The conclusion was obvious: sometime in the early 1700s, Georg had left Germany for the Netherlands and changed his given name from "Georg" to "Juriaan."

Among the things I learned from Bert van Arkel about the van Arkel family was that there had long been two wings of the family, one consisting of well-to-do businessmen and professional people, including ministers, the other consisting of common laborers. My grandmother came from the latter wing of the family. I wondered whether economic considerations had, after all, been a factor in the family's decision to emigrate.

A couple of months after Bert van Arkel had presented me with the results of his research on the Wolterstorff genealogy, I received another call from him. He had told one of his second cousins, also a van Arkel, about me, and this second cousin was inviting me and my wife and Bert and his wife to visit them in their home outside Utrecht for an afternoon and evening.

This cousin, it turned out, had owned a brickworks on the outskirts of Utrecht. When the city expanded, he sold the brickworks and built this house out in the country. Clearly, he had sold the brickworks for a good price: the house was a large and imposing villa, beautifully furnished, with stuffed animal heads the main items of wall decoration in the expansive living room.

One of the reasons he had invited us over was that he had in his possession a trove of letters that my grandmother had sent from Minnesota, over the years, to her upper-class van Arkel relatives back in the Netherlands. (She died in 1953, at the age of seventy-nine.) The letters were fascinating. In one of them, written shortly after the end of World War II, when there were still severe shortages in the Netherlands, my grandmother asked whether she could send clothes and food. Here was a member of the lower-class wing of the family wanting to know whether she could alleviate the condition of members of the upper-class wing of the family! What she wrote was a truly amazing exercise in social decorum.

Another letter moved me deeply. Grandmother was describing life in the United States to her relatives back in the Netherlands; she had never talked with me about what life in the States was like for her. The letter was written in the mid-1930s—in Dutch, of course. She used the Dutch word *baas*, which, etymologically, is the same as our English word "boss," but has strong class connotations, whereas our English word "boss" does not. Here, in the United States, the boss of the construction gang you work for might live next door, and you might have a beer with him after work. No such camaraderie with one's *baas*. Addressing someone as "baas" is not just recognizing his position as your employer or supervisor but also acknowledging him as your social superior.

This is what Grandmother wrote: "*Hier, niemand hoeft iemand baas te noemen*" ("Here, nobody has to call anybody *baas*").

I see him yet, our father, sitting at our dining-room table in Bigelow in the long winter evenings, making pen and ink drawings (my siblings and I each have some of them). The images in his drawings were taken from some painting or illustration he had seen, never (so far as I know) directly from nature. His drawings were not, however, copies of the originals; rather, they were transpositions of the images from the medium of the original into the very different medium of pen and ink. When I look at them now, I am struck by how much visual imagination went into transposing the image from the original medium into the new medium, and by how skillfully he handled his medium. Once, when Henrietta and I were still small children, we were rummaging around in a cedar chest and came across a file of papers indicating that Father had taken some correspondence courses in drawing from an art school in St. Paul.

A story that circulated in the family was that, after one year as a student at Calvin College in the mid-1920s, he was forced to drop out because his three brothers were angry that he was allowed to go off to college while they were working on farms; to my regret, I never asked him whether the story was true. I recently learned that, though only a freshman, he had been chosen to do the illustrations for the college yearbook of that year (1926). When I mentioned this to Henrietta, she said she remembers once coming across his copy of that yearbook and noticing that a good many of his classmates had written in it to say that he should become an artist. Did he allow himself to dream of that?

I speculate that disappointment over the turn his life had taken was among the sources of his melancholy. He was forced to drop out of college, and becoming a graphic artist was out of the question. If he did indeed live with these disappointments, he never mentioned them to me.

F ather was a woodworker. That's who he was: it was his identity. When he worked in the grocery store in Bigelow, he did wood-working after hours. In the last twenty-five years or so of his life, woodworking was his full-time occupation. Woodworking was in his blood. His father had been a woodworker in Utrecht, and later in Bigelow. I have done woodworking on the side, though not much in recent years. I love everything about it: the smell of freshly cut wood, achieving precision in fitting the pieces together, everything. Our sons Klaas and Christopher also do woodworking on the side, and our son-in-law, T. J. Ryckbost, is a carpenter by profession—a superb carpenter, a woodworker-carpenter!

When I was teaching philosophy and explaining to students new to philosophy what makes for a good philosophy paper, I would sum-marize my advice by saying, "In a good philosophy paper, there is both intellectual imagination and craftsmanship." When I used the word "craftsmanship," I was thinking of woodworking. Early on, my advice was a bit more expansive: "In a good philosophy paper, there is both intellectual imagination and craftsmanship. All the dovetails are tight." I noticed a puzzled expression come over the students' faces. "What's a dovetail?" In subsequent years, I dropped that sentence—with regret. In a good philosophy paper, all the dovetails are tight!

My father taught me reverence for wood. He collected wood of many different species, would rub his hand across a piece of unfinished wood, and say, "Look, Nick, this is going to be really beautiful." I think he thought of woodworking as the process of revealing hidden beauty. He knew that wood outdoors had to be painted, but, unless it was some bland piece of pine, he never painted wood indoors. Paint concealed the beauty of its woodiness; he insisted on varnishing.

He was a perfectionist. *Good enough* was not good enough. It had to be *as good as possible.* Now and then he did general carpentry, but he was no good at it—finish carpentry, yes, but not what was then called "rough" carpentry, what is nowadays called "framing." I think he intuitively thought of rough carpentry as bad carpentry.

I well remember an episode that occurred when I was working for my uncle Chuck on his farm. Chuck needed a shed built between the silo and the barn, and he hired Dad to build it. Such a shed would normally be tossed up in three or four days; it's nothing but rough carpentry. Chuck was getting agitated, because my father had been working at it for two weeks. He was constructing the shed as if he were making a fine cabinet.

There's a passage in Kahlil Gibran's *The Prophet* that captures my father's attitude toward woodworking:

All work is empty save when there is love;
And when you work with love you bind yourself to yourself, and to
 one another, and to God.
And what is it to work with love?
It is to weave the cloth with threads drawn from your heart, as if your
 beloved were to wear that cloth.

It is to build a house with affection, as if your beloved were to dwell
  in that house.
It is to sow seeds with tenderness and reap the harvest with joy, as if
  your beloved were to eat the fruit.
It is to charge all things you fashion with a breath of your own spirit,
And to know that all the blessed dead are standing about you and
  watching....
Work is love made visible.

Ingrained in our modern way of thinking about art is the distinction between art and craft, that is, between *fine* art and craft. There's a pecking order associated with the distinction: art is superior, craft is inferior. From the time I was first introduced to modern philosophy of art, I have resented and opposed this put-down of the so-called crafts, no doubt because, as a child, I was inducted into both the fine arts tradition and the crafts tradition. The pen-and-ink drawings my father made were fine art, art meant for contemplation; the cabinets and other items of wood that he made were craft. He never indicated that he thought of the former as superior to the latter. The fact that cabinets are useful in ways that pen-and-ink drawings are not, did not mean, for him, that cabinets were inferior to pen-and-ink drawings.

Mother Jen revealed the beauty in old rags. From Mrs. Yeske she learned a technique of making eight-strand braided rag rugs that is, so I am told, extremely unusual. The rugs were either circular or oval, and the braiding was done in such a way that it resulted in a swirl—a single swirl in the case of the circular rugs, a double swirl in the case of the oval rugs. Mother Jen had an unerring sense of color: the succession of colors in the swirls is stunning, and she mixed bright colors with muted colors in such a way that the bright colors accentuated the design. She was also skilled at getting the tension exactly right and even, so that the rugs would lie flat instead of curling up.

One of my cousins, David Schelhaas, is, among other things, a poet. Here is a poem he wrote about one of the rugs made by my mother, his Aunt Jen:

On the dining
room floor in front of the door
lies a woven rug a gift from Aunt
Jen a circle of love made of rags from our lives a
jumper a skirt and a jacket of yours a pants and a sport
coat of mine. The rug like our marriage was fashioned with
unfinished pieces and the pattern could not be imagined before
it was made. She chose from our rag box odd pieces matched barely
but in placing and bending these pieces her blending made beauty
one weaving. The rug which is almost as old as our marriage has
been washed shaken out and stomped upon some yet the colors
are bright and the weaving's just right not too loose not too
tight supple enough to lie flat on the floor but stiff
enough still to fulfill all the purposes rugs are
made for. A beautiful functional thing
this circle of love this rug in a ring.

Let me jump ahead to Edgerton, the hometown of Mother Jen, where we moved when I was twelve. David's family lived in the village, about a block and a half from where we lived. His mother, my aunt Trena, was one of the most wonderful human beings I have known: warm, always welcoming, generous of spirit, intellectually curious, open-minded. Sadly, she died of cancer in 1963 at the young age of forty-nine.

Every weekday morning, at precisely ten o'clock, Mother Jen walked over to Aunt Trena's house for coffee. She stepped inside, picked up a broom, and swept the entry, whether or not any dirt or dust was visible. That didn't matter. Many would have viewed this as an implicit criticism of their housekeeping. Aunt Trena accepted it as one of her older sister's many acts of thoughtfulness. She—Trena— was busy tending to several small children.

One Saturday afternoon I walked into her house and heard the Metropolitan Opera playing on her radio. To me, as a young teenager, it was caterwauling. So I asked her, no doubt in a snarky tone of voice, "Why are you listening to *that*?" Her answer remains for me a marvel and a parable. "Nick, this is my window onto the world.[2] Sit down and let me explain it to you." Because of the Depression, she had not gone to school beyond the eighth grade; at the time, she was finishing high school by correspondence.

I have used what she said to me as the "text" for some graduation addresses I have given. What is education but a window onto the world? Sit down, and let me explain it to you.

Family life was deeply religious, as was the family life of our relatives and neighbors. Those of Dutch ancestry attended either the church we attended, the local Christian Reformed Church, or the local congregation of the Reformed Church in America. Those not of Dutch ancestry—we called them "Americans"—attended the local Presbyterian church. In his book on English dissenting movements, the poet and critic Donald Davie observes:

> It was … John Calvin who first clothed Protestant worship with the sensuous grace, and necessarily the aesthetic ambiguity, of song. And who that has attended worship in a French Calvinist church can deny that—over and above whatever religious experience he may or may not have had—he has had an aesthetic experience, and of a pecu-

---

2. Her son David, who was present, remembers her as saying, "It's my window onto the world *out of this dusty little village*."

liarly intense kind? From the architecture, from church-furnishings, from the congregational music, from the Geneva gown of the pastor himself, everything breathes simplicity, sobriety, and measure.[3]

That was it exactly: simplicity, sobriety, and measure. We dressed up on the Lord's Day, dressed up *for* the Lord's Day, and entered church well in advance of the beginning of the service to collect ourselves in silence, silence so intense it could be touched. The interior was plaster painted white, ceiling pitched to follow the roof, peak high but not too high, the only decoration a bit of carving on the pulpit and the communion table, which had been made, I was told, by my grandfather Wolterstorff. No stained glass windows, no visual representations. Most people perceive such a church interior as empty. Some years ago, when I was teaching at Yale, a colleague in the history department who specialized in Reformation history, Lee Wandel, mentioned to me that John Calvin believed that light, being uncircumscribable, is the best symbol we have for God, and that that explains why the churches built and renovated by Calvin's followers were typically so bright inside. They weren't empty; they were full of light. I remember our little church in Bigelow as full of light. Before I understood a word of what was said, I was inducted into the tradition by its architecture—and by the deportment of the worshipers.

When the service was to begin, the elders and deacons entered, men dressed in black or blue suits, faces bronzed and furrowed from working in the fields, shiny from scrubbing. Behind them came the minister; before he ascended the pulpit, one of the elders shook his hand. At the end of the service, all the elders shook his hand—unless they disagreed with something he had said in the sermon. We sang hymns from here and there, nineteenth-century America and England, sixteenth-century Germany, and so forth. And we sang psalms.

3. Donald Davie, *A Gathered Church* (New York: Oxford University Press, 1978), 25.

Every service included psalms, sung lustily, always to the tunes in the Genevan psalter. My image of the hymn tunes was that they jumped up and down; my image of the Genevan psalm tunes was that they marched forward in stately, unhurried majesty. When the service was conducted in Dutch, many of the older people sang the psalms from memory.

There was no aversion to repetition. The notion that only the new and innovative is meaningful had not invaded this transplant of the Dutch Reformed tradition in Bigelow. Through repetition, elements of the liturgy and Scripture sank so deep into one's soul that nothing thereafter, short of senility, could remove them. "Our help is in the name of the Lord, who made heaven and earth," intoned the minister, invariably, to open the service.

The minister preached at length, often with passion, sometimes with tears. Some ministers adopted what was called in Dutch a *preektoon*, that is, a preaching tone, an altered form of speech located somewhere between ordinary speech and chant. The minister also led in what was familiarly known as "the long prayer," during which the elders and deacons stood, eyes closed, swaying back and forth. The stereotype of Calvinism is that everything pivots around the doctrine of election. But I don't recall any sermons about election; if there were some, they weren't memorable. It was not prominent in the tradition as it was handed down to me.

Four times a year we celebrated the Lord's Supper. In a long preliminary exhortation the previous Sunday we were urged to prepare ourselves by contemplating the depth of our sins and the unfathomable love of God in atoning for our sins through the death and resurrection of Jesus Christ. Then, on "communion Sunday," the bread and wine were distributed in silence—the bread, cut into bite-sized pieces, on silver platters, the wine in silver cups from which everyone drank. The minister communicated last.

There were two services every Sunday, morning and afternoon, the cycle for one of the two sermons fixed by the Heidelberg Catechism. This catechism, coming from Heidelberg, Germany, during the Reformation, is divided up into fifty-two "Lord's Days," and the minister preached straight through the catechism in the course of the year, taking one Lord's Day per Sunday. It was doctrine, but doctrine peculiarly suffused with emotion—perhaps because, as I now know, the catechism had been formulated in a city that was, at the time, full of French refugees. The first question and answer set the tone, and decades later, they continue to echo in the chambers of my heart and in the hearts of many in my religious tradition.

Q. What is your only comfort in life and death?
A. That I, with body and soul, both in life and death, am not my own but belong to my faithful savior Jesus Christ.

Pervading the liturgy was the deep concern that we appropriate what God had done and was doing for our salvation. We were exhorted to discern and receive the actions of God in the liturgy (this did not happen automatically). And we were exhorted, as we went forth, to live gratefully.

In his famous analysis of the origins of capitalism, the great German sociologist Max Weber argued that the energetic activism of the Calvinists was aimed at securing the financial success that they took to be a sign of membership among God's elect. I understand how it might look that way to someone on the outside, and possibly there were some on the inside—English Puritans, for example—who did in fact think and speak thus. But it's a caricature of the tradition as I experienced it. The activism I experienced was the activism of gratitude: sin, salvation, and gratitude was the overarching scheme of the "Heidelberger." My father intuitively regarded wealth as a sign of shady dealing rather than divine favor.

The portrait here of devotion would be incomplete without mention of the liturgy of the family. Every family meal—and every meal was a family meal—was begun and concluded with prayer, especially

prayers of thanksgiving, including thanksgiving for means of sustenance. We did not take the means of sustenance for granted; food,
housing, clothes—all were interpreted as gifts from God.

Before the prayer at the conclusion of meals there was a reading.
The reading after breakfast and the reading after noontime dinner
were usually from Scripture, occasionally from a devotional tract. The
reading after supper in the evening was almost always a chapter from
a children's Bible story book. The piety in which I was reared, both
church and family, was centered on the Bible—Old Testament and
New Testament together. And at every point, it was communal: we
prayed together, we read Scripture together. There must have been
talk about "a personal prayer life," but I don't remember it.

Many of those who have been reared in some religious tradition
eventually leave because they find it too confining. Not so for me.
By being inducted into the Reformed tradition of Christianity, I became a member of a community, spread across time and space, whose
ways of thinking and acting have, over the years, grounded, nurtured,
instructed, guided, and disciplined me. I have often argued with the
tradition as I received it; but my arguments have been from within,
not from outside. Belonging to this people has been and remains an
essential part of my identity. Belonging to the American people is
also an essential part of my identity. These two identities have not
always fitted neatly together.

Why have I continued to embrace the tradition in which I was
reared while others who were reared in the same tradition have rejected it—sometimes bitterly? I think it's because the tradition, as I
received it, was life-affirming rather than life-negating. It was less
about theology and about getting to heaven than it was about living gratefully, joyfully, and responsibly in this world. There was art
in the family, books, music, and games, visiting with relatives and
friends. There wasn't much that was off-limits. Our denomination
in those days forbade attendance at movies on the ground that they
were "worldly amusements." But since there was no movie theater

in town, the prohibition was irrelevant. *Nobody* in Bigelow went to movies.

The move to Edgerton, the home of Mother Jen, came in the fall of 1944, when Henrietta and I were twelve. Father had taken a job as manager of one of the two lumberyards in the village. Since the war was still going on and lumber was scarce, the job paid poorly; I helped Dad stack the small amount of lumber that came in. The family now included Ivan, born in 1941.

Edgerton, with a population of about a thousand, felt much larger than Bigelow. Initially, I found its size intimidating, but it wasn't long before I came to love both the village and the people; I still do, and I try to get back at least every other year. These people are my people, they formed me, and I don't want to lose touch with them, especially not my relatives—aunts, uncles, and cousins.

When I get back, I make a point of going with my cousin Paul, about seven in the morning, to "The Booth," a small room at the back of one of the downtown establishments, so-called because about half the space in the room is taken up by a booth. Every morning, four or five men from the village meet at The Booth and, over fried eggs, toast, and coffee, exchange village news and gossip, talk politics, discuss world problems, and tell stories, most of them true, though embroidered. A few years ago I noticed a sturdy birdhouse attached to the wall of the building outside The Booth and asked who made it. "Oh, Matt made that," one of them replied. "It's got to be forty or fifty years ago by now." Matt, my father, had worked on the second floor of the building for the last twenty-five years or so of his life.

When we moved to Edgerton, downtown consisted of several blocks of stores and shops: two restaurants, a bank, a bakery, a meat market, a drugstore, a dry-goods store, a couple of auto repair businesses, a bowling alley, a pool hall, the office of the local dentist, the offices of the local newspaper, *The Edgerton Enterprise*, and more. Bigelow had none of those. Though the establishments in Edgerton are fewer now than they were when we moved there, downtown remains to this day the center of village activity.

Probably all small villages, in the days before mass communication, were quirky, each in its own way. Edgertonians took delight in odd and quirky nicknames. I remember some of them, but by no means all. So, on a recent visit, I asked the men in The Booth for the nicknames they remembered. Here are the more memorable ones: "Mutt" (for Marion), "Ap" (for Albert), "Fat" (for Florence), "Kell" (for Caroline), "Flop" (whose real name was John), "Tiny" (who was huge), "Jumbo" (who was stocky but not huge), "Big Jumbo" (who was really huge), "Lugs" (for Lugene), "Dumbo," "Punky," "Sleep," "Snake," "Crowbar," "Oinky," "Squeaky" (who had a squeaky voice), "Bear," "Snap," "Satch," "Speed" (who was very slow at his auto-repair business), "Dinky," "Tink," "Buckshot," "Yurdie," "Catchem" (the town cop), "Cheeseball," and "Doo-Dad." Cheeseball got his name when he walked out of a local restaurant without paying for his beer and cheeseball, and the waitress called down the street after him, "Hey, Cheeseball!" Doo-Dad was so named when he made the high school basketball team and went to the local department store to buy a jockstrap. The clerk, an elderly widow known around town as a character, asked what size he needed. He shrugged and said he didn't know. She said, "Well, what size is your doo-dad?" He made the mistake of reporting this exchange to his buddies!

Back in Bigelow, we saw our relatives on Dad's side every Sunday after church; we saw our relatives on our birth mother's side, the Feenstras, less often, maybe once a month on average. They lived in and around Worthington, ten miles away, which, in those days, seemed quite a distance. Upon moving to Edgerton we had a new set of relatives, the Hanenburgs, and we now saw our Wolterstorff and Feenstra relatives only infrequently.

The Hanenburgs were and are a remarkable family. We lived in the village, as did Uncle Ap and Aunt Trena and their family; the rest of the Hanenburgs were farmers. After morning church, they all came to our house—aunts and uncles, cousins, everybody—a boisterous crowd. There were home-baked sweets in abundance, a lot of coffee, and the most dazzling intellectual experience possible for a young teenager. Enormous discussions and arguments erupted in our living room, no predicting the topic: about the sermon, about theology, about politics, about the herbicides that were then being introduced on farms, about music, about why there weren't as many fish in the lakes as there were before, about the new dam in South Dakota and what it would do to the Native Americans in the area, about the local schools, about the mayor, the town cop, the Dutch Festival, Harold Stassen, Hubert Humphrey. Everyone who wanted to take part took part: women, men, teenagers, grandfather. Sometimes it became intense. When it was time to go, they all embraced and went their way.

What strikes me now, in retrospect, is that an intellectual life was being lived out in our living room, a life of the mind. It was there that I acquired the ability to separate the person from the argument. To disagree with something someone said is not to attack the person who said it—provided, of course, one's disagreement is respectful.

The ability to separate person from argument is essential to my profession of philosophy. Philosophy lives on disagreement; consensus would kill it off. When I taught an introduction to philosophy course, it almost always turned out that there were a few students in the class who had not acquired the ability to separate person from argument. Someone would say something in class discussion, another member of the class would disagree with what he or she had said, whereupon a look of dejection would cross the face of the first person, sometimes tears. I took it as part of my calling to help those who were not able to separate person from argument to develop the

31

ability to do so. Every now and then I also had to teach a student how to disagree respectfully.

The fact that they all embraced before going their separate ways indicated that the Hanenburgs loved and cared about each other. Their love and care took the usual forms of helping out with work when someone was shorthanded, taking care of someone who was sick, bringing over a freshly baked pie, and the like. Now and then it took an extraordinary form.

Jump ahead some years. Uncle Dewey Hanenburg and his wife, Christine, lived in Chicago; Aunt Clara, the youngest sister of Dewey, and her husband, Bill, lived in Cleveland. Dewey and Christine were very conservative in their social and political views; Clara and Bill were very progressive. One year, Dewey and Christine invited Bill and Clara to ride with them to visit the relatives in Edgerton. On the way, Dewey and Clara got into a ferocious argument about politics, in which Dewey insulted Clara. When they got to Edgerton, Clara, still feeling hurt and bruised, told the relatives what had happened. This breach in the family had to be repaired. So three or four of my cousins got Dewey and Clara together, had them sit facing each other, and made Dewey apologize to Clara for what he had said. Clara accepted Dewey's apology, they stood up, and embraced, tears flowing.

At that time, Edgerton had a considerable number of eccentrics, their eccentricity encouraged, no doubt, by the insularity of village life in those days. These people did what they wanted and said what they thought; they had no filter between thought and tongue. Considerateness was often combined in them with thoughtlessness in the most baffling way.

There were and are many good storytellers in Edgerton, the men in The Booth among them. Some of my cousins are the best. "Did you hear about?" or "Do you remember when?"—and off they are on a story about some barely credible marvel, some oddity, some hilarity. Most of their stories are about something that really happened, usually embellished a bit.

Many of my cousins' stories are about Grandpa Hanenburg, whom we grandchildren called "Grandpa Pete," and his good friend Mr. Lobbes, the retired Christian school principal. Both men were lovable eccentrics, and both were devout. Members of the family still remember Grandpa Pete's long and eloquent extemporaneous prayers before meals in which he addressed God as if the two were on intimate terms with each other. Mr. Lobbes often preached in neighboring churches.

Grandpa Pete was widowed in 1927 and had retired from farming by the time I got to know him. He made no secret of the fact that he had never liked farming, and the lore in the family was that he did only enough farm work to get by. He much preferred reading and discussing Dutch theology. There was a deep love of learning in him, as there was in most of his ten children. Only Dewey went to college, and, of the others, only the two youngest, Clara and Ted, finished high school; the Depression had forced the others to drop out of school early. The love of learning that I came to recognize in them took the form of regret and longing: regret that their schooling had ended so early, and longing to know what lay behind those doors that had been closed to them. It was with deep pride and gratitude that they saw their own children graduate from college.

The Grandpa Pete stories that circulate among his grandchildren call for oral telling: when written down, they lose their inimitability, in good measure because Grandpa's Dutch accent is lost. That said, allow me to narrate three of them, the second and third about episodes that I personally witnessed. Many of the Grandpa Pete stories are long and winding, in the manner of the best of Garrison Keillor's stories. But these are short.

Mr. Lobbes was Grandpa Pete's favorite fishing buddy. Grandpa enjoyed alcohol in its many forms; Mr. Lobbes was a teetotaler. On the way back from fishing one Monday afternoon, Lobbes remarked, as they were driving past a roadside tavern with a bad reputation in the area, "They should take a stick of dynamite and blow that place to smithereens." Grandpa Pete replied, "Yah, Lobbes, you don't make sense. On Sunday you try to preach 'em into heaven and on Monday you want to blow 'em all to hell."

Our family walked to church. We would arrive twenty minutes or so before the service began, seat ourselves in our customary pew near the front, and sit in silence. As others entered, they too sat in silence. Grandpa Pete always sat in the pew ahead of us, usually arriving about ten minutes before the service began. One Sunday, shortly before the beginning of the service, when almost everybody had taken their places and silence filled the sanctuary, he became agitated. He wiggled back and forth, raised himself a bit, sat down, wiggled back and forth, raised himself a bit, sat down. After a minute or so of this agitated behavior, Mother leaned forward and placed her hands firmly on his shoulders in an attempt to get him to calm down. He pushed her hands away, stood up, turned around to face her, and said, in a loud voice, "Jen, it's me bowels, it's me bowels." I put my face in my hands. A look of horror must have crossed the faces of the adults in the church; the children would barely have been able to contain their laughter. Everybody knew that Mr. Hanenburg was eccentric, but this was over the top!

Grandpa Pete was very hard of hearing. He tried hearing aids, but the ones that were available in those days didn't help much. The pew ahead of us was wired for sound. After seating himself, Grandpa would put on the earphones, plug them into the device on the back of the pew ahead of him, turn it on and adjust the volume. One Sunday, he could not get the device to work. After putting the earphones on and off several times and fiddling with the dial, he stood up, turned halfway around, and, waving the earphones, said in Dutch, in a voice that everyone could hear, "Wat is 't met dit God-verdomde ding?" ("What is it with this God-damned thing?"). After church, the relatives appointed Uncle Jack, a son-in-law, to take Grandpa aside and tell him that he had to stop talking out loud in church. It did not go well. Grandpa's response was, "What, am I the only sinner?"

My aunts and uncles regarded the telling of Grandpa Pete stories as mockery; they didn't join in. Not even in retrospect did they find his behavior in church humorous; they found it deeply embarrassing. After a few stories they would say, "But you have to remember that Pa was more than just an eccentric." They were right about that, of course; but I can testify that, for us, his grandchildren, telling Grandpa Pete stories is not mockery but our way of affectionately keeping alive and honoring the memory of someone who was one of a kind. In him, unrestrained earthiness was combined with deep piety in the most astonishing way. In him, there was no guile. He died in 1975, within three weeks of his ninety-eighth birthday.

In the spring of 1945, early in my thirteenth year, Father announced that I would be working for Uncle Chuck, a younger brother of Mother Jen, on his farm. He said that Chuck's own children were still young and that he needed help with chores and farm work. Dad did not ask me whether I would like to work for Uncle Chuck on the farm; he simply announced that I would be working for Uncle Chuck on the farm. I don't recall resenting this peremptory announcement. That's just how it was. A few months later, Dad announced to Henrietta that she would be doing housework for Aunt Agnes—another of Mother Jen's siblings—on their farm.

Uncle Chuck and Aunt Kell lived about three miles north of town. I was to do morning chores, take the bus to school, return on the bus after school, and do evening chores. On weekends and during the summer I would do farm work in addition to chores. Essentially, I was what was called, in those days, a "hired man," the pay in my case being room and board—nothing more. My other obligations included babysitting my young cousins when Uncle Chuck and Aunt Kell visited relatives or friends and when they went to town once a week to shop for groceries.

I never again lived at home for any length of time. When I worked for Uncle Chuck, I would spend Sundays at home; in later years, I would occasionally live at home for a few days, sometimes for a few weeks. But those were interludes. From my thirteenth year on, I was "out of the house," supporting myself.

Uncle Chuck gave me a great deal of responsibility. The farm had not yet been electrified; electricity came a couple of years later. (I vividly remember the excitement of a sudden blaze of lights on a May evening. In anticipation of the current being turned on, we had flipped all the light switches to ON.) After I had learned to milk cows, initially by hand, I did most of the morning chores alone: I milked and fed the cows and fed the pigs and chickens; Chuck stayed in bed for an hour or so after I was roused by the alarm clock. I also did most of the evening chores alone. When it came to chores, I had the basic responsibility.

In retrospect, Uncle Chuck was a demanding taskmaster, not hard or harsh, but demanding, though I don't recall thinking of it that way at the time. I do recall feeling resentment now and then over the fact that, while I was doing morning chores, he was lying in bed; but I didn't dwell on it. I also recall feeling some resentment when I asked, one summer, whether I could take swimming lessons in the village once a week—and was told that I could not be spared on the farm. I learned to swim when I was a graduate student at Harvard and took swimming lessons along with those freshmen who had not yet learned to swim. In those days, you had to be able to swim in order to graduate from Harvard College.

In the summer, my responsibilities multiplied. Between morning and evening chores I did farm work: pitched manure, shocked oats, cultivated corn, whatever needed to be done. I worked alone much of the time. In the nature of the case, cultivating corn is solo work.

Not so for installing and repairing fences; two can work together at fencing. But Uncle Chuck taught me how to install and repair fences and then set me to doing it by myself.

One summer, Uncle Chuck, Aunt Kell, and their children went on vacation for a week, leaving me behind to take care of the farm. Between morning and evening chores I was to shingle the barn. In those days, shinglers did not secure themselves with ropes. Apparently, nobody—including me—gave any thought to the real possibility that I might fall off the roof, be severely injured, and be unable to call for help.

But there was more to Uncle Chuck than a demanding taskmaster. He loved the land. When he bought the farm, a few years before I began working for him, the soil had been depleted in many places by bad farming practices. He took great pride in improving it and bringing back its fertility. He openly disliked chickens, and he put up with dairy cows and pigs—but horses he loved. He gave them royal names, such as Prince, Queen, Lord, and so on. When I worked for him, farming was in transition from horsepower to tractor power, and Chuck was extremely reluctant to let his work horses go. One of his horses was a riding pony named Lady. I rode Lady often, always bareback—to get the cows from the pasture, and just for sheer delight after supper in the summer. On a few occasions I rode her the three miles to school in town, where I was the envy of my classmates: no one else rode a pony to school.

Did I enjoy farm work? Much of it I didn't mind, and I got satisfaction from doing well whatever I was assigned to do. But I don't think I ever really enjoyed most of the work. A good deal of farm work in those days was hard, onerous, tedious, dirty, dusty, and stinky. It could be bitterly cold in the winter and excruciatingly hot in the summer. Farm work today is different: the labor is highly mechanized and much less strenuous. Tractors now have heaters and air-conditioners.

What I did miss for a while, and still do miss sometimes, is the contact with nature: the look and feel of the soil, the smells and sounds of animals, of chickens chasing bugs, the sting of the wind, fierce thunderstorms, ferocious blizzards, dew across the pasture, the greening of the fields in the spring, the ripening of grain in the summer, the sweet smell of new hay, the sour smell of fermented silage, the sight of pheasants, barn cats, swallows.

After my senior year in high school, I never again worked on a farm. Every now and then I hear city-dwellers talk rhapsodically about buying a small farm somewhere, leaving behind the noise and stir of the city, and becoming a gentleman (or gentlewoman) farmer. They have no idea of what they are getting into.

Uncle Chuck died of melanoma on January 13, 1989, at the age of eighty. (Teaching responsibilities prevented me from attending his funeral.) Though the news of his death was not unexpected, nonetheless it was, for me, a blow. He and my father were the most influential figures in my life as a teenager. The years I worked for him were deeply formative. I learned a lot about farming, of course, but more important, I absorbed his deep love for the earth and for its fecundity. And I learned to take responsibility.

Every time I got back to Edgerton, after leaving for college and places beyond, I would go out to the farm to visit him and Aunt Kell. He was always interested in what I was doing. Once, as we were leaning on the gate to the barnyard, watching the cows, he turned to me and said, "Nick, you're in philosophy, right? Tell me, what is philosophy?" I remember his response, after I had done my best to explain what philosophy is: "I think I get it. That's really interesting. I'm glad I asked." And he wrapped his arm around my shoulder.

In September 1947, I enrolled as a junior in Western Christian High School in Hull, Iowa, about sixty miles due south of Edgerton. In those days, the Christian school in Edgerton, which my siblings and

I attended, did not go beyond the tenth grade—hence my enrollment in Western Christian High.

When the US Supreme Court, in *Brown v. Board of Education* (1954), ordered the integration of public schools, private schools sprang up in the American South to offer segregated education to white students whose parents wanted them to remain in whites-only schools. Some of those schools called themselves "Christian." In recent years, schools calling themselves "Christian" have been established across the country with the aim of protecting students from modern science and American culture. Students are taught that the earth is six thousand years old, that evolution is a myth, that climate change is a hoax perpetrated by a cabal of scientists, and so forth. The Christian schools that my siblings and I attended had very different origins from those of the former, and they operated with a very different philosophy from that of the latter.

In the last decades of the nineteenth century, the Dutch theologian and politician Abraham Kuyper led what came to be called "the school struggle." Kuyper and his followers in the Netherlands were convinced that the worldview shaping education in the Dutch public schools was secular, and they wanted an education shaped by a Christian worldview as an alternative. Their aim was not to protect students from the surrounding society and culture but to equip them to engage society and culture as Christians. They argued that justice required that the state support both forms of education. Eventually they won the struggle.

When followers of Kuyper immigrated to the United States in the latter decades of the nineteenth century and the early decades of the twentieth, they viewed the American public school system through Kuyperian eyes. They perceived that education in American public schools was being shaped by a secular worldview, and they wanted their children to have an alternative education shaped by a Christian worldview. So they set about establishing Christian schools, foregoing public funding. The system of Christian schools that they established is comparable to the Catholic and Lutheran school systems, not to the segregated schools of the American South or the protectionist schools of recent years.

Western Christian High was founded in 1919. For many years—and still when I attended in the 1940s—it was the only four-year Christian high school in the area, drawing students not only from northwest Iowa but also from southwest Minnesota and eastern South Dakota. Early every Monday morning during the school year, about fifteen of us from Edgerton rode the sixty miles to Hull in a Western Christian school bus, returning home on Friday afternoons. In my junior year, I roomed and boarded in town; in my senior year, I worked for room and board for a farmer a few miles outside of Hull who raised minks for their pelts. We fed them mainly horse meat, and now and then we, too, ate horse meat.

My father told me at the time that a donor was paying my tuition, but to this day, I do not know who that was. Much later, I learned that Mother Jen was very upset over the fact that I was being given the privilege of attending Western whereas no one was making it possible for Henrietta to attend. She attended the public high school in Edgerton. Mother was right to have been upset—it *wasn't* fair. Though I now know that Henrietta was envious, and rightly so, I don't recall her saying so at the time. She was a year behind me in school because, when she and I were in the fifth grade back in Bigelow, our teacher came by early in the school year to suggest to my parents that I be skipped ahead to the sixth grade, and my parents agreed. If there was any discussion of the effect this might have on Henrietta, I do not recall hearing it.

Dad set great store on our doing well in school. I consistently got good grades, as did my sisters, both of whom went on to become nurses, and my youngest brother, Ivan. Cornie (Cornelius) did not. Cornie is very bright: he became a supervisor for a firm that built water-treatment and sewage-treatment plants across Iowa and South Dakota and learned to read complicated blueprints with ease. But he chafed at the routine of school. And whereas Dad was sparing in words of praise for our good grades, he was unsparing in scolding Cornie for his poor grades: "Why aren't you working harder and getting better grades?" Cornie must have heard an implicit "like Nick" in that admonition. Dad never understood that Cornie was one of that considerable number of people who cannot stand the routine of school and who are unmoved by being scolded and told to work harder.

I loved Western, though at the time I probably would not have been able to explain why. Looking back, three things stand out. From my schooling up to that point, I had acquired the idea that school education consists of covering the material. Whether or not that metaphor was ever explicitly used, the idea conveyed was that, in each course, there was a discrete body of material to be covered and that, if all went well, by the end of the semester we would have covered the material for that semester. Next semester, we would be presented with a new body of material to be covered.

The image that comes to mind when I look back on my education at Western Christian High is that of vistas being opened up rather than material being covered. In my American and English literature courses, which I remember well, I had the sense of getting a glimpse of the vast landscape of American and English literature. No doubt what contributed to this was that we were assigned to read works that were not in the textbook; I got the sense of *more, much more*. The same was true for my course in American history, which I also remember well; I got a glimpse of the vast landscape of American history. There was *so much more*.

When I became a college professor, I learned, to my surprise, that a good many of my colleagues worked with the metaphor of *covering the material*, some of them consciously so. That was especially true of those in the natural sciences. When curricular revisions were up for consideration, and a dean would suggest that the hours of class time in their courses be slightly reduced, they would protest that, if that were to happen, they would not be able to "cover the material." I cynically thought—but never said—that what they called "the material" was what some Ivy League professor, sitting in his summer home in Vermont, had decided to put into the textbook he had been commissioned by some publisher to write.

In philosophy, it makes no sense to think in terms of covering the material. What would it be to cover the material in a course in modern philosophy, or in a course in ethics? There's always more. One opens up a vista, hoping that some students will find that vista sufficiently attractive to want to explore it further, knowing in advance that others will decide that their initial glimpse is enough.

What I also loved about my time at Western was the camaraderie. I had not realized that I was lonely. Before I went to work for Uncle Chuck, Henrietta and I had seldom been separated; after that, I saw her and the other members of my family only briefly, on Sundays. During the week, I lived with Uncle Chuck and his family, well aware that I was not a member of their family but a hired man who happened to be a nephew. From the time I was thirteen, I had had no sustained contact with my parents and siblings. And as for my classmates in Edgerton, the only chance I got to associate with them was during school hours. Immediately after classes were over, I got on the bus to do chores on the farm, leaving no time to "hang out" with friends. I was never good at athletics, but even if I had been, I would almost certainly have been told that I could not participate in after-school athletics because I was needed on the farm.

Now I was experiencing the wonderful camaraderie of riding together with classmates for an hour and a half twice a week. And in my junior year, when I was boarding in town, there was the additional camaraderie of hanging out after school with classmates who were also boarding in town. I was no longer lonely.

Third—connected to this point about camaraderie—was the fact that, whereas previously I knew only people from Bigelow and Edgerton, the classmates I now came to know were from far and wide. The human community was opening up to me, just as vistas of learning were opening up. Edgerton, much as I loved it, was beginning to feel confining.

I was pleased to be invited back to Western Christian High School to give their commencement address in May 2015. I entitled my address "Looking for Good Work," and I discussed what kind of work the graduates should look for when they looked for work. A cousin of mine, whose daughter was in the graduating class that year, talked to me before the ceremony began and reported that his daughter was worried that she would not understand what I said. She came up to me afterwards and said that she had understood every word. I was gratified.

TWO

Vistas

There was never any question *whether* I would go to college, or *where*: I would go to Calvin College in Grand Rapids, Michigan, the college sponsored by the denomination to which my family and I belonged, the Christian Reformed Church. The earnings I got from a job as a carpenter's assistant during the summer (1949) between my senior year of high school and my freshman year of college paid for my tuition, which was low in those days; a part-time job during the academic year at Baker Book House in Grand Rapids paid for room and board.

I was assigned to the shipping department at Baker. After a few months—whether because I had proved incompetent at packing books or because it was judged that my abilities could be put to better use elsewhere—I was assigned to assist in preparing used book catalogues and to do proofreading. I worked at Baker for the entirety of my college career. That, plus summer jobs as a carpenter's assistant, enabled me to work my way through college with only a couple thousand dollars of debt when I graduated. That was not unusual in those days.

I had entered a world of dazzling brightness—exhilarating and intimidating. It was my great good fortune to have Henry Zylstra, a master teacher, for freshman English. He came from my neck of the woods, North Dakota, and had an imposing presence: he was tall and lean, with a craggy face. On the first day of class he used several words I had never heard before: I remember one of them, "chivalrous." Nobody in southwest Minnesota or northwest Iowa used the word "chivalrous." I wrote it down, along with two other words I had never heard before, went to the bookstore, bought a dictionary, and looked up the words when I got back to my room. I copied out their meanings and memorized them. The next class he again used words I had never heard before, and the next, and the next. So I took to carrying a pad of lined paper to class on which I wrote down the unfamiliar words, looked them up in the dictionary when I got to my room, wrote out their meanings, memorized them, and reviewed the meanings of the words I had previously written down. The English language was proving to be vastly more expansive than the idiolect I was familiar with. Vistas!

Zylstra's class proved humbling in another way as well. Each week we had to write an essay, and each time mine came back with the same grade, B. I was not used to getting anything less than A– on papers. Zylstra would write a number of specific comments in the margins; then, at the end, he would write a comment to this effect: "Your essay feels labored." The words varied, but the message was always the same. He was right, I'm sure. My essays felt labored because I had labored over them. Finally, toward the end of the semester, I got an A, then another. I was learning to write.

In subsequent years I took a number of other courses from Zylstra, the most memorable of them being a course in Shakespeare and a course in nineteenth-century English prose and poetry. He made literature come alive, even the gnarly prose of Thomas Carlyle. He lived and breathed poetry. When we were studying a passage in Shakespeare, he would be reminded of another passage in Shakespeare, or a passage in Spenser or Milton, and he would proceed to recite the passage from memory. Or if a passage came to mind that he had not memorized and had not taken along to class, he would single out a student—Berghuis, for example—and say, "Mr. Berghuis, would you go to the library and get book so-and-so for us." The library was nearby and the stacks were open, so in no time Mr. Berghuis would be back with the book. Zylstra would turn to the page and read the passage he had in mind. My fellow students and I wondered to what extent he had planned in advance to send someone to the library and to what extent he decided to do so on the spot.

The faculty acknowledged Zylstra as one of their leaders: when he spoke, they listened—listened because he elevated their thinking. The title of a small volume of essays that he published during the time I was a student says it all: *Testament of Vision*. The book is a testament to the vision of a culturally engaged Christianity, an eloquent call for Christians to be engaged in culture, especially literature, rather than being culture-despisers

In December 1956, at the age of forty-seven, after spending the semester teaching at the Free University of Amsterdam, Zylstra collapsed and died of a heart attack while waiting with his wife for a bus on a street corner in Amsterdam. At the time, I was on a postdoctoral fellowship in Cambridge, England, so it took some time for the news of his death to reach me. When it did, I was shaken. He was one of my heroes.

Toward the end of my freshman year (1950), I was invited to join the staff of the college newspaper, *Chimes*. I later learned that this was at the suggestion of Zylstra. The *Chimes* writers were bright, high-minded, opinionated, literate, raucous, caustic, hilarious—critical of the college administration, of the church, of the government. The repartee was fast and witty. I had received some preparation for this in our living room in Edgerton, but this was of a different order altogether. Though the staff wrote news stories, they weren't really interested in news. Opinion was what they cared about, especially their own. They inserted opinion into news stories, and each week the editor wrote a lengthy editorial delivering his opinions. I became editor in my junior year.

In 2007, all the living former *Chimes* editors and writers were invited back to celebrate the hundredth anniversary of the first publication of *Chimes*. Someone had the idea that each of the former editors should take a bound copy of the *Chimes* for their year, go off somewhere, read through the editorials he or she had written, and offer the group his or her impressions of the editorials they had written—these many years later. I found myself appalled at the long-winded, self-important pomposity and ponderousness of many of mine. One of them began like this:

Modernity is an age of adolescence. Our lives are lived in the immediate passions of the moment.... We try to be daring, but we have not
yet progressed beyond the adolescent daring of wearing the bottoms
of our trousers rolled.

On the other hand we are old, tired, and bored. The happy aban-
don of youth has disappeared from our lives, and we see the comic
spectacle of boys in their teens walking about with gloomy faces
and studied stride as if bearing the burdens of the world upon their
backs.

Truly awful—a T. S. Eliot knockoff! Why had none of my professors taken me aside and suggested that I lighten things up a bit?

At that 2007 gathering I proposed a pomposity competition: each
of the former editors would read aloud the passage from his or her
editorials that they judged to be the most pompous, and a vote would
be taken. I assumed I would win, hands down. To my surprise, my
predecessor as editor, Rod Jellema, tied with me for most pompous
editorial. I had to admit that the vote was fair; Rod was my equal in
pomposity!

Ever since we first met, in the *Chimes* office in the fall of 1950,
Rod and I have been dear friends. He's a wonderful conversationalist,
loves a good story, has a sharp eye for the wonders in this world of
wonders, and is deeply attached to the place on the eastern shore of
Lake Michigan where he grew up. He has had a very distinguished
career as a poet.[1]

I took my first philosophy course in the first semester of my sopho-
more year; Henry Stob was the teacher. I took the course because
all students had to take two philosophy courses, not because I knew

1. Rod Jellema died on May 11, 2018.

what philosophy was and was interested in it. But it was love on first contact. We were about thirty minutes into the first class session when I said to myself, "I don't know whether I'm going to be any good at this, but if I am, this is it." I did not choose philosophy; philosophy chose me.

What was it in those first thirty minutes that gripped me? I don't know. I remember nothing of what Stob said; all I remember is that I was mesmerized. Did he explain what philosophy is? It's a reasonable guess that he did, since the course was entitled Introduction to Philosophy, but I don't remember. I do remember later class sessions in the course, especially the three weeks we spent on a close reading of Augustine's *Confessions*. I had never before witnessed such a close reading of any text, and I was amazed at what Stob found in the text to comment on—amazed also at the *Confessions* themselves. If this was philosophy, I wanted more of it.

I went on to take a number of courses from Stob beyond that first one. He, too, was a master teacher—the equal, in his own way, of Zylstra. Unprepossessing in appearance, he was a magician with words, speaking in beautifully composed sentences, apparently without effort. His eccentricities were as mesmerizing as his speech. He found it impossible to stand for any length of time behind the podium, so he would walk around at the front of the room for a while, and then, without missing a beat, climb onto the desk on which the podium was resting, cross his legs, and continue lecturing from that position.

Close and sympathetic readings of texts was his forte. I think especially of a seminar I took from him on Aquinas's *Summa theologica*. The *Summa* consists of hundreds and hundreds of "questions." By the end of the semester we had gotten through the first twenty or so of these. In my edition of the *Summa*, that comes to about 120 pages. For Catholics, Aquinas is one of the "sainted doctors" of the church. Stob emphasized to us that Aquinas belongs just as much to the intellectual and religious heritage of Protestants as to that of Catholics. Voice your Protestant criticisms if you will, but only after you have acknowledged Aquinas as one of your forebears in the project of Christian thought and only after you have worked hard to understand what he is saying.

Superb teacher though he was, Stob could be sharp with students to whom he took a dislike or who expressed an opinion that he found disagreeable. The faculty acknowledged him, along with Zylstra, as one of their leaders, essentially for the same reason: he articulated a compelling vision of a culturally engaged Christianity.

C ollege proved to be, for me, a journey into self-understanding. Here, in this college of the religious tradition in which I had been reared, Reformed Protestantism, I began to understand the tradition, and thus myself, by watching it at work in some remarkably gifted and dedicated professors. I learned how to live with integrity within the tradition, within any tradition: how to discern and embrace its fundamental contours while treating its details as matters of indifference; how to appropriate what in the tradition is capable of nourishing life in one's own day while leaving the rest behind; how to criticize the tradition from within, expand its scope, celebrate its accomplishments, empathize with its anxieties and its memories of suffering. I think of a passage from the Night section of Part One of Goethe's *Faust*:

> What you have as heritage,
> take now as task;
> For thus you will make it your own.

Vast expansive vistas were being opened up to the culture of the West—to its literature, its philosophy, its theology, its science, everything. Nothing was off-limits. But it was not just one thing after another; there was a vision shaping the entire enterprise. We were challenged to understand and interpret this massive cultural inheritance "in Christian perspective." More than that, we were challenged to embody Christ in culture ourselves—challenged to compose poetry, to write philosophy, to paint paintings that would breathe the spirit of Christ in some way. "There are two cities," said one of our philosophy professors, William Harry Jellema, with gripping charisma, using the terminology of Augustine. Then he would switch to the Latin: "The *civitas dei* and the *civitas mundi*. Your calling is to share in building the *civitas dei*." The recent book by the Yale law professor Antony Kronman, *Why Our Colleges and Universities Have Given Up on the Meaning of Life*, is an eloquent lament on the subject indicated in the title. When I was at Calvin, the college had definitely not given up on the meaning of life.

For me and the students with whom I associated, it was heady stuff. No doubt others were bored stiff by all the visionary talk. And the attitude of some toward the tradition was the opposite of ours: they were angry and chafed under its restrictions and rough edges. Their interest was not Nietzsche *interpreted in* Christian perspective but Nietzsche *as ammunition against* the tradition. The arguments we had were wonderful.

My friends and I were as energized and instructed by each other as we were by our professors. In my junior and senior years I was a member of Plato Club, a student club that met one evening a month to discuss philosophy. Membership was selective: to become a member, one had to apply and be voted in by the current members. At the beginning of the academic year, we chose one or two books for discussion over the course of that year; in preparation for those monthly meetings, one of us would write a paper on the assigned reading for that meeting. After spending an hour or so discussing the paper and the assigned reading, we would drift off into discussing whatever was on our minds. It was exhilarating. Henry Stob, our faculty mentor, faithfully attended every meeting, almost always staying until we broke up, usually around 11:00, after three hours of conversation.

53

Abraham Kuyper, whom I mentioned above, was the spiritual and intellectual eminence behind Calvin College. Born in 1837 (he died in 1920), he was a visionary Dutch polymath—theologian, ordained minister, politician, journalist, activist, prime minister of the Netherlands from 1901 to 1905—who located himself firmly within the Reformed tradition.

At the heart of that tradition, as he saw it, is a distinctive understanding of the interlocking significance of creation, fall, and redemption. When Reformed people survey the cosmos—along with human beings and their works within the cosmos—they see goodness, which they interpret as a reflection of God's goodness, God's excellence. Much of that goodness and excellence they interpret, more specifically, as God's gift to human beings—God's grace, God's favor. God's grace is to be seen both in what *God has created* that serves our flourishing and in what *human beings have created* that serves our flourishing. Behind the cultural products and the social institutions that serve our flourishing is to be seen what Kuyper called God's "common grace."

But when Reformed persons survey the natural world, they see not only goodness and gift, but also evil: frustration of God's desire for the flourishing of human beings, deprivation, suffering, untimely death. And when they survey what human beings have done and made, they see not only goodness and gift, but also sin: violation of the will and purpose of God. The potentials for good inherent in creation have been turned by human beings into life-squelching, oppressive directions. Always some goodness remains; but deep within the sensibility of Reformed individuals is an awareness of the ravages of sin and the pervasiveness of those ravages. Sin has etched its way into the nooks and crannies of our existence—into our art, our reasoning, our technology, everything.

Characteristic of the Reformed tradition is thus a dialectic of Yes and No: Yes to God's creation, No to the ravages of God's creation by that mysterious force that resists—in the form of deprivation, suffering, and untimely death—God's desire for the flourishing of every human creature. And both Yes and No to the deeds and works of human beings.

Corresponding to their holistic view concerning the ravages of sin, Reformed people have a holistic view of the scope of God's redemption. God in Christ did not come just to save souls for heaven; he also came to bring shalom and flourishing here in this life. There is, in Kuyper's strand of the Reformed tradition, a displacement from the emphasis on conversion typical of Anglo-American evangelicals to an emphasis on sanctification, understood holistically. We are called to live holy lives, lives that share in God's desire for the flourishing of each human being until full of years, called to pronounce a discriminating Yes and No, and then, to go beyond making such pronouncements and struggle for renewal.

Kuyper had a distinctive view of the form that struggle should take. I will now go from describing the Reformed position generally, as Kuyper understood it, to describing Kuyper's distinctive contribution. In addition to participating in the life of the church, those who are followers of Christ are called to think, feel, speak, and act as Christians within the institutions and practices they share with their fellow human beings in general. Even if it were possible, they are not to go off by themselves somewhere to set up their own economy, their own polity, their own art world, their own world of scholarship. They are to participate, along with others, in the economy of their country, its polity, its art world, its scholarship.

There is, however, no religiously and morally neutral way of participating. Everyone participates as *who he or she is.* And whatever else each of us may be, we are creatures with convictions about God and the world, about life, about the good and the right. Each of us has a worldview, and that worldview shapes—in subtle and not so subtle ways—what we do when we participate in those shared practices and institutions. It's obvious that human beings differ in their world-views, differ profoundly. Thus it is that the Christian participates—or *should* participate—*as* a Christian, just as the naturalist participates as a naturalist and the humanist as a humanist.

This is the vision that shaped my college education. When it came to the life of the Christian in scholarship, our professors encapsulated the vision in the motto, borrowed from Augustine and the medieval philosopher-theologian Anselm: "faith seeking understanding." Not faith *added to* understanding, not faith *propped up* by understanding, but faith *seeking* understanding. Later I would learn that what Augustine and Anselm meant by that motto is that it is the calling of the Christian intellectual to transmute what he or she already accepts on faith into something that he or she knows—and no longer merely *believes*. What our teachers meant by the motto was that the Christian scholar is called to participate in the academic discipline of, say, psychology by looking at psychological reality through the eyes of faith. By no means will everything in psychology look different to a Christian from how it looks to one who is not a Christian, but there will be much that does look different.

Nothing was said about constructing proofs for God's existence, nothing about assembling evidence for the reliability of Christian Scripture or evidence for Jesus's resurrection. Our professors did not explicitly oppose such projects; they simply showed no interest in them. In particular, they did not suggest that, in order to be entitled to one's Christian faith, one needed proofs or evidence. In the seminar I took from Henry Stob on Aquinas's *Summa theologica* we studied, in depth, Aquinas's "five ways," that is, his five arguments for God's existence. Never once did Stob suggest that the tenability of one's Christian faith hung on whether one or another of Aquinas's "ways" proved sound, or, if none of them proved sound, on whether there was some other argument for God's existence that *was* sound. Neither did he ask whether such arguments might have apologetic value.

This "Kuyperian" version of the Reformed tradition that I imbibed in college has remained mine throughout my life. In some of my writings I have worked it out in greater detail than any of my college professors did (my first attempt at that being my book *Reason within the Bounds of Religion* [1976]); but there have been no reversals, no big changes of mind. The vision has stood me in good stead, giving me direction and orientation throughout my life. As we shall see, it stood me in good stead in my graduate studies at Harvard University.

A few pages back I used the word "charisma" when speaking of William Harry Jellema, known by colleagues and friends as "Harry." He violated almost all the criteria for good teaching that one finds on standard teacher evaluation forms. Did he arrive at class on time? Never. Did he announce tests and examinations well in advance? Never. Were his reading assignments clear? Often not. Did he hold regular office hours? He did not. And so forth, down the line. Yet he was the most charismatic teacher I have ever had. He was handsome—that may have contributed to his charisma—but he was so much more.

In his lecture courses he would arrive two or three minutes late— he had been talking with colleagues in the faculty room—close the door behind him, say in a firm voice as he was striding to the podium, "As we were discussing last time," and off we were for the next fifty minutes. It was gripping. In his lecture courses he mixed lecturing with Socratic-style questioning. Holding a sheaf of cards that had the names of the students in the class typed on them, he would shuffle through it and settle on a name—"Mr. Vander Meer," let us say—and proceed to conduct a Socratic dialogue with Mr. Vander Meer for the next ten or fifteen minutes. It could have been terrifying; perhaps for some it was. But he did it gently, sometimes with humor.

In the first semester of my junior year I met Alvin Plantinga, who had spent his freshman year (1950–51) at Harvard University. Having

learned about Jellema's reputation from his father, Cornelius Plantinga, who had just begun teaching psychology at Calvin, Al sat in on
several of Jellema's lectures during Harvard's spring break. He decided on the spot to transfer to Calvin at the end of the academic year.
We immediately became friends, and have remained so ever since.
Jellema regularly taught a course in Kant's *Critique of Pure Reason*; in
my senior year, Al and I were the only students in the course. He and
I have both given the Gifford Lectures at St Andrews University in
Scotland, the famous lecture series whose origins go back to the late
nineteenth century, and we've remarked that Jellema would have
chuckled had he known that all the students in one of his courses
would be Gifford lecturers!

Jellema had received his graduate training in philosophy at the
University of Michigan in the 1920s and had begun teaching philosophy at Calvin immediately after receiving his doctorate. When I arrived at Calvin, a considerable number of his former students were
teaching philosophy around the country, most notably William Frankena at the University of Michigan and O. K. Bouwsma at the University of Nebraska. In the late 1930s, tensions had arisen between
Jellema and the president of the college, Ralph Stob, who accused Jellema of theological liberalism. The lore that circulated in the college
when I was a student was that this accusation was cover for a conflict
of personalities. No official charges were ever filed against Jellema,
but the controversy led him to resign and take a position in the philosophy department of Indiana University. The year before I enrolled
as a student, he had returned to Calvin in triumph. Ralph Stob had left
the office of president (under considerable pressure), a new president
was in place, and the faculty regarded Jellema as vindicated.

Why did he return? I never asked him, but I'm sure I know. He
was deeply committed to the cause of Christian thought in general,
and to the cause of Christian philosophy in particular. At Calvin, he
could advance those causes in a way that would have been impossible at Indiana University.

Heroes have clay feet. Jellema was chairman of the philosophy department when I returned to Calvin to teach. In my second year, I had a student in my logic class of whom Jellema was, I knew, quite fond and admiring. This student was definitely capable, but she failed to turn in some of the assignments, so I gave her a final grade of C in the course, without giving a thought to the fact that my chairman liked and admired her. Shortly after the grades came out, he called on the phone and asked me to come over to his house. He was angry, and gave me a stern dressing down. The student deserved better than a C, so I would have to learn to do a better job of assigning grades. He insisted that I change the grade. Bruised and cowed, I drove to the college, went to the registrar's office, and filed a change-of-grade form.

Jellema did not write much, and what he did write was convoluted and ungainly. It was his speech that was compelling, and his bearing, both intellectual and personal, had a grandeur that carried great authority. His legacy is to be found in the thought and lives of his students and *their* students.

College was not all high seriousness. I formed warm friendships, many of which endure to this day. And there were pranks. The largest building on campus, containing the main administration offices along with the chapel and some classrooms, had a cupola, with steps leading up into the cupola from the second floor. The lore among students in my day was that, a few years back, some students had led a cow up those stairs at night. When students and faculty arrived the next morning, a mysterious mooing came from somewhere above. Eventually, the janitors discovered the source of the sound. I am told that one can lead a cow up a flight of stairs but that she will refuse to go back down. The cow was too heavy to carry, so the janitors had to kill and dismember it up in the cupola. That was the story. I have no idea whether it was true.

I participated in one of the pranks. A plaster replica of Michelangelo's *Moses*, about three feet high, stood on a pedestal outside the chapel. One night a group of us partly disassembled a Model T Ford, got it through the wide entry doors into the lobby of the administration building, reassembled it, put Moses in the driver's seat, strung a braided rope around the assemblage to deter people from touching it, and put up a nicely lettered sign:

> Mount Sinai Express
> Reduced Round Trip Fare $1.00
> Place Money in Container

Some of the conspirators had been assigned to see to it that the night watchman was not on the scene, but I never learned how they managed to do that.

We, the conspirators, showed up shortly after the doors opened in the morning and gleefully witnessed the amazement that crossed the faces of students and faculty as they entered the lobby. Word spread rapidly, and soon there was a huge crush of people and great hilarity. The janitors set about dismantling what we had wrought, though they proved much clumsier at getting the Model T out of the building than we had been at getting it in.

All went well until early afternoon, when all of the conspirators were summoned to appear at four o'clock in the president's office (we never discovered how the president learned of our involvement). The president, William Spoelhof, had us stand against the wall around the large table in his conference room—I think there were about twelve of us—and proceeded to chew us out. But what caught my attention was not what he was saying but his tone of voice: his tone seemed to me to indicate that he thought this was all jolly good fun, but that it was his duty, as president, to reprimand us. Our only punishment was his verbal scolding.

Ours was the first in a series of pranks involving Moses over the next couple of decades. Eventually, a faculty member on the college disciplinary committee became so exasperated that he took a sledge hammer to Moses and smashed him to bits.

I first met Claire Kingma in the *Chimes* office, shortly after the beginning of my junior year and her freshman year (1951). She got my attention immediately: she was beautiful and had flair—a flair in her bearing, a flair in how she dressed—but not a flamboyant flair, a restrained flair, if that makes sense. She did not look around to see how other women dressed and then dress that way. She decided *for herself* how she would dress. Of course, someone might decide for herself how she would dress and the result might be appalling. Not so with Claire. Nothing eccentric: a scarf worn in an unexpected way, an unusual fabric, an unusual style of jacket. Flair, but never flash. I learned later that she sewed most of her clothes herself. She still does, and to this day, people come up to her and tell her how much they admire something she is wearing, always something she has sewn herself. Later I came to see that her way of dressing was just one mark of her talent for putting a stamp on things in her surroundings. She has an eye for the distinctive and the beautiful.

For a couple of years she considered a career in medicine, but she ended up majoring in English literature. Reading is—and always has been—one of her great loves. I sometimes tease her by saying that the Platonic form of The Reader Itself has been fully instantiated in her. Though it was her dress and the way she bore herself that initially drew my attention, it was her character, her "inscape," that soon evoked my love. I borrow the term "inscape" from the early twentieth-century English poet Gerard Manley Hopkins, who used it to refer to the distinct character of individual things. There is a moving passage in one of his letters in which he laments the felling of a tree in his garden because an inscape that he had come to love was now forever gone.

Vistas

The ash tree growing in the corner of the garden was felled. It was lopped first. I heard the sound, and looking out and seeing it maimed there came at that moment a great pang and I wished to die and not to see the inscapes of the world destroyed any more.[2]

For reasons that go beyond not only telling but understanding, each of us finds something about the inscape of certain persons that attracts us and draws us to them. We find ourselves loving them. Each of us develops a distinct contour of such loves, loving one person for her particular inscape, another for his, loving one more than another. What was it about Claire that made me fall in love with her? What is it about her inscape that makes me continue in love? Words fail—it's ineffable.

Claire is a person of strong emotions, with a unique gift for conversation in which another person opens up to her, and she to them. Over and over, someone who sat next to her at some function will remark to me afterward how memorable they found their conversation to be. She is drawn to those who are troubled, and they to her. She has an extraordinary gift for saying what they find helpful.

Ours has been a traditional marriage, in the sense that my profession has determined where we have lived. Each time I have been offered a certain position, we have discussed together whether I should take it, and each time we have come to agreement. But the effect has been that she has accompanied me. She spent her junior year of college at Vassar, then an exclusively women's college. There she felt affirmed as a woman in a way she had not felt affirmed before; later, with the rise of the feminist movement in the mid-1970s, she became an ardent and active feminist and remains so to this day. I have strongly affirmed and supported her in that. Both of us are mystified, and somewhat hurt, by the fact that feminism is not an

2. John Pick, ed., *A Hopkins Reader* (New York: Oxford University Press, 1953), 57.

62

issue for many of the women we know in the generations that have followed ours.

For me, feminism has been not only a cause I have supported but a learning experience. I have been sensitized, by Claire and others, to the ways in which women are put down, many of them ways in which I was complicit but to which I had been oblivious. By language, for example. I open my book *Art in Action* (1980), and in the table of contents I find these headings: "Artistically Man Acts," "Man as Earthling," "Man's Vocation," "Man's End." I am now appalled and embarrassed by such sexist language. I wish I had been awakened earlier and had never written those words.

We entered the covenant of marriage as two persons in love with each other. Soon our identities became inextricably intertwined, so that neither could answer the question "Who are you?" without referring to the other. I plan in the light of her plans, and she plans in the light of mine. I rejoice in her rejoicing and grieve in her grieving, and she in mine. We have become two in one. The love has endured, sustained and nourished by commitment.

If the gift for conversation is inherited, Claire got it from her father, Jan Willem Kingma. He was the most gifted conversationalist I have ever known, seemingly on any topic, politics excepted, often to the family's dismay: "Can't he ever stop talking?" The Kingmas were as remarkable in their way as the Hanenburgs were in theirs. The family had recently moved to Grand Rapids because Claire's father had taken a position as instructor in Dutch language and literature at Calvin College. Before moving to Grand Rapids, they had lived for a good many years in Philadelphia, where, for ten years or so, Claire's father had held a job in a tobacco shop in downtown Philly. But I doubt that tobacco, in any form, ever crossed his lips.

Claire's mother, Gezina, was an artist. She made, among other things, stunningly beautiful and imaginative embroideries; all of the five children have inherited some of them. Claire's father, though not himself an artist, was an art lover. During the years that he worked in the tobacco shop, from the mid-1930s to the mid-1940s, he would use his free time on Fridays to attend auctions in downtown art galleries, looking for bargains. He concentrated on oriental art, got himself deeply informed, and built up a truly remarkable collection at small cost. He could talk at length about each piece, telling you when and where it had been made and, with great enthusiasm, drawing attention to what it was about the piece that called for admiration and enjoyment. The love of art I had acquired from my own father was now joining forces with the love of art I was acquiring from Claire's parents.

How did Jan Willem go from working in a tobacconist's shop in Philadelphia to teaching Dutch language and literature at Calvin College? I know only fragments of how it came about. He had emigrated with his parents from the Dutch city of Amersfoort when he was seven, so he grew up speaking Dutch. When I got to know him, it became evident to me that he had a deep love for both Dutch and English literature and, though he had never done graduate work, was well-informed in both. In the mid-1940s he felt called to become a teacher. So he resigned his position at the tobacco store and began teaching English in nearby high schools. It became clear rather soon that he was not cut out for teaching high-school students, so he began to look for some other kind of teaching position.

That is the background, but it does not explain how Calvin came to offer him a position as instructor in Dutch language and literature. Perhaps the position was advertised and he applied (there would not have been many qualified applicants). Or perhaps the administration at Calvin had heard about him through the grapevine. In any case, he was not entirely happy teaching at Calvin either, partly because he had not done graduate work and felt insecure teaching at the college level. So, after three years, he resigned and spent two years doing graduate work at the University of Michigan. He was then offered a position in the English department at Westmont College in Santa Barbara, California. At the same time, Claire's mother was offered a position in the art department there. Westmont proved a perfect fit for both of them, and they were much loved by students and faculty alike.

Though I loved philosophy, and graduated from Calvin in 1953 with a philosophy major, throughout my college years I seriously entertained the possibility of attending seminary and becoming a theologian. When I was in my senior year, I had to choose: Would I spend my life as a philosopher or as a theologian?

Sometime during the course of that year, my philosophy professors urged me to apply for admission to the graduate program in philosophy at Harvard, and also to apply for a couple of fellowships. They knew that I was considering seminary, but they made the point that, even if I did eventually decide to go into theology, some graduate training in philosophy would stand me in good stead. I could postpone the final decision for a few years. Their advice was persuasive, so I applied to Harvard, was admitted, and was awarded the two fellowships. Off I went to Harvard in the fall of 1953.

The first year I worked extremely hard. The training in philosophy I had received at Calvin was excellent: it had opened up the vast vista of the Western philosophical tradition. But whereas at Calvin we *studied* philosophy, immersing ourselves in the great philosophical texts of the past, at Harvard the talk was all about *doing* philosophy, that is, thinking philosophically for oneself. Since doing philosophy requires that one be au courant with what is going on in philosophy at the time, the graduate program at Harvard was heavy on contemporary philosophy and light on the history of philosophy. At Calvin I had studied no contemporary philosophy, so I had a lot of catching up to do.

What added to the pressure was that "prelims" (preliminary examinations) were given at the end of the first year of graduate study. In most American philosophy departments, prelims are given after two years of course work, and are used to determine whether the student should be allowed to complete the doctoral program by writing a doctoral dissertation, or should instead be invited to leave with a master's degree. The prelims are so called because they are preliminary to writing a dissertation. Nobody ever explained to us why, in the Harvard philosophy department in those days, prelims were given after only one year of course work.

There were, as I recall, twenty-one of us in that first-year class, only one of whom was a woman. The prelims consisted of four three-hour written examinations, two a day over two days. When the results were posted a few days later, four of us were allowed to continue in the doctoral program, one was allowed to continue for a master's degree, and the others, including the one woman, were sent packing with nothing to show for their year-long effort. The gloom could be sliced with a knife.

The purpose of giving prelims after one year of course work was now clear. Instead of admitting to the doctoral program only students who could be expected to finish the degree—which, to the best of my knowledge, is what all graduate programs do today—the Harvard philosophy department was being lax in its admission criteria and using the prelims to winnow down the class to those who could be expected to complete the doctoral program. It was cruel.

Those were the glory days of the Harvard philosophy department. Willard van Orman Quine, Karl Hempel, C. I. Lewis, Nelson Goodman, and D. C. Williams were all on the faculty, to name just the five most prominent figures.

There was a lot of buzz about so-called logical positivism, a movement I had not heard about at Calvin. One of the claims of the positivists was that sentences that purport to be about God are in fact meaningless—not false, but meaningless. It wasn't long before I discerned that this claim was not a drinking in of objective facts about meaning but was, instead, an implication of the positivist worldview. The "take" on philosophy that I had absorbed at Calvin, namely, that philosophy is, at bottom, the articulation of worldviews, was now standing me in good stead.

At the heart of the positivist worldview was the conviction that modern natural science is the only mode of inquiry that holds genuine promise for human progress. Religion and the speculative philosophical subdiscipline of metaphysics are dead ends. If that is one's view, it is then incumbent on one to offer some criterion for demarcating natural science from those dead ends. The positivists proposed, for this purpose, a thesis concerning the meaning of sentences. To have meaning, they said, a sentence must be either empirically verifiable or analytically true or false. Examples of the latter sort of sentence are "All bachelors are unmarried" and "2 + 2 = 4," the idea behind calling them "analytically" true being that they are true, so it was thought, by virtue of the meaning of the terms, analysis of their meanings then being sufficient to establish their truth. The sentences of modern natural science (and mathematics) satisfied their criterion of meaning, so the positivists claimed, whereas the sentences of religion and metaphysics did not.

In the past, religion and metaphysics had sometimes been dismissed on the ground that there was no way of determining whether what they claimed was true or false. Now they were dismissed on the ground that nothing was being claimed: the sentences were meaningless.

Not for a moment was I tempted by the faith of the positivists in natural science. So, rather than being cast into religious doubt by their claim that speech that purports to be about God is meaningless, I found myself viewing their claims about meaning with a mixture of annoyance and bemusement. I was supported in this posture by D. C. Williams, whose attitude was, "This, too, shall pass." As indeed it did. Though positivism appeared robust at the time, it was in fact near death, collapsing a few years later from difficulties internal to the program.

Some positivists worried that their criterion of meaning was too narrow. The sentences of ethics—"Murder is wrong," for example— are neither empirically verifiable nor analytically true or false. Are they then to be dismissed as meaningless? Clearly that would not do. But what proved decisive for the death of positivism was not that problem, but the fact that the positivists found themselves incapable of explaining the concept of "empirical verifiability" so that it would do the work they asked of it. When they explained the concept in such a way that the sentences of religion and metaphysics were not empirically verifiable, it turned out that much of theoretical physics was also not empirically verifiable, and hence not meaningful. When they explained the concept in such a way that theoretical physics as a whole was empirically verifiable, it turned out that most religion and metaphysics was also empirically verifiable, and hence meaningful.

The mentality of logical positivism hangs on today among a few very liberal theologians and among some vocal opponents of religion—Sam Harris, for example, and the other so-called new atheists. But it can safely be said that there are no longer any logical positivists among professional philosophers. In the *New York Review of Books* of December 21, 2017, Jim Holt writes: "Today logical positivism has a whiff of the ridiculous about it. It conjures up a priggishly narrow-minded style of philosophy—scientistic, hair-splitting, at once arrogant and naïve."[3] Exactly.

I made no secret of the fact that I was a Christian; yet, despite all the buzz about positivism, no one ever attacked or belittled me on that account. Perhaps they thought, "There's something odd about

3. *New York Review of Books*, December 21, 2017, 74.

this Wolterstorff fellow, he's religious, but he seems bright, so he's likely to get over it."

In my second year, another philosophical movement, in competition with logical positivism, appeared on the scene, namely, so-called *ordinary language* philosophy. It was the view of the ordinary language philosophers that a great deal of confusion in philosophy is caused by philosophers using words in ways that never occur in ordinary language, and without assigning to them any clear alternative meaning. The ordinary language philosophers delighted in pointing to egregious examples of this sort of confusion: they bandied about the sentence, supposedly found in the German philosopher Heidegger, "The not nothings itself." It was further their view that embedded in ordinary language is a certain way of seeing things, and that that way of seeing things often represents deep wisdom and insight. With the aim of bringing that wisdom to light, they looked closely, for example, at how such words as "voluntarily," "intentionally," and "acting freely" are used in ordinary speech. In the background was Ludwig Wittgenstein's *Philosophical Investigations*, which had been published not long before.

J. L. Austin, professor at Oxford and one of the leading ordinary language philosophers, was visiting Harvard during my second year as a grad student and delivering the lectures that were later published as *How to Do Things with Words*. I well remember attending what was advertised as a debate between Austin and the prominent Harvard behaviorist B. F. Skinner. Skinner led off, expatiating at length on how behavioral psychologists had discovered that there is no such thing as free will: behavior can be manipulated and predicted. In his response, Austin did not directly dispute anything Skinner had said. Instead, he called attention to some of Skinner's sentences in which he had used the word "voluntary," and then said, "But one wouldn't say that." A bit later he called attention to some other of Skinner's sentences in which he had used the word "freely," and again said, "But one wouldn't say that." And so it went. A look of total bewilderment crossed Skinner's face. Perhaps he was thinking, "But I just did say that." What Austin meant, of course, was that one wouldn't say that if one were speaking ordinary idiomatic English. Skinner never caught on—not that evening anyway. My guess is that, if he had caught on, he would have shrugged and said, "So what? I never claimed to be speaking ordinary English."

Whereas I had been repelled by logical positivism, ordinary language philosophy intrigued me for a time. I wrote a few course papers in which I made some comments on what one would and would not say. On one of them, D. C. Williams wrote: "I discern the slimy trail of the linguistic serpent across these pages." His attitude toward this new movement was the same as his attitude had been toward logical positivism: "This, too, shall pass." He was right again. After a brief day in the sun, ordinary language philosophy disappeared.

I took a couple of courses in Greek on the side. The one I remember best was a course offered by Werner Jaeger, the illustrious émigré German scholar of ancient Greece. At the time, Jaeger was editing the writings of the church father Gregory of Nyssa. Two other students and I met for the course in his office in Widener Library, working our way through his edited text of Gregory.

Claire and I were married in June 1955, the summer between my second and third year of graduate school. The ceremony was held in Grand Rapids, with Henry Stob officiating. While I was waiting for the ceremony to begin, Stob regaled me with what had transpired when he was waiting for his own wedding to begin. Henry Zylstra, his best man, had arrived with a bottle of whiskey and a brush, the whiskey to calm Stob's nerves and the brush to deal with his dandruff.

I was grateful that my days of living in a dormitory were over. Whereas most of my grad school colleagues prolonged their stay in graduate school as long as possible, I did not. I very much enjoyed my days as a graduate student, but I had no desire to prolong them. I resolved to finish my dissertation, if at all possible, by the end of my third year. D. C. Williams, my favorite Harvard professor, taught and wrote on classical metaphysics; under his tutelage, metaphysics became my first love. Metaphysics was very much out of fashion at the time, regarded as a relic of pre-positivist days. So what? I loved it! Early in my third year, my prospectus for a thesis on the metaphysics of Alfred North Whitehead was accepted by the department. Williams was to be my supervisor; I was his only directee at the time. I worked diligently on the dissertation and finished writing it the following July.

In writing the dissertation, I became disillusioned with Whitehead. After submitting it to the philosophy faculty, I have never looked at it again, nor have I ever read Whitehead again. In one of Williams's courses I had read some of Whitehead's early writings and found them fascinating; it was on the basis of those early writings that I chose his work as the subject of my dissertation. Now I had to take into account his later work as well, which I had foolishly never looked at. I found it vague and obscure.

Be that as it may, in the letter Williams wrote to me, after I had submitted the dissertation, he was exceedingly complimentary and typically witty: "I doubt if Whitehead has ever before had a commentator and interpreter at once so industrious, penetrating, ingenious, and withal respectful and sympathetic as you.... Your treatment of him is comparable to Russell's treatment of Leibniz." Williams went on to note that my work was not, however, without significant flaws. "There are some things in the other column of the ledger. Two main kinds of faults.... The first is a certain immaturity or prematurity, an unlickedness and lack of finish.... Your style occasionally throws too coltish heels in the air." Second, "a lack of connected flow. We continually stop and start and it is not always plain that the next station is even on the same line with the last one. To change the metaphor: the mortar is not always as good as the stones."

At some point in the course of my third year, Williams called me into his office, handed me a pamphlet about a Harvard fellowship, the Sheldon Traveling Fellowship, and suggested that I apply. I looked over the description of the fellowship, noted that its purpose was to support graduate students whose dissertation topic required them to do research abroad, and observed to Williams that my dissertation topic did not require research abroad: the writings of Whitehead were readily available in local bookstores and in the Harvard library. And in any case, I expected to finish writing my dissertation by the end of the summer. "None of that matters," said Williams. So I applied for the very substantial fellowship and was awarded it.

Shortly after the awards were announced, the other recipients and I were invited to a reception hosted by the classicist J. P. Elder, the chair of the committee that awarded the fellowships. It was a cozy little sherry party for the six new Sheldon fellows. During my conversation with Elder, it became clear to me that he knew I would not be using the fellowship to do research on my dissertation topic. At a certain point in our conversation he patted me on the shoulder and said, "Wolterstorff, you should use this money to sample European culture." His exact words—I have never forgotten them. I thought, if Harvard wants to give me this money to sample European culture, who am I, a boy from the farm country of Minnesota, to question them?

American philosophers were flooding Oxford at the time, since Oxford was then the epicenter of ordinary language philosophy. A contrarian streak in me led me to decide to go to Cambridge instead. Since I still had in mind the possibility of going into theology, the plan was that, after a term in Cambridge, Claire and I would go to Amsterdam, where I would take in some theology lectures. In those days, the Free University of Amsterdam was regarded as *the* place to go if one wanted to study Reformed theology. We purchased boat tickets for early October, New York to Southampton.

Claire was pregnant with our first child, due in early September 1956. After spending the first part of the summer in Grand Rapids with Claire's parents, who had not yet moved to Santa Barbara, we drove to Minnesota to visit my parents. Before we headed back to Grand Rapids, in late August, Claire got an appointment with the village doctor in Edgerton to ask him whether it was safe to travel eight hundred miles by car so late in her pregnancy. "No problem," he said. "If you feel pain or discomfort, you'll know what ails you." I don't know what we would have done had he said it would not be safe.

Amy Elizabeth was born in Grand Rapids on September 9, a beautiful infant with lots of curly dark hair. I luxuriated in the experience of holding her, watching her move, kissing her, carrying her out of the hospital and placing her in Claire's lap in the car, picking her up again when we got to Claire's parents' house, putting her to bed, watching closely as she was baptized a week or so later. It was exhilarating. The obstetrician noticed that one of her ankles was somewhat deformed due to the position of the foot in the womb. Nothing serious, he said. A series of casts would correct the problem. We should consult a physician in England or the Netherlands.

I had received notice from Harvard that my dissertation defense was scheduled for the end of September, a few days before we were scheduled to sail for England. So we decided that I would take the train to Boston for my dissertation defense; then, a few days later, Claire would take the train with Amy from Grand Rapids to Grand Central Station in New York, where we would meet. The luggage containing the things we would need for a year in Europe would accompany Claire. A dear friend, Lew Smedes, who was pastoring a church in New Jersey at the time, would meet us in Grand Central and drive us to their home in New Jersey, where we would stay the night with Lew and his wife, Doris.

I traveled to Boston, as planned, and defended my dissertation before the entire philosophy faculty. I had the sense that it did not go well; some of the faculty intimated that they did not approve of metaphysics. My sense that it did not go well was reinforced by the fact that, after I was asked to leave the room, the faculty deliberated for what seemed to me a very long time. But eventually Williams came out and announced that I had passed.

I was staying with a friend in Arlington, a suburb of Boston. The next day, he and I were tossing a football in the street when my left foot got caught in the opening of a storm sewer and was badly injured. He drove me to the Harvard health clinic, where they diagnosed the injury as a severe sprain, bound up the ankle, prescribed a painkiller, and gave me a pair of crutches. I took the train to New York the next day and hobbled on my crutches to our agreed-on meeting point in Grand Central. There was Claire, holding our tiny Amy, surrounded by a heap of luggage. Shortly, Lew found us and we headed for New Jersey.

We had arranged that, the next day, Lew would drive us to the home of another friend, Gene Callendar, who lived in mid-Manhattan. We would stay the night with Gene and his family, and Gene would then drive us to the boat the following morning. Obviously, we could not get a passport for Amy before she was born, so as soon as possible after her birth we had a photograph taken of Claire holding Amy, and got the office of our Michigan congressman, Gerald Ford, to order the expedited issuance of a passport. We were informed that the passport would be waiting for us in the passport office in Rockefeller Center; on the way to the boat, I would pick up the passport.

Gene was a laid-back sort of fellow, and I was getting antsy.

"Isn't it time to be on our way?" I asked.

"No need to rush," said Gene.

When we did get under way, we discovered that the streets were jammed with traffic because of a strike by the subway workers. We did eventually arrive at Rockefeller Center, and I hobbled on my crutches up the exterior steps and took the elevator to the passport office, a good many floors up. They had the passport, but they needed Claire's signature. So I took the elevator back down, hobbled on my crutches down the steps to where Claire was waiting in the car, got her signature, and made the trip up and down a second time.

By the time I got back into the car, passport in hand, I was a nervous wreck for fear that we would miss our boat. Gene was still laid back: no need to rush. We got to the dock thirty or forty minutes before the boat was scheduled to sail. I could not find the tickets. The woman at the desk analyzed the situation and said, "Why don't you sit down in that chair there and relax? I'm sure you'll find them." I sat down, and almost immediately I found the tickets. She looked at them, then at us, and said: "We have some empty first class staterooms on this sailing. We are putting you and your family in one of them."

Off we sailed—in luxury!

We docked in Southampton and took the train to London, where we caught the train to Cambridge. In the train to London we found ourselves in a compartment seated across from two elderly British women who were chatting with each other. It was impossible not to overhear their conversation: they were discussing the recent death of a mutual friend, Michael. At a certain point one of them said to the other, "So sad about Michael—he died before he got his pension." We had entered a different world. Never before had I heard someone's death lamented because he died before he got his pension!

We asked a cab driver in Cambridge to take us to a hotel that he could recommend. He took us to the Royal Hotel, which turned out to be the grandest hotel in the city. Our room was cavernous, maroon the dominant color. Our dinner in the hotel that evening featured a fixed menu: boiled potatoes, boiled cauliflower, cod with a white sauce, served on a white plate with a glass of white wine, white table-cloth. White on white on white. To this day we laugh about it. Claire loves color, as do I.

Since we had made no prior arrangements for living in Cambridge, I asked the hotel for assistance in contacting a reliable housing bureau, and the bureau they recommended gave me four or five possibilities. With a map in hand of the bus lines in Cambridge, I set out to look them up. I was still on crutches. Nobody had ever mentioned to me how exhausting it is to walk on crutches. I decided to take the first apartment that seemed acceptable—no shopping around. The ones I looked at in the center of the city were all dingy, so I took the bus to one on the edge of town. The walk from the bus stop to the address was long and, on crutches, difficult. But the apartment, in a handsome brick Victorian house, looked promising:

The woman who answered the doorbell introduced herself as Miss Ansell. Yes, she did have an apartment that was available for the two and a half months that we needed one. It consisted of a rather large living room and a small kitchen on the second floor, and a bed-room on the third floor. The bath and toilet on the second floor were shared with two other renters, an Israeli couple and a single English-man who, in the course of the term, introduced me to the delirium of British soccer. This would definitely do. I signed a contract, returned to the hotel, and got a taxi to move the family and our luggage to our new abode.

After three years of extremely hard work in grad school, I took it easy during our stay in Cambridge. Once I was off crutches, I took great pleasure in exploring Cambridge with Claire, doing what J. P. Elder had instructed me to do—sample European culture. We needed a baby carriage, so when Claire saw an ad for one in the newspaper, she hired a cab to get it. She returned with a truly enormous "perambulator," as the Brits called it. Neither of us had ever seen anything like it. But it served us well. Claire usually put Amy on her "tummy," another British locution, since that's what Amy seemed to prefer. To the English, this was all wrong, and women regularly undertook to instruct Claire that babies had to lie on their backs.

I attended lectures by a number of luminaries, among them C. S. Lewis, who had recently moved from Oxford to Cambridge and was giving some lectures on medieval poetry; the philosopher Elizabeth Anscombe, deeply influenced by Wittgenstein and very eccentric; and the philosopher John Wisdom, who imitated the eccentricities of Wittgenstein. He would suddenly stop lecturing, lean over the podium, close his eyes, grimace, clasp his forehead, say nothing for half a minute or so, look up, and say, "No, no! That's all wrong. Let me start over." Lewis came across as stiff and formal, never smiling. Everybody knew of the public debate, some years earlier in Oxford, between him and Anscombe about a chapter in Lewis's book on miracles, a debate, it was generally agreed, that Anscombe had won hands down.

I managed to get an invitation from the philosopher C. D. Broad for afternoon tea in his rooms in King's College. Broad was a superb metaphysician; I had studied some of his writings with D. C. Williams and had in mind a number of issues in metaphysics that I wanted to discuss with him. He made it clear to me, however, that one did not talk "business" over tea. So we chatted. He asked me where I had received my undergraduate training. He knew the reputation Calvin College had for producing excellent philosophers, and he speculated that that was because of an affinity between the style of argumentation in analytic philosophy and the style of argumentation in Dutch Reformed theology. In the course of our rather rambling conversation he also told me that the English and Frisian languages are sufficiently alike that English and Frisian fisherman were able to communicate with each other in the harbors along the North Sea. I have no idea whether that is true.

In the fall of 1956, the Russians were threatening to invade Hungary. Miss Ansell's "drawing room" was in the front of the house on the ground floor, just off the entry. It was dark—maroon being the dominant color—and felt like the interior of a coffin. She spent all day every day writing letters to world leaders urging them to do what they could to stop the Russians. She mentioned to me that she had written the British prime minister, Harold Macmillan, offering to lay her body across the tracks between Russia and Hungary, provided the British government paid for her way there and, in case she survived, paid for her way back. I never learned whether she received the courtesy of a reply from the prime minister's office.

There was a rather large apple orchard behind Miss Ansell's house; it was fall, and the apples were dropping. I happened to be standing in the entry one day when the Israeli couple stepped into the drawing room to ask Miss Ansell if they could pick up some of the apples that had fallen. It was evident to Claire and me that they were very poor. Miss Ansell tartly replied that the garden was off-limits to renters. Empathy for the distant Hungarians, a cold shoulder for renters in her own house. Some time later I read Charles Dickens's novel *Bleak House*, in which Dickens draws a satirical portrait of Mrs. Jellyby. Mrs. Jellyby is deeply invested in a mission project in Africa: helping the "poor Africans" is her all-consuming passion. Meanwhile, her own children are dressed in rags and left to fend for themselves. I had met a living Mrs. Jellyby there in a Victorian house on Hills Road in Cambridge. She remains my image of cheap liberalism.

In mid-December we headed for the Netherlands: first by train to the English coast, then by boat across the English Channel, with our considerable quantity of luggage and our enormous baby carriage, Claire carrying Amy. Our plan was to stay with Aunt Clara and Uncle Bill in their apartment in The Hague for a few weeks until we found an apartment in Amsterdam.

Aunt Clara was the youngest sister of Mother Jen. During the last years of World War II, she had worked in Manhattan and, on the side, had taken piano lessons at a conservatory and had become an accomplished pianist. On Sundays she played piano for the worship services in a seaman's mission in Hoboken, New Jersey, where she met her future husband, Bill Kogeler, a Dutchman. Trained as an engineer, Bill was employed by Dutch Shell and stationed in Curaçao. Toward the end of the war he was sent, for some reason, to the States, and wound up on a Sunday in the seaman's mission in Hoboken. After Bill and Clara married, they moved to The Hague, where Bill worked in the headquarters offices of Dutch Shell.

Uncle Bill met us at the boat at Hook of Holland, and though we had never met, we recognized each other from photographs. We took the train to The Hague, then a taxi to their apartment. They had three small children of their own, Ellen, Jeanette, and Willem, so when the three of us joined the five of them, the apartment was crowded. Nonetheless, Bill and Clara were wonderfully warm and welcoming. We came to love the whole family, and we have remained close over the years.

While staying with them, we joined them in attending their church on Sundays. Though I found speaking Dutch difficult, my passive grasp of spoken Dutch was quite good—so I could keep up with the liturgy and the preaching. One Sunday, after the worship service, Clara, in characteristic American fashion, greeted the woman who had been sitting behind her by introducing herself. The woman straightened her back, said, in an icy tone, "Ik heb niet de eer om U te kennen" ("I do not have the honor of knowing you"), turned around, and walked off.

Not many years after we stayed with them, the family moved to Cleveland, Ohio, where Bill had secured a position with an engineering firm that specialized in designing oil refineries. It's dangerous to pick out favorites among one's relatives, but I will do so anyway. Bill and Clara were our favorite uncle and aunt: intellectually curious, open-minded, life-affirming, always interested in what we were doing. We felt a deep affinity with them. Clara was in her nineties when we visited her in Cleveland and found her with my recently published book, *Justice: Rights and Wrongs*, in hand. "Nick," she said, "I've been reading this, and I like it a lot, but I've got some questions for you." This was typical! She had never been to college. She died on June 22, 2017, three months short of her hundredth birthday. Bill had died ten years earlier, on January 7, 2007, at the age of ninety-five.

One Saturday, while we were staying with them, a truly amazing performance took place in Bill and Clara's apartment. It was Ellen's seventh birthday, and there was to be a party in the afternoon and evening. Most of the guests had arrived when in strode a distinguished-looking elderly gentleman, tall and portly, in a three-piece black suit with a gold watch chain, followed by an equally distinguished-looking woman wearing a striking hat. These were Uncle Bill's father, the *burgemeester* (mayor) of Middelburg, the provincial capital of the Dutch province of Zeeland, and his wife, Uncle Bill's mother.

The *burgemeester* took over as master of ceremonies and choreographed the remainder of the day. He welcomed everybody and declared how happy he was to see that so many people had come to join in celebrating the birthday of his granddaughter Ellen. Then, since it was a bit nippy outside, he proposed that we all have a *borrel* (a small glass of Dutch gin). After we had savored our *borrels* and chatted a bit, he announced that it was time for some singing. So we sang some songs. After some more chatting, he announced that it was time for tea. So tea was made, and we all had tea and cake. Then he announced that the time had come for the poetry. What I learned later was that it is the custom at Dutch birthday parties and weddings for the guests to compose poems for the occasion. The poems are, of course, doggerel—but comical doggerel, often hilarious. The guests at Ellen's birthday party read the bits of "poetry" they had composed, to peals of laughter. So it went for the remainder of the day, until the guests left after dinner.

I had never witnessed anything like it. In the United States we have birthday parties, of course, but they are not choreographed group performances. Later I learned that what Claire and I had witnessed that Saturday afternoon in The Hague was a rather extreme example of the ceremonial quality that is typical of Dutch birthday parties, wedding receptions, and other occasions. In general, ceremony has a far more prominent and pervasive role in Dutch life than it does in American life.

Thirty years after that birthday party in The Hague, when I was teaching philosophy at the Free University of Amsterdam, I participated in the final oral examinations of some candidates for the doctoral degree and in the awarding of the degree. Before I describe how that went, let me recall how it went in my own case at Harvard. I was examined for an hour or so by the faculty in a room in Emerson Hall, the building of the philosophy department, and then was dismissed and told to wait outside the room some distance away. After the faculty had deliberated and my director, D. C. Williams, had come out to invite me back into the room, the chairman announced the decision and I shook hands with the faculty members. The next June I received by mail a printed announcement of the official awarding of the degree at the annual graduation ceremony, which I had not attended.

At the Free University, the oral examination of a candidate on his or her dissertation is open to the public: friends and relatives of the student being examined, faculty members, fellow students, and interested members of the public—all attend. The candidate is questioned by three or four examiners, one of them the candidate's supervisor, and always at least one from another university. Shortly before the proceedings begin, the philosophy faculty, along with the outside examiners, all dressed in academic garb, assemble in a chamber near the auditorium. They are then led into the auditorium by a beadle bearing a mace (staff).[4] The examiners take their places at a long table, and the rest of the faculty members take the front seats in the auditorium. The candidate, dressed in formal attire and flanked by two so-called paranymphs (also dressed in formal attire), stands facing the examiners, about fifteen feet away. (My dictionary defines "paranymph" as "a friend going with a bridegroom to fetch home the bride in ancient Greece.") The official function of the paranymphs in the Dutch system is to assist candidates in answering the questions put to them. It would be disastrous, of course, for any candidate to actually consult the paranymphs on any question. It never happens.

The proceedings begin with the candidate giving a brief summary of his or her dissertation, and the examiners then take turns putting questions to the candidate. Precisely an hour into the proceedings the beadle, who has been standing throughout the proceedings, holding the mace upright, stomps the mace on the floor and shouts, *Hora est* (Latin for "the hour is"). After whoever is speaking at that moment has completed his or her sentence, the examination stops and the beadle leads the faculty and examiners back to the chamber where they had previously assembled, and the faculty and

4. The Dutch term for "beadle" is *pedel*, accent on the second syllable; the English and Dutch terms have the same etymology. Merriam-Webster defines "beadle" as "a minor parish official whose duties include ushering and preserving order at services and sometimes civil functions."

outside examiners take a vote on whether to award the degree. In my experience, the vote is always affirmative. The candidate is called into the chamber to hear the decision from his or her supervisor, and the candidate then inscribes his or her name in a large book whose several volumes contain the names of all those who have received a doctoral degree from the Free University in the past. The beadle then leads the candidate, the examiners, and the faculty back into the auditorium. The candidate and his or her supervisor stand facing each other, the supervisor announces the decision, the audience applauds, and the supervisor delivers the *laudatio*, that is, a brief speech in praise of the candidate's work. The beadle then declares the ceremony adjourned. I am told that the ceremony associated with the awarding of a doctoral degree is similar at the other Dutch universities to the ceremony at the Free.

At the Free, after the ceremony has been declared adjourned, everybody moves to a large open space adjacent to the auditorium, where wine, juice, and small snacks are served, and members of the audience line up to congratulate the candidate. That evening the candidate hosts a dinner in a nearby restaurant for friends, relatives, and members of the faculty.

In mid-January of 1957, Claire and I with Amy in arms—her foot now in a cast—moved into an apartment in Amsterdam that looked out over the Amstel River. Again we did as J. P. Elder had instructed me: we sampled European culture. Claire and I fell in love with Amsterdam and have remained in love ever since, returning often.

The dominant opinion at the time among professors and students of theology in the Dutch Reformed community, both in the United States and the Netherlands, was that the finest systematic theologian then active in the Reformed tradition was G. C. Ber-

kouwer, professor at the Free University. So I began attending Ber-
kouwer's lectures.

There was much I admired in his lectures: for example, his ecumenical spirit, his nonpolemical attitude toward those with whom
he disagreed, and his deep historical learning. But I found them seriously lacking in the sort of rigor that characterized the analytic
tradition of philosophy into which I had been inducted at Harvard.
His mode of intellectual discourse was an alternative that I did not
find congenial at the time. After a month or so, I decided that, if Ber-
kouwer was the best of contemporary Reformed theologians, I could
not spend the rest of my life among theologians. I would stay with
philosophy. I have never regretted that decision.

I have, however, remained interested in theology. A good many
of my colleagues in philosophy of religion are dismissive of contemporary theology, regarding it as intellectually incompetent. I do not.
Much of it employs a mode of discourse quite different from that of
present-day analytic philosophy, but it is not incompetent.

A couple of times in the preceding two paragraphs I have referred
to *analytic philosophy*. It's likely that some readers don't know what
that sort of philosophy is, so allow me to interrupt my story for a
moment to explain, as briefly as I can, what it is. Analytic philosophy
is a way of doing philosophy that has now become a tradition, and
it's that tradition that I will be characterizing. Of course, to really get
a "feel" for the tradition, one has to spend some time reading books
and essays written by philosophers who have worked in that tradition, or who are presently working in it. It's a commonplace that, in
philosophy of the past seventy-five years or so, there are two main
traditions, commonly called the *analytic* and the *continental*. Not all
twentieth-century philosophers fit into either of these two traditions; Whitehead, for example, does not. But most do.

If one were to explain, say, Platonism to someone, one would
present to her or him the main philosophical positions articulated
and defended by Plato and by those who identified themselves as

belonging to his school. Not so for contemporary analytic and continental philosophy. Neither of these is characterized by any particular set of positions on philosophical topics; instead, each is characterized by a certain body of works that it treats as canonical, and by a certain philosophical style—using the term "style" to refer not just to a way of writing but also to a way of thinking.

The founding canonical figures of the analytic tradition were the German philosopher Gottlob Frege (1848–1925) and the British philosophers Bertrand Russell (1872–1970) and G. E. Moore (1878–1958). All three of these figures placed themselves in opposition to the so-called *idealism* that was current in philosophy at the time. They reacted to idealism's high-flown speculative character, and they attacked it for what they regarded as the lack of precision and clarity in the claims it made and for the lack of rigor in the arguments it offered. They aimed to do better in their own work on all these scores.

Their influence lives on. Philosophers in the analytic tradition typically prize argumentative rigor and rhetorical precision and clarity. What rhetorical precision amounts to, in practice, is that analytic philosophers are typically sparing in their use of figures of speech, such as metaphor, hyperbole, and simile; theirs is a dry, literal style devoid of suggestion and allusion, in contrast to the much more literary style of continental philosophers. As a result, when one analytic philosopher discusses the work of another, she devotes relatively little time and effort to interpretation, since it is usually clear what the other philosopher is saying, instead focusing on whether the claims made are true and whether the arguments offered are cogent. Vastly more time and effort are devoted to interpretation in continental philosophy than in analytic philosophy.

As for the aversion to high-flown speculation, what happens in practice is that analytic philosophers fly close to the ground, as it were, typically making much use of examples when presenting their own views, so as to assure themselves and their readers that the theses they are defending fit the relevant cases, and typically making much use of counterexamples when criticizing the views of others: sparse rhetoric combined with concreteness and specificity in content.

What I have said thus far has not yet brought to light what I regard as the "deep structure" of analytic philosophy. What's the point of prizing argumentative rigor and rhetorical precision and clarity? What's the point of preoccupying oneself with whether the claims made by oneself and one's interlocutors fit the relevant cases? The point, as I see it, is an implicit understanding of the task of the philosopher. I can best explain that understanding by briefly referring to a theme in the thought of Immanuel Kant. The rapid development of the natural sciences in Kant's day (the late eighteenth century) led him to ask—in his own way—what, if anything, would be left for philosophers to do if that growth were to continue.

The essence of Kant's answer went as follows. The heart of the scientific enterprise is the discovery of *contingencies*: that is, facts and laws that could, in principle, be otherwise. It remains for philosophers to explore *necessities*: that is, ways things are that could not be otherwise. And whereas scientists and ordinary people make and criticize judgments of many different kinds—perceptual judgments, moral judgments, aesthetic judgments, and so on—they do not typically ask about the grounds of such judgments. It remains for philosophers to do that. We all make perceptual judgments. What ultimately grounds and justifies those judgments?

The tradition of analytic philosophy is shaped by this Kantian understanding of the philosopher's task. The analytic philosopher of art leaves it to art historians and art critics to make judgments about the contingencies of art. She or he stands back from that work and asks, What is the nature of art? What is representation? What is expressiveness? What is the aesthetic dimension? And on what basis do we make judgments of artistic and aesthetic worth? These are Kant-style questions. (Some readers will notice that they are also Socrates-style questions.)

My own philosophical thinking and writings are clearly in the analytic tradition. In a couple of ways they are not, however, representative of that tradition. I have engaged major figures in the continental tradition more than have most of my fellow analytic philosophers: Gadamer, Habermas, Ricoeur, Derrida, and Adorno, among others. It was my judgment that, when these philosophers were appropriately interpreted, they had important things to say on the matters I was dealing with. And I have engaged in less of the conceptual analysis typical of analytic philosophers, and in more of the phenomenological description typical of continental philosophers, than is characteristic of philosophers in the analytic tradition.

End of interruption. When I was teaching at Yale, in the 1990s, my philosophy of religion students were required to take a course in systematic theology. At the time, the syllabus for the course included substantial selections from the writings of the twentieth-century Swiss theologian Karl Barth. Students who had been trained in analytic philosophy would often throw up their hands in despair and come to my office to vent. I told them that they must not read Barth as if they were reading a text in analytic philosophy. Barth was not a failed analytic philosopher. They had to acquire and practice an alternative way of reading, one that fitted Barth's continental style. Relax, I said, be open, set your presuppositions off to the side, and gradually you will discern what it is that makes Barth one of the great theologians of the Christian church. Most of them eventually managed to do just that.

Sometime in the spring of 1957, I received a letter from my father suggesting that we visit Uncle Charlie Feenstra and his family in Nijmegen. I didn't know that I had an Uncle Charlie; nobody had ever mentioned him to me. But I made contact, using the address Dad gave, and one day Claire and I, with Amy in arms, took the train from Amsterdam to Nijmegen to visit Uncle Charlie and his family. When we arrived at their house, it was clear at a glance that they were desperately poor: the house was tiny and the food meager. But they welcomed us warmly as members of the family and ooh-ed and aah-ed over Amy.

The next day we met Uncle Charlie's cousin Andreas, who employed Uncle Charlie as a truck driver for his firm. Andreas, who lived in a large and stately house, hosted us to a superb dinner that evening and invited us to stay for the night. We were reluctant to accept, for fear that Uncle Charlie would regard this as snubbing him; but Andreas contacted Uncle Charlie and gave him some explanation that Uncle Charlie accepted.

Andreas was obviously very well-to-do. So what, we thought, is going on? Why was he living high off the hog while Uncle Charlie, his cousin and employee, was living in penury? It all came out in the course of the evening. When he was a young teenager, Uncle Charlie had immigrated to the United States with the rest of the Feenstra family. In his early twenties he had committed some petty crime and was jailed. While in jail, he got into a fight with one of the other inmates and wounded him with a knife. He was deported to the Netherlands, where he repeatedly got into more scrapes with the law. He would be jailed, Andreas would get him out of jail, he would be jailed again, Andreas would get him out again, and so it went. We were standing outside as Andreas was telling us Uncle Charlie's sad saga. He pointed to the moon and said, "Charlie is loony."

I now knew why no one in the family had ever mentioned Uncle Charlie: he was the black sheep, and they were ashamed of him. They didn't want to talk about him; indeed, they wanted to put him out of mind. I understood that. But why, when Dad suggested that we visit Uncle Charlie, had he not given us some background? Why had he left it to us to figure out the situation? In June, when Claire and I got on the boat in Rotterdam for the trip back to the States, Uncle Charlie was at the dock to say goodbye, weeping copiously.

Some years later, Uncle Charlie flew to the United States to visit a daughter who was living there. He drove around in a rental car and conned a sizable number of people, including relatives, into giving him money (though he did not contact Claire and me). He was a charmer, a genius at evoking empathy. His key to success as a con artist was that he didn't seem like a con artist: he wasn't at all oily or insinuating; instead, he seemed like a wonderfully warm and caring human being, which perhaps he really was, in his own complicated way.

THREE

Yale

In late March 1957, when we were still in Amsterdam, I received a letter from the chair of the philosophy department at Yale University, Brand Blanshard, offering me a position as an instructor in the Yale department of philososphy. He did not invite me to apply for the position; he offered me the position. Claire and I discussed it briefly, and I wrote back my acceptance. Blanshard, when I met him in late August of that year, proved to be rather formal, so I never felt comfortable asking him how it came about that, out of the blue, I had received the offer from Yale. But I was pretty sure I knew how it had gone. He had called up the chair of the philosophy department at Harvard and asked whether Harvard had any recent graduates they could recommend for the position at Yale. The Harvard chair had recommended me. It was the old boys' network in operation. Not much of that network is left today, and it's a good thing—because the network was unfair. But at the time, I did not reflect on the unfairness; I was just surprised and honored to be offered a position at Yale.

The philosophical atmosphere at Yale was very different from that at Harvard. Analytic philosophy ruled the roost at Harvard; at Yale, it was marginal. Contemporary continental philosophy and the history of philosophy were strong, along with the dying remnants of British and German idealism. Arthur Pap, the only analytic philosopher on the permanent faculty when I arrived, was mocked and shunned by his colleagues. The following year, the analytic philosopher Wilfrid Sellars joined the faculty. Sellars was older than Pap, considerably more prominent, and much feistier. Nobody abused him.

Yale was my introduction to full-time teaching. In my third year at Harvard, I had been a teaching assistant for Raphael Demos in his lecture course, Introduction to Ancient Philosophy. The course was enormously popular, enrolling about three hundred students each semester. At the conclusion of many of the lectures, the students stood and applauded. Demos was not charismatic in the way Jellema was—not for me, anyway—but his lectures were beautifully crafted and merited the applause.

Being a teaching assistant in a lecture course was a way of being eased into the teaching profession. The course was organized, and the lectures delivered, by a senior professor. The class was divided up into discussion sections of about twenty students each, and once a week the teaching assistants would lead discussions in these sections on the reading material assigned for the week. At Harvard, nobody gave us teaching assistants instructions on how to lead the discussions; nor did they offer more general instructions on how to teach. Apparently, it was assumed that we had learned how to teach by having been taught. Nor did I receive any instructions on how to teach when I started at Yale.

At Yale, I was a teaching assistant for Brand Blanshard and for Wilfrid Sellars. But the principal assignment—of those who were instructors—was to teach sections of Yale's Directed Studies Program. Freshmen and sophomores applied for admission to the program, and about 150 were admitted each year. The students in the program had a common syllabus of great texts from across the humanities: philosophy, literature, religion, history. At the beginning of each week they assembled for a lecture on the readings assigned for the week; then, twice a week, they met in small discussion groups. I was the instructor for two of those groups.

It was a heady experience. The Directed Studies Program attracted the cream of the crop of Yale freshmen and sophomores, so the students were very bright. And they were intensely engaged with the material. They read and discussed the assigned readings without worrying about what good their studies might do them in their future lives.

I had acquired the relevant skills for teaching the philosophical texts that were included in the syllabus, but not the skills for teaching the literary texts: Dostoyevsky's *Notes from Underground*, Diderot's *Rameau's Nephew*, E. M. Forster's *Passage to India*, selections from Dante's *Inferno*. Feeling uneasy and incompetent, I sought the advice of my fellow instructors in the program who had done graduate work in literature and knew, better than I did, how to teach literary texts. And I worked hard. Yale was then, and is now, incredibly rich in cultural offerings, probably richer than any other university in the country: concerts, lectures, museums, and so forth. I had to ignore almost all of it.

Teaching was exhausting. When it went well, which it usually did, I was exhausted from the exhilaration; when it went poorly, I was exhausted from the disappointment. Teaching, in those beginning years, was an emotional roller coaster. After a few years I learned to steady my emotions by reminding myself, when it went well, that it was bound to go poorly again down the road, and when it went poorly, that it was likely to go well again later on.

What remains one of the most unsettling teaching experiences of my entire career occurred in the spring of my first year at Yale, in a course I taught at the Yale Psychiatric Institute. A number of patients at the institute were Yale students, and the Institute was offering them college-level courses. The previous year Richard Bernstein had taught a course in philosophy that was, by all reports, highly successful. Dick and his wife, Carol, were spending the year in Israel, so he was not available to repeat the course; I was invited to take his place. When Dick and Carol returned at the end of the year, we became good friends and have remained so ever since, sharing many enthusiasms over the years—including Japanese ceramics and mid-century Danish furniture. From the time we first met, Dick has been one of my favorite discussion partners.

I was apprehensive about teaching a course at a psychiatric institute. But we needed the money (my Yale salary was only $4,000 for the year), so I accepted, and decided to do what Bernstein had done, namely, present to the students highlights from the history of Western philosophy. I was given no instructions on how to teach this unusual group of students. I made nothing of that at the time; now, in retrospect, I find it both astonishing and irresponsible.

When I arrived for the first class session, I introduced myself to the person at the reception desk, and he took me to the gymnasium, where the class was to be held, and introduced me to an attendant, who locked us in. About fifteen students were waiting for the class to begin. They were seated on metal chairs arranged in a circle in the center of the cavernous space. Scattered around the gymnasium were padded mats. One of the students had taken one of those mats, placed it within the circle of chairs, and was lying flat on his back on the mat. The attendant appeared to think nothing of this unusual behavior, so I said nothing.

Plato was first in the syllabus that I had drawn up. With great enthusiasm I presented Plato's theory of forms: The Good Itself, The Beautiful Itself, The Bed Itself—eternal, unchanging, invisible, outside of time and space. Fascinating ideas! Suddenly the student lying on the mat sat bolt upright and exclaimed, in a tone of total incredulity, "Plato said WHAT? He said WHAT?" I knew what he meant. *This is crazy talk. A bed that takes up no space? The guy is off his rocker.* My universe teetered as roles threatened to reverse. Who were the "crazies"? Who were the sane ones? My attempt to whip up enthusiasm for Plato's thought had been felled by a single three-word question.

With the wind out of my sails, I carried on as best I could for the remainder of the hour. If I had had more teaching experience under my belt, I might have been amused rather than rattled. But I was just beginning.

Deflated, I mentally reviewed the syllabus on the drive home. "Aristotle next. No problem there. Somewhat boring; but nobody would think he was crazy. Aquinas, the same. Then Descartes and his reasons for doubting the existence of an external world. No, no, I won't risk it. I decided to play the coward. At the beginning of the next session I would announce that there was a change in the syllabus. We could not possibly cover all the great philosophers in the Western tradition; we would skip Descartes.

A few years later, when I was reading Ludwig Wittgenstein's *On Certainty*, I was reminded of this episode when I came on the following passage: "I am sitting with a philosopher in the garden; he says again and again, 'I know that's a tree,' pointing to a tree that is near us. Someone else arrives and hears this, and I tell him: 'This fellow isn't insane. We are only doing philosophy.'"[1]

Those early years at Yale were not only formative for my career as a teacher but formative in another way as well. I was leaving behind my days as a student of philosophy and entering the guild of American philosophers. The senior professors at Yale were rather distant, and I had little contact with them; but there was a sizable contingent of young instructors, and of advanced graduate students serving as teaching assistants, and we talked philosophy incessantly —in the halls, on walks between classes, in coffee shops, at dinner parties. One of these was my good friend from Calvin College, Al Plantinga, now my colleague at Yale. After graduating from Calvin, Al had spent a year doing graduate work in philosophy at the University of Michigan, and then had transferred to Yale. In my first year as an instructor at Yale, Al was completing his dissertation. It was a great delight to be with him again.

Most of the instructors were, like me, from other universities. From them I got a sense of what was going on in philosophy around the country. We joined the American Philosophical Association

1. Ludwig Wittgenstein, *On Certainty*, passage numbered #467.

(APA) and traveled together to conventions of the association, where we met other young philosophers. A far-flung camaraderie was being formed. Each time we met we would briefly renew our acquaintance, and then we'd ask each other, "What are you working on?" Philosophy was in our blood.

Active participation in the guild of philosophers has remained, for me, an important part of my identity. As I indicated when I described the "Kuyperian" vision that I caught when I was a student at Calvin, I saw it as my calling as a Christian scholar not only to be in dialogue with other Christian scholars but also to participate, as a Christian, in the long-enduring, ongoing, social practice of philosophy. Over the years, I have written both for my fellow Christians and for my fellow philosophers, Christian or not—written with both my right hand and my left hand, as it were.

I was honored to be elected president of the American Philosophical Association (Central Division) for the academic year 1991–92. I was even more honored to be invited, in 2006, to give the inaugural lecture in the association's newly established series, the Dewey Lectures. The idea of the series was to have senior philosophers reflect on their philosophical careers. I titled my talk "A Life in Philosophy."[2] That same year I was elected as a fellow of the American Academy of Arts and Sciences.

Almost accidentally, Claire and I followed in the footsteps of her parents and began collecting art. Somehow we heard about the International Graphic Arts Society (IGAS). The mission of IGAS was to promote contemporary graphic art: original woodcuts, etchings, engravings, lithographs, silk screens, aquatints, and so forth. The soci-

---

2. Included in Steven M. Cahn, ed., *Portraits of American Philosophy* (Lanham, MD: Rowman and Littlefield, 2013), 5–23.

ety commissioned prints by important artists from around the world, and every other month sent out a small brochure containing black-and-white photographs of fifteen or so new prints, along with brief biographies of the artists. The prints were published in rather large editions, typically between fifty and a hundred impressions, and were priced amazingly low—on average, about fifteen dollars.

IGAS was based in Manhattan, and whenever possible, Claire and I would take the train into New York to see the actual prints. Many were aesthetically superb. From IGAS we acquired prints by Ben Shahn, Karel Appel, Corneille, Sadao Watanabe, Shiko Munakata, and a good many more. We liked the idea of helping to support the work of living artists. And we were, of course, attracted by the low price; we could acquire original works of art at low cost (each impression of a print being an original, not a reproduction). What also appealed to us was the fact that we shared the very same work of art—the very same print—with all the others who owned an impression. Whereas a painting can have only one owner, the same print is owned by all those who own an impression. Prints are "for the people" in a way that paintings are not.

What additionally appealed to me, given my background in woodworking, was the fact that graphic art prints inhabit the border between art and craft. They are clearly "fine art"; but the way the plate is produced, then inked and run through a press, resembles woodworking more than painting. Perhaps what also contributed to my attraction was the memory of my father sitting at our dining room table in Bigelow on winter evenings, doing pen-and-ink drawings. Unlike prints, pen-and-ink drawings are one of a kind; but like etchings and engravings, they are lines on paper.

But why *collect* prints? Why not take the train into Manhattan every other month, go to the offices of IGAS, look at the new batch of prints, enjoy them, and return home? Why own them? It's not *ownership* as such that appeals to me; it's *living with* works of art that appeals. Our prints are part of my everyday life, present in my environment; I don't have to travel somewhere to see them. Just now I have gotten up from sitting in front of my computer, walked around our house, and once again enjoyed the prints on our walls: three Chagall prints, two Rouault prints, three Watanabe prints, three Peterdi prints, two Corneille prints, a Johnny Friedlander print, a Ben Shahn print, two prints by our brother-in-law Paul Stewart. These are friends of long standing.

Those that are not framed I can touch. For me, there is something indescribably wonderful about feeling the texture of an etching or engraving, following the trace of the hand of the artist.

Yale proved to be a brief stop. In the spring of 1959, my second year at Yale, I received a letter from Harry Jellema offering me a position in the philosophy department at Calvin. Claire and I were at once strongly inclined to accept, but we thought it wise, before we made our decision, for me to talk it over with some of the senior members in the Yale philosophy department, especially Brand Blanshard, who had hired me.

Blanshard was perplexed that I would even consider leaving Yale. My prospects were good for staying on, he said, so why would I think of leaving, especially to go to a small college like Calvin? He seemed annoyed that I would even consider the idea. The implication of his remarks—though he never quite said it—was that there was no more prestigious institution of higher education than Yale: Yale was at the top of the academic ladder. Why would anyone in his right mind leave if he could stay?

Prestige meant little to me. My decision would be based on where I thought I could best develop and flourish as a Christian philosopher. Blanshard had nothing to say that was relevant to that decision. Wilfrid Sellars, with whom I also discussed the matter, was more understanding. His father, Roy Wood Sellars, had spent his career teaching philosophy at the University of Michigan, where he had had Harry Jellema as a graduate student. Wilfrid was well acquainted with Calvin, and with its reputation for graduating a sizable number of students who later became professional philosophers, and he pointed out something that I was only vaguely aware of: the Yale philosophy department had a reputation for being erratic and unpredictable in promoting people from within their ranks. (This was to be confirmed a couple of years later by the department's utterly irrational decision not to extend Dick Bernstein's appointment, a decision that produced an uproar among Yale students.) If it was important to me that I teach at Yale, Sellars said, it would be best for me to come in at the top, as he himself had done.

I told Claire about my discussions, and we decided that I should accept the offer from Calvin. I accepted partly out of affection for my alma mater, but mostly because I had a sense of calling, in the classic Protestant sense of a vocation, a *Beruf*. I felt called to be not just a good philosopher but a Christian philosopher, following in the footsteps of those who had inspired me at Calvin, particularly Harry Jellema and Henry Stob. I judged that I could develop and flourish in that way much more at Calvin than I could at Yale, at least at the beginning of my career.

Our family now included Eric, who was born in the early morning of January 31, 1958. We had arranged in advance with our landlady, who lived on the floor below, that she would take care of Amy when we left for the hospital for Claire to give birth. It was snowing heavily when Claire went into labor, the evening before. The hospital wasn't far away, but, so far as I could tell, the snowplows weren't out, and I was desperately worried that we would get stuck. The streets were empty of traffic, so I went straight through stop signs and traffic lights, never stopping, barely able to see through the windshield. We made it.

Eric was born with an abundance of red hair that stuck straight up, so we affectionately called him our little *stekelvarken* (Dutch for "porcupine"). His birth was just as precious and exhilarating as Amy's was. As I was holding this tiny infant for the first time, the conviction swept over me that he had been placed by God in my hands and Claire's for safe-keeping, love, nurture, and guidance, so that he might flourish. The same was true of Amy, of course.

FOUR

Teaching in Turbulent Times

I n September 1959, I began what would prove to be thirty years of teaching and practicing philosophy at Calvin College. This was my calling, and I loved it. And Calvin was, for me, an ideal venue.

What I call "practicing philosophy" is what the people at Harvard called "doing philosophy." Most people think of philosophy as what philosophers have thought—some of that preserved in philosophical texts. There is that, of course. But, more basically, philosophy is a social practice, an ongoing activity of a certain kind, specifically the activity of thinking philosophically, of writing philosophical texts, and of teaching and discussing philosophy. Philosophical thought contained in texts emerges from the social practice. The practice is basic.

What kind of thinking is philosophical thinking? I once heard Wilfrid Sellars give an explanation of philosophy that seems to me as apt as any. Philosophy, he said, is about how things—in the broadest sense of the term "things"—hang together, in the broadest sense of the term "hang together." How is justice related to love? How are God's commands related to God's love? What makes a thing beautiful? Philosophical thinking is thinking about such matters.

What do I love about thinking philosophically? I love both the understanding that results from it and the process of achieving the understanding. Sometimes the understanding comes easily, as when I read some philosophical text that I find convincing and illuminating. But often it comes after struggle and frustration. My attention has been drawn to something I do not understand, which makes me baffled and perplexed. Questions come to mind that I cannot answer. I love both the struggle to understand and the understanding itself—if it comes. The love of understanding and the love of achieving that understanding are what motivate and energize my practice of philosophy. For me, practicing philosophy is love in action.

Striving to understand something that one does not understand pervades the lives of all of us, at one time or another. Often those attempts are motivated by considerations of utility: there are certain things we have to understand if we are to achieve the goals we have set for ourselves. But not always. Sometimes our attempts to understand are motivated by the sheer love of understanding: the love of understanding a Shakespeare sonnet, the love of understanding what Plato was getting at in one of his dialogues, of understanding genetic structures, of understanding the causes of the Reformation. The love that motivates and energizes the practice of philosophy is mostly like those loves: *disinterested* love of understanding. If such love disappeared, philosophy would die, because, as the old saying has it, philosophy bakes no bread.

Someone once remarked to me, after listening to a few of my public lectures, that he was struck by the fact that it was my strategy to plant a question in the minds of the audience and then invite them to pursue, along with me, the answer to the question. Though I wasn't aware that that was my strategy, his comment made me realize that it *was* my strategy, not only in public lectures but also in classroom teaching. My goal in teaching philosophy was, of course, to open up to students the vast vista of philosophical thought, but, in addition, to get them to think philosophically along with the philosopher we were studying: not just to learn what Descartes thought, but to follow Descartes in his line of thought—or to think along with me as I explored some philosophical topic. If things went well, students would begin to think philosophically on their own.

The disinterested love of understanding that keeps philosophy alive is to be found throughout the arts and sciences. The pervasiveness of that love says something important about what it is to be human: we are creatures who bear the unique dignity of longing and loving to understand—and of being capable of understanding— God, the world, and ourselves. Today, that love of understanding is under threat, both in Europe and in the United States. Colleges and universities are being asked to justify what they teach by reference to its benefit to the economy. Are we to be reduced to cogs in the economic machine? Reality is mysterious—deeply and endlessly mysterious. Are we to renounce our longing to penetrate some of the mystery?

Every now and then, understanding evokes wonder and awe at what one has come to understand, wonder and awe at the astounding immensity and amazing intricacy of God's creation, wonder and awe at some product of human creativity, such as J. S. Bach's *B minor Mass*. Sometimes what is evoked is not wonder and awe but horror, horror at what human beings have done to other human beings, horror at what human beings have done to the earth and its inhabitants, horror at the tragedies that have befallen human beings. I write these words a few months after I visited the Holocaust Museum in Washington, DC, where I experienced horror.

If a student, in the course of her education, never loves understanding for its own sake, and never experiences wonder and awe before what she has come to understand, there is something seriously wrong—either with the student or with her education. The same is true if she never feels horror. Education, when it goes well, engages not just the mind but the heart.

The sources of wonder and awe are many. I remember being struck with wonder and awe when our third child, Robert Paul, was born on August 9, 1960, perhaps because of something I had been reading—I don't remember. Once again, exhilaration, but now, especially, wonder and awe at the intricacy of the new life I was holding in my hands, and at the intricacy of the transition from life in the womb to life outside. The psalmist of ancient Israel already had some intimation of the intricacy of human life. He wrote, addressing God, "I praise you, for I am fearfully and wonderfully made ... intricately woven" (Ps. 139:14-15). I knew vastly more than the psalmist would have known about the astoundingly intricate weaving of the human life I was holding in my hands. Wonder and awe.

The times were becoming turbulent, as they had never been up to that point in my lifetime—and have never been since. The nation was traumatized by the assassination of President John Kennedy on November 22, 1963; and again, a few years later, by the assassination of Martin Luther King Jr., on April 4, 1968; and yet again, on June 6 of that same year, by the assassination of Robert Kennedy. The Vietnam War was dragging on, generating enormous controversy and unrest in America. Across the country people marched in protest; protesters were shot by police and members of the National Guard; students seized control of university buildings and staged sit-ins; riots erupted, where whole sections of cities were set on fire and widespread looting became the norm. A peace treaty between North Vietnam and the United States was finally signed in January 1973.

The civil rights movement was taking place at the same time, dating from December 1, 1955, when Rosa Parks, in Montgomery, Alabama, refused to give up her seat on a bus to a white person. Her refusal sparked many years of widespread protest against segregation, and Martin Luther King Jr. eventually became the acknowledged leader of the movement.

The feminist movement was also gaining momentum. There had been an earlier feminist movement in the United States, which culminated in the passage, on August 26, 1920, of the Nineteenth Amendment to the US Constitution, guaranteeing women the right to vote. Betty Friedan is often credited with initiating the second feminist movement with her 1963 book, *The Feminine Mystique*. She helped organize a nationwide Women's Strike for Equality on August 29, 1970, the fiftieth anniversary of the passage of the Nineteenth Amendment. Large marches took place across the country in support of women's rights.

Institutions everywhere were under pressure to reform: colleges and universities, churches, the police, the military, businesses, political parties. Many of these institutions resisted. Anger was everywhere, often erupting into shouting matches, sometimes into violence. The social fabric was being frayed. This was the social context in which I began my career as a philosopher. It was heady and menacing, exhilarating and alarming.

I was a vocal opponent of the Vietnam War. I spoke at rallies against the war, both on-campus and off-campus. Telephone calls came in the middle of the night, threatening me and my family. I was also a firm supporter of the civil-rights movement. Though I did not travel to the South to participate in any of the marches there, I did participate in marches and rallies in Grand Rapids. And I was a supporter of the feminist movement, though, as I observed above, I was much too slow to catch on to some of the many ways in which women are demeaned.

The philosophy department at Calvin had its own conflicts. Harry Jellema identified himself as standing in the line of Abraham Kuyper, as did his former student and younger colleague Henry Stob. There were, at the time, two additional lines of Kuyper's influence on philosophers: Herman Dooyeweerd and Dirk Vollenhoven at the Free University in Amsterdam were the leading representatives of one of those lines; Hendrick Stoker, at the University of Potchefstroom in South Africa, was the leading representative of the other. The leaders of the first two of these three philosophical branches of the Kuyperian family did not get along well with each other. As for Stoker, he was pretty much ignored by the others.

Dooyeweerd and Vollenhoven were both extraordinarily systematic thinkers, Dooyeweerd in systematic philosophy (his home field was philosophy of law), and Vollenhoven in the history of philosophy. Together, they were the originators of a philosophical system they called the "Philosophy of the Law-Idea" (in the 1950s it came to be called "Reformational philosophy").

Jellema chafed at systems. He had no interest whatsoever in

constructing a system, or in systematizing the history of philosophy. What drew his interest was how the pagan worldview of the ancients shaped and came to expression in ancient philosophy, how the Christian worldview of the medievals shaped and came to expression in medieval philosophy, and how the worldview of modernity shaped and came to expression in modern philosophy.

But it was not merely the preoccupation of Dooyeweerd and Vollenhoven with system that Jellema found off-putting. Whereas Jellema spoke of philosophy as shaped by worldviews, Dooyeweerd spoke of philosophy as shaped by what he called "ground motifs." No significant difference there. It was over the way in which Dooyeweerd used the idea of a ground motif that substantial differences emerged. After rejecting the ground motif of the ancients and that of the moderns as both antithetical to Christianity (as did Jellema), Dooyeweerd went on to identify a distinctly Christian ground motif, and to claim that the Philosophy of the Law-Idea was the first to be shaped exclusively by the Christian ground motif. In other words, this was the first truly Christian philosophy. The medieval philosophers had some apprehension of the Christian ground motif, but, failing to see that it was antithetical to the ground motif of the ancient pagans, they combined the pagan ground motif of nature with the Christian ground motif of grace into the synthetic ground motif of nature/grace. The result was "synthesis philosophy."

Jellema was deeply annoyed by a number of things in this scheme: he was annoyed by the triumphalist claim that the Philosophy of the Law-Idea was the first truly Christian philosophy; he was annoyed by the dismissal of medieval philosophy as synthesis philosophy (he thought and taught that the medieval philosophers were our Christian philosophical forebears); and he was annoyed by the habit of Dooyeweerd, Vollenhoven, and their followers of studying other philosophers only to uncover the ways in which their false ground motifs had led them into error and distortion. Jellema thought and taught that there were things to be learned from Plato, from Aristotle, from Aquinas, from Descartes, from Kant. They should not simply be studied and then dismissed because of the error of their ways.

When I was still a student at Calvin, Evan Runner was appointed to the philosophy department at Calvin. Runner was an "American" (as my Minnesota relatives would call those who were not Dutch), but he had received his graduate training in philosophy at the Free University and was an ardent adherent of the Philosophy of the Law-Idea. In his teaching, he expounded the system with great enthusiasm. Many students found him as charismatic as I had found Jellema, especially those who had emigrated, with their families, from the Netherlands to Canada or the United States after World War II.

Even the most winsome representative of the Philosophy of the Law-Idea would have provoked Jellema's ire. Evan Runner was not winsome, and he did not conceal his disdain for Jellema's approach to philosophy; Jellema returned the favor by not concealing his disdain for Runner's approach. The conflict was intense. By the time I began teaching at Calvin, in 1959, their conflict had escalated to the point where they did not speak to each other unless absolutely necessary. It was obvious to me that there was nothing I could do to mediate the conflict. I would have to endure it.

As chair of the department, Jellema assigned the courses that the members of the department were to teach. When Runner was assigned a course, he would often refuse to teach what the catalog described as the content of the course. Assigned to teach logic, for example, he instead taught Dooyeweerd's philosophy of logic. One semester, when I was still a student, I enrolled in the course in modern philosophy that Runner had been assigned to teach. In his opening lecture, he argued that one could not understand Descartes without understanding his medieval background; in turn, one could not understand Descartes's medieval background without understanding the classical ancient philosophers; in turn, one could not understand the classical ancient philosophers without understanding the pre-Socratic philosophers; and one could not understand the pre-Socratic philosophers without understanding Hesiod, one of the earliest of the Greek poets, writing centuries before anything appeared on the scene that would be, for us, recognizable as philosophy. So the course began with Hesiod, and was heavy on philology. A week or so from the end of the term, we had gotten up to Aristotle. So Runner leaped ahead and gave two lectures on Descartes to conclude the semester. Jellema, we students heard, was furious. I remarked above that, when I arrived at Harvard, I had had good training in the history of philosophy. I must qualify that remark: I did not have good training in the history of *modern* philosophy.

Once Jellema and Runner retired, the atmosphere changed. Though the Jellema branch and the Dooyeweerd-Vollenhoven branch continued as two distinct branches of Kuyper-influenced philosophy (along with the South African branch), the animosity dissipated. I had long been good friends with some members of the Dooyeweerd-Vollenhoven branch, particularly Calvin Seerveld, Henk Hart, and Lambert Zuidervaart. Now our friendship deepened. I taught a course jointly with Hart at the Institute for Christian Studies in Toronto, where he and Seerveld were on the faculty, and Zuidervaart joined the philosophy department at Calvin. In the future, I would also become good friends with Dutch representatives of the Dooyeweerd-Vollenhoven branch, especially Bob Goudzwaard, Sander Griffioen, and Johan Vander Hoeven.

I was no more than three years into teaching at Calvin when I began talking with other young faculty members about reforming the college curriculum. Were we reflecting the turbulence of the times? Perhaps. But mostly, I think, we were motivated by the approach to academic learning that we had imbibed in graduate school. At Harvard, I had been inducted into the social practice of doing philosophy—into the craft of philosophy. My young colleagues had similarly been inducted into the crafts of their disciplines: the craft of history, the craft of sociology, and so forth. We were excited by the prospect of inducting our own students, at a beginning level, into the crafts of our disciplines. Of course, our older colleagues had likewise been inducted into the crafts of their disciplines; they, too, had done doctoral work. But when we looked at the curriculum, and looked over their shoulders at how they taught, it struck us that they, rather than inducting students into the crafts of their disciplines, were teaching them the results—that is, teaching what is to be found in philosophy books, in history books, in sociology books. No doubt that was because, for the most part, they were themselves no longer practitioners of their disciplines; they were devoting their energies almost exclusively to teaching. It seemed to us too passive, too backward-looking. It rubbed against the activist attitude we had acquired in graduate school.

After talking among ourselves for a year or so, we decided to present a motion to the faculty to form a curriculum revision committee. In the course of the discussion, some of the senior members of the faculty recalled that the basic structure of Calvin's curriculum had been taken over from the University of Michigan in the 1930s, and noted that it had never been revised. Our motion passed. Whenever I reflect on this, I am amazed once again at the graciousness of the senior faculty in accepting a motion to revise the college curriculum coming from a band of young Turks. Would I have been so gracious? Would I not, instead, have bridled at the audacity of it? In any event, a committee was elected at a subsequent faculty meeting, and the committee chose me as its chair.

Early on, we decided that we could not do a responsible job of proposing a revised curriculum without first reflecting seriously on the entire project of Christian liberal arts education. Thus our final report had two main parts: foundations of Christian liberal arts education, and curriculum of a Christian liberal arts education. I spent the summer of 1965 writing it. The faculty discussed and debated it during the following academic year, and the faculty adopted our curricular proposals, with some revisions, in the spring of 1966. The report was subsequently published by Eerdmans under the title *Christian Liberal Arts Education: Report of the Calvin College Curriculum Study Committee* (1970). In the preface to the published report, William Spoelhof, then president of the college and a member of our committee, wrote:

> Reforming a college curriculum is the most daring and yet the most rewarding work in which an academic community can engage. On the one hand, curriculum reform may be fraught with frustrations, fears, and forebodings, while on the other hand it can be the occasion which produces the noblest and best in faculty thought and feeling.
>
> The curriculum reform which this study describes prompted more exhilarating moments than exhausting ones. In retrospect, we may judge that in many respects our faculty community reached its grandest hour during the process of weighing, evaluating, and deciding on the proposals which refashioned the Calvin College curriculum....
>
> The series of faculty meetings held in 1965–66, at which the basic six or seven committee proposals were debated and acted upon, were the most exciting, dramatic, and proudest moments we ever experienced as a faculty, for we indeed came to grips with the basic principles of Christian higher education and with the issues which lie at the very heart of our existence as a Christian and as a Reformed college....

My writing of the curriculum report was the first of many forays on my part into philosophy of education. Though I have never taught the subject, I've written a good many essays on education and given a number of talks, many of which are now collected in two volumes, *Educating for Life: Reflections on Christian Teaching and Learning* (Baker, 2002) and *Educating for Shalom: Essays on Christian Higher Education*

(Eerdmans, 2004), both edited by Clarence Joldersma and Gloria Stronks. Most professors teach without reflecting much on the activity of teaching and on its institutional basis. I have felt impelled to reflect on the activity and to work actively for the health of the institutions in which I have taught.

I was thankful that the semester was over when our fourth child was born—on December 15, 1962. We named him Nicholas Jan, Nicholas after me and my paternal grandfather, Jan after Claire's father. We have always called him "Klaas," the Dutch nickname for Nicholas. He was born in the wee hours of the morning, a couple of weeks before he was due. We had been to a party the night before, and Claire thinks it was her standing for much of the time at the party that induced early labor. (Claire reminds me now that we hoped he would be born before the new year so that we could take him as a deduction on our 1962 income tax return!) At the party, one of my colleagues in the English department, Tom Harper, insisted that I call him if we needed someone to tend the other children when Claire went into labor and when she and I would be headed for the hospital. I called Tom a few hours later, about 3:00 in the morning, and he came right over. Amy and Eric were now old enough to enthusiastically welcome their new brother. Robert, who was only two years old, seemed, as I recall, a bit bewildered.

In the fall of 1963, Alvin Plantinga joined our department. Al had left Yale when I did and had taught for a few years at Wayne State University in Detroit. He was as committed as I was to the project of Christian philosophy and to *practicing* philosophy, not just *studying* philosophy. Though writing about Whitehead's metaphysics for my dissertation had disillusioned me about Whitehead, it did not disillusion me about metaphysics. In fact, I was at that point beginning to work on the book that would become *On Universals* (1970). Al had written his dissertation on Jean Paul Sartre, but he had similarly dropped Sartre and was working on a book that would become *God and Other Minds* (1967). Al read chapters of my manuscript and offered comments, and I did the same for him.

After one or two years of doing that, we decided to make our exchanges more regular and to invite the other members of the department to join us with their work. We proposed that every Tuesday afternoon we meet for two hours to discuss something one of us had written and distributed in advance. Cliff Orlebeke, already a member of the department, joined us; Rich Mouw joined us when he became a member of the department in the fall of 1968; Pete de Vos, a bit later, and then, somewhat later still, Ken Konyndyk, Greg Mellema, Del Ratzsch, Lee Hardy, and Steve Wykstra. Others joined as they became members of the department. For the remainder of my career at Calvin we met for two hours every Tuesday afternoon, sometimes even through the summer, going page by page through the article or chapter that one of us had written and distributed in advance. "Any comments about the paper as a whole? Nothing more about the paper as a whole? Then let's turn to page one. Any comments about page one? No more comments about page one? Then let's turn to page two. Any comments about page two?" So it went. More than anything else, it was my participation in these Tuesday discussions that helped me master the craft of philosophy. The same was true, I would guess, for the other participants.

It was tough love. We genuinely cared about each other and wanted to assist each other at what we were working on. And we were united in the project of practicing philosophy as Christians: we were a true community of Christian philosophers. Still, a flurry of critical comments could leave one feeling bruised. After our Tuesday meetings had been under way for a few years, I made a point of assuring new members of the department beforehand that critical comments were never meant personally; we did genuinely want to help each other.

Our department was a community in another way as well: every summer we got together on an evening to discuss how we could and should be serving various constituencies: Christian philosophers, philosophers in general, the Christian Reformed Church, the church generally, Christian colleges, and so forth. We identified issues we thought should be addressed, considered the venues in which they could best be addressed, and parceled out assignments. Rich Mouw remembers that, one year, Al Plantinga volunteered to write some articles for *The Banner*, the weekly publication of the Christian Reformed Church, whereupon the rest of us jumped in: "No, no, there are others of us who can do that better than you can. And in any case, it's not a good use of your talents." In retrospect, setting an agenda for ourselves in this way seems rather grandiose; at the time, it was exciting.

My students at Calvin in the 1960s and 1970s were extraordinary: bright and feisty, articulate, confident, nothing shy about them, respectful but not deferential, occupied with the big questions, seemingly unconcerned with finding jobs after graduation. I suppose it was, in part, a reflection of the social turbulence of the times. It's unfair to the others to mention any of them, but I will do so anyway. In addition to the considerable number who have gone on to distinguished careers in philosophy, there was Dale Van Kley, who has had a distinguished career as a historian; Paul Schrader, as a screenwriter and film director; Jeannine Oppewall, as an art director and production designer in film; Marlin Van Elderen and Jon Pott, as editors; Dennis Tolsma, as a health administrator; and Neal Plantinga, who has had a distinguished career as a theologian. The list could go on and on. My students since then have been just as gifted, but in those days there was a buzz in the air—an excitement and an intensity—that later disappeared.

There was an intensity and excitement among the young faculty as well. No doubt this, too, was a reflection of the social turbulence of the times. But I think it was also a continuation of the discussions and debates about the nature and future of Christian higher education that the work of the curriculum committee had inspired. We shared the sense of an open and beckoning future. After faculty meetings, we would get together at someone's house for beer, and there were lots of dinner parties. Those were golden years. Claire and I became especially close friends of Lew Smedes (theology) and his wife, Doris; of Jim De Borst (political science) and his wife, Julie; of George Marsden (history) and his wife, Lucie; of Ed Van Kley (history) and his wife, Elaine; and of Ed and Ervina Boevé.

Especially the Boevés. Ervina taught theater and directed plays; Ed was a painter who taught both painting and art history. His teaching of art history was masterful. I remember tagging along with him once when he was leading a group of Calvin students through the New York Metropolitan Museum, opening their eyes to the art they were seeing. I became aware that the group was gradually increasing in size. I looked around, and saw that people in other groups were drifting away from their guides to listen to Ed.

In those days, doing things with one's hands was regarded by the administration as inferior to just using one's mind: making art was inferior to studying art history, directing theater was inferior to studying theater, and so on. The Boevés were regularly the brunt of putdowns. I deeply resented that and often spoke up and acted in their defense. We cried together—and sometimes laughed together. Both the theater department and the art department were weak fledgling departments when the Boevés began teaching at Calvin; within ten or fifteen years they were thriving, in spite of the put-downs, due in good measure to the determined and energetic efforts of Ed and Ervina. Ervina died in July 2006. Ed remains a dear friend.

~

Was I neglecting my family? I think not, though they will have to say whether they felt neglected. Apart from those occasions when I was attending a conference or giving a lecture out of town, our entire family always ate dinner together; we usually had breakfast as well, and, when possible, lunch. Dinner was the occasion for everybody to talk about what had happened during the day. At the conclusion of dinner we had family devotions around the dinner table. On Sundays, we attended church together.

I used my office at the college for meetings with students and faculty, not for reading, preparing lectures, or writing. I did those things in my study at home, and that meant that I was home a good deal of the time. The door of my study was always open. If Claire or one of the children had something to say, they could walk right in.

The children were all bright and good at school; they did not need prodding. Klaas has revealed that he never liked school, and I take his word for that. But he did his schoolwork just as assiduously as if he had liked it. Naturally, the children had to be consoled every now and then because of something that had happened during the day. Claire was much better at that than I was.

None of them ever gave us any serious trouble. They never used drugs, they never abused alcohol, and none of them had any serious health problems. Though they got into the usual sorts of arguments with each other, their arguments were never bitter and never lasted long. Helping each of them to mature in her or his own way was a great joy. Klaas once asked me why I didn't give him more advice than I did. My reply was that I gave him as much advice as I thought he needed—which wasn't much. Later, I realized that what he was really saying was that he wished I had been more forthcoming than I was about my hopes and ideals for him and the others.

During the summers they devised their own play. They roamed the neighborhood—on bike and on foot—fished in a nearby lake, caught frogs in a nearby pond, and so forth. Recently they remarked that often they did not reveal to us where they had been and what they had been doing. We never worried about them. When they got to be teenagers, they found summer jobs on their own. They often tease me about never going on vacations except when I was scheduled to speak somewhere and they came along. It's true that, in the summer, I did often use the occasion of a lecture I was giving out of town as the opportunity for a family vacation. But when they tease me on the matter, I list some of the times we went on a family vacation when I was not speaking. They tend to discount those.

So I was not an absentee father, not physically, at least, nor was I absent in caring for the children and caring about them. Was I emotionally absent? Perhaps. They did not often confide in me; they confided in Claire instead. I think that was not so much because I was busy with many things but because I do not open up to others the way Claire does, nor do others open up to me the way they do to her. Her emotional openness is one of her many graces.

FIVE

Beyond Teaching

Claire's sister Eulalie and her husband, Paul Stewart, called early in the summer of 1964, said that they had a proposal to make, and asked whether they could drive over to discuss it. They lived in Albion, Michigan, where Paul taught in the art department of Albion College. A college friend of Paul, Phil Doster, had contacted them a few days earlier to ask whether Paul and Eulalie were interested in joining Phil and his wife Ginny, and Phil's sister Char and her husband, Roy Stricker, in buying an eighty-acre piece of land that had just come on the market about thirty miles straight south of Grand Rapids. Phil had grown up in the area, and one of his relatives, who still lived there, had mentioned to him the availability of the property. Phil asked Paul and Eulalie whether they knew of anyone else who might be interested. They said they would approach us. We told Paul and Eulalie that we were definitely interested. The asking price for the eighty acres was $3500.

That spring I had taught a seminar in metaphysics for the philosophy department at the University of Chicago. Once a week I took the Pere Marquette train from Grand Rapids to Chicago, going there and returning the same day. (The Pere Marquette, in those days, retained some touches of its former glory: there was a dining car with linen on the tables, china and silver, waiters taking orders.) The money that the University of Chicago had paid me for teaching the seminar could be used to pay for our share of the $3500.

Soon after Paul and Eulalie had talked with us, we all met at the property to get acquainted and to walk the land. Claire and I took an instant liking to the Dosters and the Strickers, and the land was extraordinary. Very hilly, part of it a sizable unspoiled marsh, much of it wooded. The southeast corner of the property, apparently never clear-cut, was a spectacular forest of beech trees. A beautiful creek flowed through the property, cutting through high banks for much of the way. At one point there were caves in the banks. I learned some years later that these are formed of tufa, a type of limestone, and that this is one of only two places in southern Michigan that had not been glaciated.

The land had not been farmed for many years; there were some old concrete and stone foundations, but the buildings had rotted away. Almost certainly the farming had never consisted of anything other than grazing: the hills were too steep to be tilled, and there was almost no level ground in the valleys other than the marsh.

We went to a restaurant in the nearby village of Orangeville and talked excitedly about what we had seen, agreeing that such an extraordinary piece of land had to be protected from development. Phil dreamed of starting a small retreat center on the property. We decided to purchase the land at the asking price. Legal documents for a partnership were drawn up, and in January 1965 we became co-owners of the land. Garner and Paul Brown, the previous owners, had just one request: that they be allowed to collect morel mushrooms in the spring.

Let me jump ahead and continue the story of "the land," as we call it. When the purchase was made, we co-owners all lived in south-western Michigan. Some years later the Strickers moved to Colorado, the Dosters to New York State, and Paul and Eulalie to Ann Arbor, where Paul taught printmaking at the University of Michigan (about a hundred and twenty miles from the land). So we, who lived only thirty miles away, got to the land far more often than the others did, often hiking it with our children and friends. We loved the diversity of the topography and the astounding variety of native plant species.

And I loved the fact that nature was being rejuvenated. Where areas had once been cleared for grazing, trees and shrubs and wild-flowers were now springing up. Lines from Gerard Manley Hopkins's poem "God's Grandeur" came to mind:

The world is charged with the grandeur of God.
It will flame out, like shining from shook foil....
Generations have trod, have trod, have trod;

And all is seared with trade....
And for all this, nature is never spent;
There lives the dearest freshness deep down things....
Because the Holy Ghost over the bent
World broods with warm breast and with ah! bright wings.

In the summer of 1973 we all decided to build a cottage on the land. I designed it and, since we lived closest, I did most of the carpentry; my experience as a carpenter's assistant in my younger years came in handy. Over the years we greatly enjoyed spending time at the cottage. But our enjoyment was spoiled by the fact that it was repeatedly broken into and burglarized. Twice a wood-burning stove that we had installed was stolen. The farm country that I had known growing up, around Bigelow and Edgerton, was safe: houses were never locked, and everybody left their keys in their cars or pickups. In talking to our neighbors at the land, I learned that this area of southern Michigan was not safe. "Rednecks," as our neighbors called them, were a problem.

Then, in May 1988, when I was teaching at the Free University of Amsterdam, we got a long-distance call from our son Klaas back in Grand Rapids. "Are you sitting down?" he asked. "No," I said, "but I will." He then told me that the police in Orangeville had called to report that our cottage had been burned by arsonists and that nothing was left of it. At the time the call came, our good friend Dick Bernstein was having dinner with us in our apartment in Amsterdam.

Upon hearing the news about our burned-down cottage, I felt more relief than anger: we would no longer have to deal with break-ins. Though it turned out that our insurance would pay enough to rebuild, we all agreed that, if we did rebuild, the same thing was likely to happen again, and since the Dosters and the Strickers had not used the cottage in many years, they had no interest in rebuilding. So we did not rebuild.

In 2010, the Dosters and Strickers declared that they wanted to get out of the partnership. Whereas initially we had all said that we wanted to protect the land from development, they now declared that their only interest was selling the land at market value. There was no alternative but to get the land appraised and to put it up for sale. The appraisal came in at $240,000, and we put it on the market at that price.

A few weeks after we put it on the market, a woman offered the asking price. She told the realtor that she wanted to raise organic cattle on the property, and that she planned to construct a couple of buildings near the road where she and others could do psychological counseling. She proposed to buy it on land contract, but not to pay anything on the contract for five years. I felt sick. I don't know what an organic cow is, but in any case, one could scarcely imagine a more unpromising place for rearing cattle than our land: it's too hilly, too heavily wooded, too much of it consists of wetlands. I was convinced that the offer, and the description of what the land would be used for, was a front for some sort of nefarious activity—who knows what?

Claire and I discussed with each other and with our children whether we should buy the other couples out. We probably could, but should we? Was the land really as unusual and extraordinary as we thought it was? Might nostalgia be coloring our judgment? I asked David Warners, a friend who taught ecology in the biology department at Calvin, to walk the land with me and tell me whether or not it was exceptional.

Dave is a man of few words. Apart from expressing his awe at the forest of beech trees, he said little other than "Look at this sedge here" and "Look at *this* sedge" and "Here's another species of sedge." He taught me that one can identify a sedge, a type of grass, by looking at the cross section of a leaf: the cross section forms a "W." It seemed fitting that there were lots of sedges growing on our land!

On our walk, Dave did not reveal what he thought about the land. But the next day I received in my email inbox a lyrical six-page, single-spaced description. It was, Dave said, an extraordinary piece of land; he had seen nothing like it in southern Michigan. The thought came over me that God had placed this extraordinary piece of land in our hands for safekeeping and that we would be religiously irresponsible if we allowed it to be sold to someone who might spoil it. So Claire and I bought out the other three couples and formed a limited liability corporation in which we, our children, and our grandchildren are co-owners. We named the land "The Wolterstorff Land Preserve" and placed it in the Southwest Michigan Land Conservancy so that it can never be developed. The conservancy people filed the necessary papers to have the creek, which had never been named, officially called "Cave Creek."

In June 2015 a couple of botanists from Michigan State University, accompanied by some people from the land conservancy, explored the beech woods. One of the botanists wrote, among other things: "Cave Creek woods [the beech woods] was a really cool site. I listed 66 species, 63 of which were native....There were some very cool plants; in particular the Stylophorum diphyllum [celadine poppy] was the highlight for me. I had never seen it before in the wild."

Our family makes a point of seeing to it each year that we don't miss going to the land in late April and early May when the spring ephemerals are blooming, so-called because they last just a week or two. The forest floor is a carpet of white, pink, and purple: spring beauty, Dutchman's breeches, squirrel corn, trillium, hepatica, violets, May apple, bloodroot, bishop's hat, geranium, phlox, and many more. It would take Annie Dillard's gift with words, on full display in *Pilgrim at Tinker Creek*, to describe it.

Things were coming at me fast.[1] In the summer of 1964, the synod of the Christian Reformed Church (CRC) appointed a liturgical committee with the mandate to review the liturgical texts, rules, and practices of the denomination and to recommend whatever revisions the committee deemed desirable. I was asked to serve on the committee. I never learned why; at the time I knew nothing about liturgy. My guess is that those who appointed the committee knew that I was interested in art and thought that liturgy and art have something to do with each other—as indeed they do. The mandate given the committee looked interesting, so I accepted.

During the 1960s almost all mainline denominations were engaged in liturgical revision: Catholics, Lutherans, Episcopalians, Presbyterians, and Methodists—the Eastern Orthodox being the principal exception. But I doubt that it was this ferment of liturgical reform that led the CRC to appoint its own liturgical revision committee. I think it was primarily the fact that, whereas liturgical practice had once been virtually uniform across the denomination, it was no longer; plus, it was widely felt that the forms for the Lord's Supper and baptism were seriously out of date. They were long, heavy-handed forms that originated in the Netherlands in the sixteenth century and had never been substantially revised.

I took my assignment seriously and began to read avidly in the history and theology of liturgy. I found the history more interesting than the theology. The theologians operated, for the most part, at a very high level of generality. Though some of that was illuminating, I found the details the historians turned up truly fascinating—beautiful, appalling, profound, inexplicable, inspiring, bizarre.

In the introduction to the report sent to the synod of 1968, the

---

1. In the late 1960s and early 1970s, I chaired the committee that worked to consolidate the hitherto independent Christian schools in Grand Rapids. I have decided not to write about that experience, prominent though it was in my life at the time, and important though the consolidation was for the Christian school movement in Grand Rapids.

committee wrote: "It soon became apparent to the committee that its mandate could be significantly fulfilled only by way of a thorough study of the history of Christian worship in general and of Reformed worship in particular." Since none of us on the committee was a specialist in liturgy, together we undertook to educate ourselves. We gave ourselves long reading assignments as preparation for our meetings, and the meetings were then lively seminars on what we had read and on its significance for carrying out our mandate. It was a wonderful way to acquire an education in liturgy!

Our report was written by Lewis Smedes, who was by that time teaching in Calvin's religion and theology department. It's a superb piece of work. After surveying the highpoints of the history of Christian liturgy in general and of Reformed liturgy in particular, the report offered a very helpful and perceptive discussion of the principles to be used in appraising liturgical practice. It then presented a liturgy for an integrated "Service of Word and Sacrament," which it recommended to Synod for use by the churches. The structure of the recommended liturgy, and a good many of its words, were like those emerging in other denominations.

An integrated Service of Word and Sacrament was an innovation in the Reformed tradition. In 1525, Ulrich Zwingli dispensed with the Catholic Mass in his church in Zurich and replaced it with forty-eight preaching services over the course of the year and four Lord's Supper services. John Calvin protested this arrangement, insisting that the Lord's Supper should be celebrated every Sunday. But the Zwinglian practice of quarterly Lord's Supper celebrations had been instituted in Geneva some years before Calvin arrived, and the city council refused to change the practice that the people had, by then, become accustomed to. Quarterly celebration of the Lord's Supper became the near-universal practice of the Reformed churches around the world.

Our committee's study of the history and theology of liturgy convinced us that the churches of the denomination should at least be given the opportunity to celebrate the Lord's Supper weekly with an integrated Service of Word and Sacrament. The Synod of 1968 agreed, and the committee's proposed liturgy was approved for trial use; with a few revisions, it was later approved for permanent use. Since then, the denomination has continued to produce new and revised liturgical texts, all of them more or less consonant with the vision of the 1968 report.

My work on the liturgical committee of the denomination, and my reading in the history of liturgy, persuaded me that liturgy is too important—and too fascinating—to be confined to committees, synods, and seminaries. Courses in liturgy should be available to college students. So, though I was by no means a specialist in liturgy, I began teaching it. One of the innovations of the curricular revisions that the Calvin faculty approved in 1966 was the so-called January Interim: the idea was that, during the month of January, faculty members would teach intensive three-week-long courses that, for one reason or another, did not fit well into the regular curriculum. For two years I taught an Interim course on liturgy. It went well, I enjoyed it, I learned a lot, and the students were enthusiastic.

But it was a sideline for me. So I proposed to the religion and theology department that they take over the course and include it in their regular semester curriculum. Their response was that they would make it part of their course entitled "Ecclesiology—Doctrine of the Church." I was appalled. Liturgy is not doctrine; it is activity, the activity of worshiping God by singing hymns, eating bread, drinking wine, offering prayers, and the like. Then and there I resolved to do whatever was necessary to keep liturgy out of the hands of the theologians. I got approval to teach the course myself and, for a few years, taught it as a regular semester course—in the evening, so that townspeople could attend.

Though students were again enthusiastic, I felt uneasy. I knew enough about the subject to teach a brief Interim course, but I did not feel equipped to teach a semester-long course. Furthermore, I was not prepared to change careers—from philosopher to liturgical scholar. So, after two years, I gave it up, whereupon liturgy disappeared from the college curriculum for a couple of decades, only to reappear in 1997. John Witvliet, a student in one of my evening liturgy courses, was fascinated by the subject and went on to get a doctoral degree in liturgy from the University of Notre Dame. John is not only a very fine scholar but also an unusually gifted academic entrepreneur. In 1997 he returned to Calvin to teach liturgy on a regular basis and to inaugurate the Calvin Institute for Christian Worship. The Institute does extraordinary work. It uses large grants from various foundations to support liturgical projects by a wide variety of churches and academic institutions, and each year, at the end of January, it hosts a liturgy conference at Calvin. In recent years the conference has drawn more than sixteen hundred attendees from around the world. It is deeply gratifying to me to see that, from those small beginnings in an evening course, there has blossomed this extraordinary flowering of interest in liturgy.

I did not put liturgy out of mind after no longer teaching it. Just as my work on the college's curriculum revision committee provoked me into thinking and writing about education, so my work on the denomination's liturgy committee provoked me into thinking and writing about liturgy and to become deeply involved in liturgical practice, as we shall see shortly.

By 1967 we had outgrown our house. We had bought it when we had three children; now we had five. Christopher Matthew, our fifth child, was born shortly after the beginning of the school year, on September 23, 1967. His middle name, Matthew, was my father's name. We had already been feeling the need for more room; now, that need was clear and pressing.

I remember feeling nervous when I first held each of the other children. Each time they were so much smaller than I had imagined, and seemed so delicate and vulnerable. With Christopher, it was different; I felt relaxed, confident, perhaps overconfident, that I had gotten the hang of how to hold a newborn infant and how to do my share in taking care of him. The other children were excited to have a new brother and welcomed him warmly into the family; I discerned no touch of jealousy in any of them. They were each beginning to show their own distinct inscape. What would Christopher's inscape be?

Under the guidance of a realtor we liked, Claire looked at thirty or more houses for sale, and I looked at the ones she judged to have some promise. We rejected all of them: they were out of our price range, did not fit our needs, or were architecturally dismal. One day, in the summer of 1967, when we were taking a walk with the children, we came upon a "For Sale" sign on an attractive lot on a cul de sac. It took us no time at all to decide to buy the lot and to build.

I had long resolved that, if we ever did build, we would employ an architect. I began developing what I anticipated would be the program for the architect we chose. We knew by now what we wanted for the life of the family, and I had some design ideas, so I began making sketches of floor plans and elevations. After a good deal of trial and error, I came up with a design that fitted our needs, that we liked, and that was sufficiently detailed for a builder we consulted to give us a rough cost estimate. No need for an architect!

What we did need, however, were architectural drawings for the builder to use. I had never had any architectural training and thus did not know how to make architectural drawings. What I had drawn was nothing more than sketches on graph paper of floor plans and elevations. So I went to a nearby lumberyard and asked if they knew of someone who would make architectural drawings from my sketches. They did. His initial drawings failed to realize some of my design ideas; for example, what I had intended as vistas were not vistas in his drawings. But soon he came up with drawings that did capture what I was after. We built the house during the summer of 1968.

It is, unmistakably, a mid-century modern house (what some would call a "California-style ranch"): single story, flat roof, big openings to the out-of-doors, and so forth. Some people, when they see it, say it reminds them of Frank Lloyd Wright's "prairie style" architecture; others say it reminds them of Scandinavian architecture, and still others, of Japanese architecture. In each case, I recognize what it is about the house that leads them to see it as they do, but when designing it, I had none of those styles in mind. I was just "doing my own thing."

The house is designed as an "L" around some large black willow trees that were already on the property. The leg of the "L" facing the street contains the living areas; the leg of the "L" at right angles to the street contains the sleeping quarters. Whereas windows in most houses are punctures in the walls, I thought it would be interesting to make the windows interruptions in the walls instead. So in the corners of the rooms there are windows going from floor to ceiling; adjacent to that strip of windows is a slab of uninterrupted wall; then, in several of the rooms, there are sliding glass doors with transoms above them. Thus a rhythm is established of light from ceiling to floor, then uninterrupted wall, then light from ceiling to floor again, and so on. I designed the trim work around the windows and doors in such a way as to enhance the rhythm of strip of light/slab of wall. The large uninterrupted slabs of wall have proved ideal for displaying our collection of graphic art prints.

Another feature of the design is that, between the two legs of the "L," there is a reversal of solids and voids. When one enters the house, one is presented with a solid element containing a closet and part of the kitchen; rooms rotate around this solid element, open to each other: entry, living room, kitchen, family room, and study. In the back leg of the "L" there is a void at the center, and the closed bedrooms and bathrooms rotate around it. The ceilings in the front part of the house are ten feet high, to reflect the fact that this is where daytime activity takes place; the rooms in the back part have eight-foot ceilings—to reflect that these spaces are for the quiet of sleeping. Throughout the house there is a great deal of natural wood; the ceilings in the front part of the house are all natural cedar, as are the walls in the "family room" and in the back hallway and baths. (This reflects my upbringing, of course.) I did most of the finish carpentry myself.

I think of architecture as, essentially, the shaping of space and the control of light. I have described the "envelope" of our house, which shapes the space and controls the light. I don't know how to describe the space itself, nor the light. Suffice it to say that we have greatly enjoyed living in this house, and visitors often express their admiration.

From the time we built the house, Claire said that she missed a screened-in porch. There was an obvious place to add a porch, but all the designs I came up with seemed clunky to me. Then, when we redesigned the entrance to the house, about thirty years after we had built it, I saw how the porch had to be designed. I had been attempting to echo the design of the house; the porch had to echo the redesigned entry.

Constructing the porch required that we build about a foot closer to the lot line than the zoning regulations permitted, so we requested a variance, and were given a hearing before the city zoning commission. A member of the commission who had been assigned to go out to look at the situation spoke enthusiastically in favor of our request, as did our neighbors. Another member of the commission spoke vigorously against it, however; I guessed that he was a developer. I explained to the commission that the reason the house had been built close to the lot line, forcing us now to seek a variance, was that I wanted to save the big black willow trees on the property. He refused to accept this. "Houses last longer than trees," he said. "You should have cut the trees down."

I feared that our request for a variance was going nowhere. So I pulled out all the stops. I explained that, ever since we built the house, my wife had regretted the absence of a screened-in porch. Just recently I had come up with a design that we liked. I would now like to present to her, as a gift on her seventieth birthday, a screened-in porch. (Claire had in fact recently celebrated her seventieth birthday.) The motion to grant a variance passed by one vote.

What I have been calling a "porch" is not really a porch, but rather a north-facing solarium. It's been a wonderful addition! A couple of years ago, when I was sitting in the solarium on a spring evening, someone drove up and rang the bell. The visitor told me that he had long admired our house and that, as he was driving past this time, he noticed that I had white hair. He wondered whether we were thinking of selling.

I n October 1969 I was invited to join the editorial board of *The Reformed Journal*. I had already published thirteen pieces in the *Journal*, the first in October 1960; by the time the *Journal* ceased publication, in 1990, I had published eighty-nine pieces. Over those thirty-one years, I was not only thinking and writing as a professional philosopher, but also thinking and writing for the church, the *Reformed Journal* being the principal venue for that second side of myself. I wrote about political issues in the United States, apartheid in South Africa, the plight of the Palestinians, the Vietnam War, the civil rights struggle in America, theological conflicts in the church, education, school choice, art and music, liturgy, the ordination of women, and more.

The *Reformed Journal* was a remarkable publication: it occupied a unique position within American religious journalism and spoke with a voice all its own. It appeared monthly (except for two double-month issues in the summer) for forty years, from 1951 to 1990, financially supported and published by Eerdmans Publishing Company.

The subtitle of the *Journal* was: "A periodical of Reformed comment and opinion." What that subtitle did not indicate was that it was a periodical of *progressive* Reformed comment and opinion. In an early issue, one of the editors, James Daane, declared that the postwar world required "a Reformed theology bristling with vitality and restless with creative energy."

Its subscribers were intensely loyal, but there were never many of them, never more, as I recall, than 2,800. But despite the small subscriber numbers, the Journal was surprisingly influential, read and referred to by many more people than actually subscribed to it. The editorial board regularly fretted over the small number of subscribers and discussed what steps could be taken to expand it. Those discussions never came to anything. On one occasion, the board hired a professional firm for advice; their advice was to dumb down the writing. They did not, of course, use the term "dumb down," but that was clearly the idea. The board rejected the advice out of hand: better critical esteem and broad influence than a dumbed-down publication with lots of subscribers. In fact, one of the things readers often said they liked about the Journal was that the articles were well written without being dumbed down. Anyone interested in getting a firsthand sense of what the writing in the Journal was like should browse among the ninety pieces that James D. Bratt and Ronald A. Wells selected for their collection of essays entitled *The Best of the Reformed Journal* (Eerdmans, 2011).

The Journal was founded by five friends: Harry Boer, James Daane, George Stob, Henry Stob, and Henry Zylstra, all of them, with the exception of Zylstra, ordained ministers in the Christian Reformed Church. Born out of intramural quarrels within the denomination, the Journal, in its early years, commented mostly on theological and ecclesiastical issues of concern to members of the denomination. Bratt and Wells do a good job of describing the changes that took place in the topics the Journal addressed over the forty years of its existence: "For its first dozen years the magazine centered on in-house disputes in the Christian Reformed Church in opposition to the denomination's entrenched defenders of orthodoxy. The 1960s and '70s brought a quickening of sociopolitical concerns—issues of war and peace, race and civil rights, American foreign policy and Christian Zionism—along with responses to radical new proposals in theology and the erosion of the old 'mainline' in American Protestantism. In the Journal's last dozen years, the triumph of conservative politics in the presidency of Ronald Reagan prompted the magazine to offer a coherent, yet supply expressed version of critical Reformed thinking in the Niebuhrian as well as Kuyperian tradition over against claims by such organizations as the Moral Majority and the Christian Coalition to speak for biblical Christianity."

Bratt and Wells go on to observe: "To many, the most striking aspect of the magazine was its combination of distinctive point of view and expansive range of commentary. Articles on theology and the deliberations of church assemblies spread out on the Journal's pages, as befit a religious magazine, but so did reviews of literature and film, essays on higher education and aesthetic theory, and articles on philosophy and science—and sometimes the philosophy of science. The Reformed Journal gave persistent attention to important social trends like the civil rights movement and the rebirth of feminism, as it did to political controversies attending the Vietnam War and the rise of the Christian Right. It was also marked by ecumenical concern in giving space to the plight of Christians in Palestine and especially (sometimes almost uniquely) in publishing the leading Christian voices—black, white, and colored—in the resistance to South African apartheid. All this added up to a consistent body of reflection refracted through theological commitment, engaged with the state of the academic disciplines, and intent on articulating fresh positions above hardened predictable habits of opinion."

The Journal became "a noted presence on the evangelical Protestant scene.... [It] served to make traditional Protestant conviction more reputable in mainline precincts while also setting a standard among evangelicals of top-notch, venturesome commentary on the whole range of concerns of modern public life."

In 1960 the editors introduced an opening section called "As We

See It." It was here, especially, that the *Journal* spoke with a distinctive voice. Let me quote Jon Pott from his "Publisher's Note" in the Bratt and Wells collection: "Whatever the importance of the articles and reviews, it was the opening 'As We See It' section that probably most defined the magazine for its readers. This section also produced some of the *Journal*'s best (and journalistically most awarded) writing, its eclecticism and diversity, in form and substance, reflecting the omnivorous curiosity of its contributors. Akin, to speak a bit grandly, to *The New Yorker*'s fabled 'Talk of the Town,' the pieces ranged from classic editorials ... to quietly reflective personal commentary that would sink home in the reader's shared human experience."

I loved writing for the *Journal* and being a member of its editorial board. I had the sense of being an active member of a religious intellectual community that was creatively using its tradition to address the events and issues of the day. I knew many of the contributors. We did not take our bearings from the standard categories of left/right, liberal/conservative, but thought for ourselves from our own distinct orientation. There was an indescribable buzz in the air. It was exciting.

By the time I joined the editorial board of the *Journal*, only two of its founding members were still active in the monthly editorial meetings, namely, Henry Stob and Harry Boer. Henry Zylstra had died, James Daane had taken a position at Fuller Seminary in Pasadena, and George Stob was a pastor in New Jersey. Henry Stob I already knew, of course; now I got to know Harry Boer. When I joined the board, my good friend Lewis Smedes was a member; among later additions was Richard Mouw, my colleague in the philosophy department at Calvin.

Harry Boer was one of the most memorable persons I have ever known: he had inscape! When I got to know him, he had retired from serving as a missionary of the Christian Refomed Church in a theological college in Nigeria. Harry hated anything that smelled of compromise, deception, or evasion. He preferred going down fighting for his views on a board or in an assembly to accepting a squishy-worded compromise that each party could interpret as they pleased. At one point, when he was still a missionary, he discovered that the denomination was secretly funneling its mission funds for Nigeria through an agency in Canada in order to avoid certain restrictions imposed by the US government. As it turned out, there was nothing illegal about this. Nonetheless, Harry was furious and created a public furor, because the practice was deceitful even if not illegal.

One of the confessional standards of the Christian Reformed Church is the Canons of Dordt, adopted in 1619 by a synod of Reformed churches—mainly Dutch—held in the Dutch city of Dordrecht. Harry ardently disagreed with the doctrine of double predestination taught by the Canons, the doctrine that God "predestines" some persons for salvation and others for damnation. So, one year he filed an appeal to the annual synod of the CRC in which he argued, at some length, that the section of the Canons that taught the doctrine of double predestination should be repudiated as bad theology. Synod appointed a committee to study the matter, and asked me to serve as one of its members.

Though I had never read the Canons of Dordt with care and had never thought hard about the doctrine of double predestination, I intuitively shared Harry's conviction that the doctrine was wrong, and I expected to come out supporting Harry's position. But after carefully reading the Canons and Harry's protest, I found myself forced to conclude that Harry had misinterpreted the Canons on some crucial points; the text did not say what Harry took it to say. One could make a compelling case that the Canons did teach the doctrine of double predestination, but Harry had not made that case. My view was shared by the other members of the committee, and we wrote our report accordingly.

Harry was extremely upset with me and phoned to say that he wanted to come to my office to talk. He showed up at the agreed-on time and said, "Hello, Nick." Then, without a further word, he took two cups out of a pack he was carrying, set them on a corner of my desk, took out a thermos, unscrewed the top, poured tea into the cups, took out a small tin box, opened it, took out some Oreo cookies, and sat down.

"Nick," he said, "we have to talk." And talk we did—at length. At one point in our conversation, the thought crossed my mind: "How fitting—Oreo cookies when double predestination is the topic! I wonder whether Harry had that in mind." I didn't ask him.

A l Plantinga and I were friends and acquaintances of a number of philosophers our age at the University of Notre Dame. We regarded them as coworkers in the project of Christian philosophy. So, sometime in the late 1960s or early 1970s, we proposed that the Calvin philosophers get together every now and then with the Notre Dame philosophers to discuss what we and they were currently working on. A member of each department would write a paper and distribute it in advance. We met twice a year, alternating between Calvin and Notre Dame. The camaraderie was great.

After a few years of these meetings, the suggestion emerged of opening up our discussions to others by forming a society of Christian philosophers. We brought other Christian philosophers into the planning: I think especially of the late William P. Alston and Marilyn Adams, and of Robert Adams, Eleonore Stump, Peter van Inwagen, and George Mavrodes. The Society of Christian Philosophers was officially organized in 1978, and it took off at once—like a dam bursting and the river now surging forth.

Today the society has about nine hundred members, making it the largest affiliate of the American Philosophical Association (APA) and a major presence on the North American philosophical scene. As one would expect, many members of the society hold teaching positions at the Christian colleges and universities of this country;

but there are also a good many who hold positions in major "secular" universities. At least ten members of the society have served as presidents of the national APA. The society is ecumenical in its membership, requiring only that a person declare that she or he is a Christian. It publishes a quarterly journal, Faith and Philosophy, now in its thirty-fifth year of publication (2018). The formation of the society has spurred the organization of similar societies in other countries—in Korea, for example.

When I was a graduate student at Harvard, I was aware of a handful of Christian philosophers who held positions at major universities: John Wild, for example, one of my professors at Harvard; William Frankena, a Calvin graduate, teaching at the University of Michigan and well known for his work in ethics; O. K. Bouwsma, another Calvin graduate, teaching at the University of Nebraska; and Jesse de Boer, also a Calvin grad, and teaching at the University of Kentucky. But few of the philosophers that I knew to be Christian wrote much that was recognizably Christian, the major exception being Bouwsma. The latter was famous for his uncanny ability to devise humorous little stories that held up to the light of day the implausibility of one or another philosophical position. The story he told to highlight the implausibility of logical positivism, in a plenary address he gave in the early 1960s at the annual convention of the APA (Central Division), held that year in the grand old Palmer House Hotel in downtown Chicago, has become a classic.

Bouwsma gave his address in the main ballroom. I can see the scene as if it were yesterday. The seating was semicircular, and off to my right, sitting together a few rows ahead of me, were the philosophers from the University of Minnesota, several of them well-known positivists. I could see their faces. Recall the central claim of the positivists: if a sentence is neither empirically verifiable nor analytically true or false, it is meaningless. Here is the story Bouwsma told (in my words):

It happened one day that a housewife answered the knock of a vacuum-cleaner salesman on her door. The salesman said that he was selling a new type of vacuum cleaner, and asked whether he could come in to demonstrate it. The woman said that she was very satisfied with her present vacuum cleaner. But the salesman was persistent, and she eventually gave in. The salesman plugged in his vacuum cleaner, turned it on, and ran it across the carpet. The woman said, "But it's not picking up the dust." The salesman replied, "Lady, if this thing don't pick it up, it ain't dust."

A glance over at the University of Minnesota positivists showed that they were not joining in the laughter.

A sister-in-law of Bouwsma lived in Grand Rapids. Each summer, when Bouwsma came to visit her, he would invite the younger members of the Calvin philosophy department over to his sister-in-law's house for an evening of conversation. Each time, Bouwsma would manage to trap Al Plantinga into being his straight man for the evening, or into saying something foolish, and each time the next year, as we were driving over together, Al would resolve not to take the bait. It never worked. I remember Bouwsma asking, on one of those occasions, why we studied the history of philosophy. The consensus emerged that we did so, in part, because we learned things from our philosophical forebears. Bouwsma turned to Al at that point and asked him what he had learned from reading Plato. On the spot now, and a bit flustered, Al mentioned some rather bland point Plato had made. Bouwsma saw his opening: "You didn't know *that* before you read Plato?"

Why was it that, after being virtually invisible for many years, Christians became prominent in the guild of professional philosophers in the late 1970s and have remained prominent there ever since? I think the main factor was the death of logical positivism. Recall that an implication of the positivist doctrine of meaning was that God-talk is meaningless. When positivism died in the early

1960s, no other movement emerged to take over its "policing" function of telling believers what they could and could not think or say. For a couple of centuries, Kantians had been claiming that concepts have no function beyond experience; but Kantianism never enjoyed the popularity among American philosophers that it did among European philosophers. The thought police were gone. Philosophers began talking freely and openly about God.

One of the many gratifying strands of my life has been sharing in the founding of the Society of Christian Philosophers, watching it flourish, participating in its activities, and serving a term as president. Each time I have attended a meeting of the society in recent years, I have been surprised and delighted by the number of young philosophers in attendance and by the enthusiasm of their participation.

The social turmoil of the 1960s had the effect on many young people of making them critical of the churches they were members of. They wanted a more participatory liturgy, more intense fellowship, a less top-down authority structure, a serious commitment to social justice, a voice for women equal to that of men, an open discussion of the ethics of war. Claire and I were among these young people advocating for change.

When we moved to Grand Rapids in 1959, we became members of LaGrave Avenue Christian Reformed Church, an old, well-established, and prosperous congregation in downtown Grand Rapids. It turned out that most of the church's members did not welcome the changes that we and others were now advocating. They found the social turmoil threatening rather than energizing. We had not realized, when we joined, that the congregation was as socially conservative as it now proved to be.

In the mid-1960s, a number of us who were advocating for change in our various churches began to find each other. We got together in our homes for worship and fellowship, and we talked excitedly about a new form of church. The group grew in size, and we could no longer meet in someone's living room, so we decided to hold open public worship and fellowship services on a regular basis on Sunday afternoons. Our first open meeting was in the YMCA in downtown Grand Rapids. To our astonishment, hundreds of people showed up. The excitement—something new was happening—was palpable. Not long thereafter a name emerged: "Fellowship of the Acts."

Our family continued to be faithful attendees of the Sunday morning worship services at LaGrave, and in 1967, I was elected to the church council as an elder. I regularly informed my fellow council members about my participation in Fellowship of the Acts, and I invited them to tell me to stop if they disapproved of what I was doing. None of them did.

The Fellowship of the Acts found itself in the unsatisfactory position of being forced to move around from one hall or school gymnasium to another. So I proposed to the worship committee of LaGrave, of which I was the chairman, that we invite the Fellowship to meet at the church on Sunday afternoons. There was plenty of available space in the church's building, and it would be a form of worship alternative to LaGrave's Sunday morning worship service that would be attractive, I said, to many people who would otherwise never darken the door of a church. The worship committee agreed, and sent the proposal on to the entire council, where it was accepted—though with evident apprehension and some reluctance. The Fellowship was invited to meet in the basement of the church.

A large crowd of young people showed up for the first assembly, some dressed in ways that had never before been seen at LaGrave, a few riding up on motorcycles. There were not enough chairs, so some people sat on the floor. The members of the council who had been designated to attend and report back to council were shocked at this lack of decorum. That was the end of the experiment. There would be no alternative worship at LaGrave Avenue Christian Reformed Church.

I mentioned above that the 1968 Synod of the Christian Reformed Church had recommended to the churches, for trial use, the integrated Service of Word and Sacrament that the denominational liturgical committee had proposed. In the fall of that year, I proposed to the LaGrave worship committee that the church use the proposed liturgy for a couple of months. The committee thought the entire council should be brought in on the decision, and the full council accepted our proposal. The pastor was on sabbatical in England that fall and was not present at those meetings. Upon returning, just before Christmas, he single-handedly reinstated the liturgy that had been in place before we introduced the new liturgy. He did not consult me, as head of the worship committee, on the matter; he simply discarded the new liturgy and reintroduced the old one. I realized that I had been naïve.

It was this episode—combined with the shock of the council at what transpired when Fellowship of the Acts used the basement for worship that infamous Sunday afternoon—that persuaded me that there was no hope of incorporating, within LaGrave, the new forms of worship and fellowship that we were advocating and experiencing in Fellowship of the Acts. Nor did anybody in the Fellowship know of any other church that would welcome us.

What to do? We could continue the side-by-side arrangement of attending our regular churches on Sunday mornings and meeting as Fellowship of the Acts late Sunday afternoons. But, slowly and reluctantly, I and others came to the conclusion that that would likely not continue for long: the divided loyalty of the side-by-side arrangement—in my case, for example, loyalty to both LaGrave and to Fellowship of the Acts—was becoming difficult. Furthermore, the great amount of volunteer activity required to keep the Fellowship going was beginning to wear us down; voluntarism, while exciting at first, eventually becomes burdensome. And third, informal groups such as the Fellowship of the Acts typically have a relatively short life-span.

We came to the conclusion that we had to do one or the other of two things: either live with the realization that Fellowship of the Acts would go out of existence in the not-too-distant future or petition to become a congregation within the Christian Reformed Church. I strongly favored the latter option, as did most members of the leadership group: we did not want what we had learned and practiced to disappear into the sand. Not everyone agreed. Some were convinced that, if we became a congregation within the CRC, we would soon become just like the churches we were critical of, and those in the group who were members of other denominations felt they would have to leave if we became a CRC congregation.

Fast-forward now to 1972. In late summer of 1972 we applied to Classis Grand Rapids East (the CRC is divided into regional classes) for permission to organize as a congregation within the denomination. The traditional reason for organizing a new congregation within the CRC is that the existing congregations are either too large or too far away. Obviously, neither of those was our reason. All of the delegates at the semiannual meeting of the classis that autumn knew that our reason for wanting to organize a new congregation was that we were critical of the existing churches. But it would have been fatal for us to come right out and say that. So those of us who were presenting our case did our best to put a positive spin on the matter.

After a great deal of animated discussion, the classis made a decision that had no precedent: they would give us permission to meet for a year "under the umbrella of classical supervision." What that meant, in practice, was that we could organize and meet *as if we were* a congregation within the denomination, and then, if things went well, a year later classis would give us permission to organize as a congregation. In the fall of 1973 we were given that permission. A member of our group proposed "Church of the Servant" as our name, and there was immediate and unanimous approval—we never even bothered to take a vote. For a few years we shared the building of a Presbyterian church; after that, we met in a succession of school gymnasiums.

The fact that we now met on Sunday morning meant that we

were faced with a decision that Fellowship of the Acts had never had to make: What would be our Sunday morning liturgy? Would we use the integrated "Service of Word and Sacrament" that the denomination's liturgical committee had recommended? I proposed that, rather than debating the issue of a weekly Lord's Supper, we try it for six months and then take a vote. My proposal was accepted. When the vote was taken, six months later, it was unanimous in favor of weekly communion.

We were full of youthful idealism. We declared that we would never employ a full-time pastor; each week we would ask a minister in the area to preach for us and celebrate the sacraments, and we would pastor each other. We declared that we would remain small and intimate; we would form a "daughter" congregation rather than become large. We declared that we would never spend more money on ourselves than on outside causes. We declared that we would never own a building.

Two years later we called a full-time pastor. We grew rapidly. We got into complicated discussions about what constitutes "spending money on ourselves." And we now own a building. Ours has been the humbling experience of having one's youthful ideals chastened by reality. Our underlying vision remains intact, but we have been led to imagine and pursue new and unanticipated ways of embodying that vision.

Participating in the founding and life of Church of the Servant has been, for me, an extraordinarily rewarding experience.

I was on sabbatical leave for the academic year 1970–71, supported by a fellowship from the National Endowment for the Humanities and by the Harbison Award for Excellence in Teaching, awarded by the Danforth Foundation. We decided to spend the year in London as a family. We flew into London Heathrow, and located an inexpensive hotel near Regent Park, our whole family of seven in one long room. I had not arranged for living accommodations for the year, so the next morning I contacted an organization we had heard about, "Universal Aunts," and in their listings found a notice for an apartment that seemed possible, in Beckenham, a suburb on the southern edge of London. I called the number. The woman who answered the phone seemed pleasant, and her description of the apartment made it sound promising. So I took a train out to look it over and decided that it would be just fine for us.

We had arranged in advance for the purchase of a Volkswagen camper, which we were to pick up in London. So the next morning I located the camper, near our hotel, as it turned out, loaded up the family and our luggage, and we set out. We were on the north side of London and had to take the Ring Road around London to the south side of the city. The drive proved to be one of the most harrowing experiences of my life. It was Friday mid-day, the traffic was heavy, and I had never before driven on the left side of the road. The Ring Road is not what an American imagines when he hears the term "Ring Road": it is not a two- or three-lane expressway; rather, it's a sequence of ordinary streets that, together, circle London. The names of the streets keep changing, and the only indication that one is still on the Ring Road is a small sign, every now and then, saying "Ring Road." By the time we arrived at our destination, I was a nervous wreck.

The apartment was on the third floor of a very large Victorian house in a pleasant neighborhood, a few blocks from the local train station. The owners, the Kinches, lived with their six children on the first two floors. We became close friends with them, Claire and I with Barb and Tony, our children with their children. We greatly enjoyed our stay.

We asked Barb and Tony for their advice about schools. They made it clear that they did not want to see our children enrolled in the ordinary run of schools. So we followed their recommendation and enrolled Amy in a nearby selective school for girls and Eric in a nearby selective school for boys. We enrolled Robert and Klaas in the local elementary school. After some initial nervousness about the new and unfamiliar situation, they all enjoyed the experience and did excellent work. In subsequent years, they have often reminisced, with much laughter, about the experience, especially Robert and Klaas about the school lunches: "bangers" and "mushy peas"! Alas, Christopher was still too young for school.

My project for the year was to begin working on the ontology of art works ("ontology" is another word for metaphysics). What, for example, is a work of music? What is its ontological status? Are works of music created, or are they discovered? And what is the nature, the ontological status, of the world of a literary work and of the characters within such a world? It's obvious that fictional characters are not persons. So what are they? Such questions intrigued me.

The book that eventually emerged from my reflections was *Works and Worlds of Art* (Oxford, 1980), written in a rather inaccessible style, which I now very much regret. The reason I wrote it as I did was that philosophy of art, in those days, was widely regarded as the weak sister among the subdisciplines of philosophy, and I wanted to show that it could be developed with as much heft as any other philosophical subdiscipline. A big mistake. It's the last book I wrote on metaphysics. I have since written essays in this area of philosophy, but not an entire book. My only regret on that score is not having thought and written at greater depth than I have about the nature of time. I don't find any of the extant theories plausible.

Sometime in the fall of that year, Claire and I made the decision to take the kids out of school in the spring and go with the entire family on a long European tour—our poor person's version of the Grand Tour. We thought it unlikely that we would ever again have an opportunity to do that. I bought maps, guidebooks, and a listing of European campsites, and laid out an itinerary. On March 31, 1971, we set out in our VW camper, by boat from England to Belgium, Belgium to France, France to Italy, by boat from Italy to Greece, Greece to Istanbul, back through Greece to Yugoslavia, through eastern Italy to Austria, Germany, Denmark, Sweden, Norway, and back by boat to England. The monuments of Europe were not yet fenced off. I have a photo, for example, of the children sitting on the steps of the Parthenon, something that is no longer permitted. Earlier in the year we had visited Stonehenge, and I have a photo of the children leaning against the stones. Stonehenge was later fenced off by an ugly chain-link fence.

We were on the road for thirteen weeks. Eric was a genius at reading maps, and he would often sit in the front seat to guide me, especially when we drove through cities. We had a tent that attached to the side of the camper; the children slept in the tent and Claire and I slept in the camper. With no lodging expenditures other than fees for campsites, and with Claire cooking evening meals in the camper, the cost of our tour averaged out to about $20 per day.

The children were wonderfully patient and well-behaved. The tour I had laid out was heavy on cathedrals. I would point out the ways in which each cathedral was different from the others we had seen: Bourges, for example, has two aisles flanking the nave on each side, whereas almost all the others have just one. Eric listened attentively and took lots of photos, the others tolerated my enthusiasms. There was a point somewhere in southern France, however, when Amy asked plaintively, "Can't we go to a beach some time? Do we always have to look at churches?" So we departed from the itinerary, drove down to the Riviera, and spent a couple of days there. We all agreed that the beach along the eastern shore of Lake Michigan was finer than the Riviera!

Greece was, for all of us, a high point: Athens, ancient Delphi, various sites in the Peloponnesus, especially Mycenae, Olympia, and the ancient Byzantine city of Mistra. But for me, personally, the high point of all high points was Hagia Sophia in Istanbul. I was overwhelmed—and baffled. I had the same experience many visitors have had, of this enormous structure appearing to cascade down rather than rise up: half-domes descending from the great central dome, quarter-domes descending from the half-domes. The sixth-century historian Procopius wrote that it was as if the central dome were suspended by a chain from heaven. How is it done? Something has to be holding it up. But what? Where are the supports? Why does the central dome look as if it's floating?

Many writers have noted that what contributes to the appearance of the central dome as floating are the windows surrounding the base of the dome, making the dome seem to float on a band of light. But there had to be something more. Finally, the answer emerged: the central dome is supported by four enormous piers; but the eye is led away from those. Standing in the center of the building, facing forward, one sees a wall between the two piers on the left and a wall between the two piers on the right. These walls are constructed of the same marble as the piers and are continuous with the piers. Only if one looks closely does one see where the piers end and the walls that connect them begin. These walls are screen walls, full of penetrations. So when one stands between them, what draws the eye are these seemingly insubstantial screen walls. The whole is a masterpiece of illusion!

On the way back from Istanbul we stopped at Meteora, in northern Greece, where a number of monasteries were constructed in the Middle Ages on towering outcroppings of rock, from there to Yugoslavia, which was then still a unified state, to visit some of the old churches there, then through northeast Italy and Austria into Germany, visiting some of the Baroque churches there, then a loop to the east to visit the Taizé community in eastern France, and on to the Scandinavian countries.

Driving in Paris, Rome, and Istanbul was almost as harrowing as driving in London that first day. In Norway one morning, as we were headed to Bergen to catch the boat back to England, driving was sheer terror. I had made a point of searching out some of the fantastic old wooden stave churches in Norway, all of them out of the way, off the main highways. Now we had to drive up from a valley to the crest of a mountain on a back road. My guidebook indicated the grade of incline: it was steep. The VW camper of those days was underpowered, so I checked the owner's guide for the maximum grade of incline the vehicle was capable of. I concluded that we should be okay, though the fact that we were loaded down made me a bit apprehensive.

We began the ascent. The guidebook had not mentioned that the surface was gravel rather than paved. Nor did it mention that, after about a quarter mile, the road became a long series of switchbacks. I put the VW in first gear. It had rained the night before, so all the turns were soft and squishy, making it impossible to get up any speed. A quick glance to my right showed a steep drop-off. The road was narrow, impossible to turn around in, so there was nothing to do but continue. It was sheer terror. "What have I done?" I thought. "I have put the lives of seven people in jeopardy. Will the family have to get out and walk up?" We made it to the summit, where there was a place to park. It was an hour or so before I had calmed down sufficiently to be able to continue on our way to Bergen.

SIX

Awakenings

At some point the late 1960s, I experienced an art awakening. It happened on a Saturday afternoon in our living room in Grand Rapids, as I was listening to the University of Michigan public radio station. Normally the U of M station played classical music in the afternoons; on this particular afternoon, the announcer said they would be playing work songs, that is, songs sung to accompany manual labor. I was fascinated—and then, the awakening.

I was teaching the Calvin philosophy department's course in aesthetics. (In the next few paragraphs, I will follow the common practice of using the terms "aesthetics" and "philosophy of art" interchangeably.) I had never enrolled as a student in a course in aesthetics, neither in my undergraduate years at Calvin nor my graduate years at Harvard. When I listened in on student conversations about these courses, the courses sounded to me more like armchair psychology of art than like philosophy, and that did not appeal to me. But when Tunis Prins, who had been teaching the aesthetics course in our department at Calvin, retired, the department tapped me to teach it—on the ground that I cared about art.

As good fortune would have it, a few years before I was tapped to teach the department's course in asthetics, Monroe Beardsley, whom I knew personally, had published his book entitled *Aesthetics*, and this was definitely philosophy, not armchair psychology, so I chose it as the textbook for my new course. Beardsley's approach to art was shaped by the widely shared assumption that art is a special sphere of life, and that leisure is required if we are to engage works of the arts as they are meant to be engaged—that is, as objects of absorbed aesthetic attention. In my teaching of aesthetics I had gone along with that assumption, and for fifteen or twenty minutes that's how I engaged the work songs being broadcast on public radio that Saturday afternoon. Then dissonance set in. The thought came to mind that, though the station was presenting these songs for absorbed aesthetic attention—and though that's how I was engaging them—that's not how they were originally engaged. They were sung as accompaniments to work.

At the time, I didn't know what to do with this dissonant thought. Could it be that Beardsley didn't know about work songs? That seemed implausible, and, in any case, I knew about work songs long before listening to a few of them on the radio that Saturday afternoon. Could it be that work songs are not art, and hence not something that philosophers of art would pay attention to? But they *are* works of music, and music is one of the arts. Isn't that enough to make them something philosophers of art would take account of? Or was Beardsley perhaps assuming—and had I gone along with the assumption—that work songs are inherently inferior and hence not worth a philosopher's attention? If so, inferior in what way? I found them fascinating to listen to, as did the station programmer, presumably, and those who originally sang them must have found them rewarding for singing while working.

It took me several years to arrive at answers to these questions. What eventually emerged from my reflections was my book *Art in Action* (Eerdmans, 1980), published the same year as *Works and Worlds of Art*. Though the two books appeared in the same year, *Works and Worlds* was virtually completed before I began writing *Art in Action*.

Works and Worlds of Art was internally motivated. The interest in metaphysics that graduate school had awakened in me, and that had led me to write *On Universals*, naturally led me to think about the ontology of art works when I began teaching our department's course in aesthetics. By contrast, it was my attempt to make sense of my unanticipated art awakening that led me to write *Art in Action*. In that respect, *Art in Action* was like my writings on liturgy: it was my unanticipated appointment to the denomination's liturgy committee that motivated me to think and write about liturgy.

The classic German philosopher, when he is, say, twenty-five years old, has a vision of a twelve-volume system, and resolves to allow nothing to distract him from working steadily at that system so that his final days see the completion of the final volume. That's a caricature, of course, but it captures a truth. A great deal of philosophical writing is internally motivated. After *Works and Worlds of Art*, my life in philosophy has been very nearly the opposite of that caricature. Most of what I have thought and written has been provoked by something that befell me.

My main argument in *Art in Action* was that, to understand art, we have to give up the idea that works of the arts are autonomous loci of meaning and significance and instead attend to the many ways in which they are embedded in action. To understand work songs, we have to attend to the fact that they are sung to accompany and enhance manual labor; to understand hymns, we have to attend to the fact that they are sung to praise God; to understand symphonies, we have to attend to the fact that they are performed for absorbed listening by the public—and so on.

That argument left me with a pressing question: If it's true that we engage works of the arts in many different ways, why did Beardsley make claims and assumptions about art that are patently false for many of the ways in which we engage works of the arts? Why have most other philosophers of art of the modern period done the same? Why had I done so as well? Why have philosophers of art often presented as universal what is true only of particular forms of art and of particular ways of engaging art? They write that art requires leisure. That is certainly true for piano sonatas, violin concertos, and the like, but it is patently false for work songs functioning as work songs. They write that art is useless, that it has "no reason for being outside itself, but possesses its entire value and the goal of its existence in itself." That has some plausibility for lyric poems, symphonies, modern dance, and the like, but it has no plausibility whatsoever for work songs, hymns, and many other forms of art.

The answer I proposed in *Art in Action* to the question of why philosophers of art write as they do, was that philosophers of art of the modern period have typically had their eye on what I called our "modern institution of high art." I argued that this institution is organized around just one way of engaging works of the arts, namely, as objects of absorbed aesthetic attention; and I observed that the generalizations made by philosophers of art of the modern period are true, or close to being true, for art as we find it in that institution. I went on to argue that those of us who are philosophers of art should expand the scope of our inquiries and take note not just of aesthetic attention as a way of engaging works of the arts but also of the many other ways in which art is embedded in action.

Why did my hearing of those work songs on my radio that Saturday afternoon, and my almost visceral feeling of dissonance between how I was engaging them and how they were engaged by those who originally sang them, lead me to rethink the role of art in life? Why did I not continue to listen to the songs aesthetically, with untroubled mind? Or why did I not dismiss them as not worth the attention of philosophers on the ground that they represented art not come into its own? Was it, perhaps, the prominence of the singing of hymns in my religious background? Hymns, after all, are a kind of work song. Or was it an inchoate sense that this was the music of the little people of the world, the people of my origins? I don't know.

Toward a Christian Aesthetic, the subtitle of *Art in Action*, indicates that I did not limit myself to making the case mentioned above, that to understand art we have to consider it within the context of the multiple ways in which works of the arts are embedded in action. I presented a Christian perspective on art, so understood. The book remains in print, and it continues to be read by new crops of students.

A couple of months after *Art in Action* appeared, I received a phone call from a woman in Pennsylvania who said she had just read the book and asked whether she could drive to Grand Rapids to talk with me about it. "Of course," I said, wondering what would lead someone to drive some five hundred miles for a face-to-face meeting. She had scarcely sat down in my office before she broke down in tears. Slowly the story came out: she was a professional dancer who had recently become a Christian, and she had begun doing liturgical dance in the church she had joined. When her professional colleagues learned about this, they minced no words in telling her that they regarded liturgical dance as slumming it. She said that reading my book was the first time she felt affirmed in both sides of her life as a dancer, and she wanted to tell me this face to face.

In the early 1970s, I received a phone call from someone who identified himself as the personnel manager of the Herman Miller Corporation and asked whether I would be willing to come to the company's headquarters in Zeeland, Michigan, about twenty miles west of Grand Rapids, to spend a day as a consultant. My immediate response was that he had the wrong number; I was a philosopher. No, he said, I was the person they wanted. They wanted a philosopher who was interested in the arts. After further discussion, I accepted the invitation, partly because I was intrigued, partly because the honorarium they offered was well in excess of any honorarium I had ever received!

Herman Miller produces meticulously crafted furniture for both the domestic and commercial markets. For more than seventy-five years it has been a leader in good industrial design. Several of its chairs have become icons of modern design, most famously the Eames Lounge Chair, designed by Charles Eames and first produced in 1956, and the Aeron Chair, designed by Bill Stumpf and Don Chadwick and first produced in 1994. Claire and I had for years admired Herman Miller furniture, and we owned a few items ourselves.

There were five of us consultants from around the country: a journalist, a lawyer, a physician employed by NASA, a freelance furniture designer (Bill Stumpf), and I; five or six of the top executives at Herman Miller were also present, along with Max De Pree, the CEO of the company. Max led off the discussion by remarking that twice a year he and his top executives took a day off from their regular work to stand back and reflect, with a small group of consultants, on what they were doing at Herman Miller. It was their experience, he said, that a reflective retreat of this kind helped them keep the big picture in mind.

Max had written down a few questions for our discussion. He didn't care in what order we discussed them, nor whether we got around to all of them; they were simply questions he had on his mind. We, the consultants, were not to concern ourselves with how our discussion might benefit the company; we were to let the conversation flow. The people from the company would discuss later what to do with what was said.

I remember three of Max's questions. First, is there a moral imperative to good design? Max explained that, ever since the mid-1930s, the Herman Miller Company had been committed to good modern design, and he told the story of how that commitment came about. At that time the company, then headed by Max's father, D. J. De Pree, was making conventional furniture. One day the designer Gilbert Rohde came through showing his portfolio of modernist furniture design. D. J. was intrigued and, so the story goes, remarked to Rohde, "Well, we're not making any money now, so we may as well try your designs." Over the years since then, there had proved to be a significant market for Herman Miller's modernist furniture. But, said Max, he had recently been asking himself whether there was not, perhaps, a deeper basis for the company's commitment to good design than that there was a niche market for it. Might it be that good design is morally required?

Is growth compatible with intimacy? Max asked. For many years the company had prized intimacy among its employees and managers and had developed a number of strategies for encouraging intimacy, but the company had gone public shortly before our meeting, and stockholders were now clamoring for growth. Hence the second question: Is growth compatible with intimacy?

The third question Max posed was: What is the purpose of business? Some of his young executives were saying that the purpose of business was to make money. He himself didn't believe that, said Max, but he thought the matter worth discussing. In the course of the discussion his own views on the matter emerged. He thought the purpose of business was to make good and useful products for the public and to provide a place of meaningful work for the employees. Obviously, the company had to make a profit in order to stay in business. But profit is to business, said Max, as breathing is to living: you have to breathe to live, but you don't live to breathe. A corporation should be a community of people in which everybody is valued and all enjoy a fair share in the fruits of their collective labor.

The breadth and depth of these and the other questions Max posed took me aback. I had expected that I, a philosopher, would be a fish out of water. But not only was this water, it was *my* water. These were philosophical questions. I have no memory of what I said that day. Whatever it was, I doubt that it was of much use to the Herman Miller people, since, though the issues raised were philosophical, they were not issues I had previously thought about. What I do remember is that I enjoyed the day enormously.

Subsequently, when I have found myself in situations where it was being said or assumed that the purpose of business is to make money, I have told the story about serving as a consultant for Herman Miller and Max's explaining that, in his view, making money is a condition for operating a business but not the purpose. Sometimes the response has been that it was possible for Max to operate with this view of things because the furniture Herman Miller produces is upscale and expensive. He could not operate with those ideals if the company were producing moderately priced furniture for the general market. On one occasion, a participant in the discussion became visibly angry and declared that Max was cheating his stockholders.

Before that consultation, I had not met Max; subsequently, we became good friends.[1] He was a remarkable person, one of the most

---

1. Max died on August 8, 2017.

remarkable in my acquaintance. He was deeply religious, a loyal life-long member of the Reformed Church in America. Though he did not reveal it at the time, it was his religious convictions that lay behind the questions he posed for us that day, as they did behind how he operated the company. He was somewhat shy, and didn't like being asked directly how his religious and moral convictions shaped his running of the company. One had to wait for it to spill out in the course of a conversation. Among the many examples I could cite, let me mention two that I found especially moving.

The state of Michigan passed a law requiring that industrial buildings be accessible to people with disabilities. Though the machinery in the Herman Miller plants had been, for some time, accessible to the handicapped, the buildings themselves were not. So the company complied with the new law by installing ramps. In one of our conversations, Max remarked to me that when he went out to inspect the work, it struck him that, while the handicapped people were going up the ramps, the able people were going up the stairs. He ordered the stairs torn out so that everybody would go up the ramps.

One of the workers got an appointment with Max one day to ask that she be excused from the Friday lunch meetings, which were a component of the company's strategy for encouraging intimacy. Max was taken aback; he was proud of those Friday meetings. Why didn't she want to participate? She explained that she had a severely disabled child at home and that uninterrupted work helped get her mind off her difficulties. "You see, Mr. De Pree," she said, "work for me is a healing experience." Max reported to me that his immediate thought was, How can I make work a healing experience for everybody?

In *Leadership Is an Art*, Max wrote: "The first responsibility of a leader is to define reality. The last is to say thank you."[2]

---

2. During Max's tenure as CEO of Herman Miller, the company was frequently cited by *Fortune* magazine as one of America's "most admired companies"

Claire's father, Jan Willem Kingma, conversationalist without peer—who taught me much about art and whom I loved and admired greatly—died in Santa Barbara, California, of cancer on July 20, 1969, at the age of sixty-five. After Claire's father and mother moved to Santa Barbara, we were not able to see them often. But as a family we did, twice, take the train to visit them, and several times they flew to visit us in Grand Rapids. In short, the children knew their grandparents rather well. The first time we visited them in Santa Barbara, Robert flew into his grandfather's arms and said, "I love plants, too." He had learned from Claire and me about his grandfather's love of plants. Our entire family flew to Santa Barbara shortly before his death and were able to say our final good-bye and attend the funeral.

Exactly four years after the death of Claire's father, on July 20, 1973, my father died at the age of seventy. His death was instantaneous and unexpected, without warning. There was no autopsy, so we don't know the cause of death. I flew to Edgerton for the funeral and was deeply moved by the broad outpouring of affection and admiration for my father, both expressed to me personally and written out in the book of remembrance that I was later given. People mentioned episodes in his life that I had never heard about. He was a pillar of the community. In the plane on the way back, I had the vivid and unsettling image of walking across a landscape with a large number of people behind me but nobody in front of me. I was now exposed.

---

and as one of the "best companies to work for." In 1981 the American Institute of Architects awarded the company its AIA Gold Medal for "dedication to excellence in design."

In the spring of 1975, I did something truly foolish: I allowed myself to be a candidate for the presidency of Calvin College, successor to William Spoelhof, who was retiring after twenty-five years of a very successful tenure as president. I am daily grateful that I was not chosen. I would have been miserable. I do not have the mentality or the temperament of an administrator, and I would have found it emotionally draining to be responsible for the well-being of thousands of students and hundreds of faculty and staff. My love is philosophy.

I had long been deeply involved in policy decisions at the college. After chairing the curriculum revision committee, I served on a number of other committees and spoke up rather often in faculty meetings. I cared about the direction and well-being of the institution. And the college was thriving: enrollment was rising, students were bright and feisty, new young faculty were being added—bright, well trained, energetic, committed to good teaching and to the flourishing of the college as well as to their own research.

When Spoelhof announced his retirement, a number of colleagues from a variety of departments urged me to be a candidate for the position. I discussed it with Claire and the family. Claire urged me to go ahead; she was immediately full of ideas as to what she might do as spouse of the president. Others warned me against it, especially Al Plantinga, and my brother-in-law, Stuart Kingma, who was at that time an administrator at the federal Centers for Disease Control. Stuart was emphatic in his warnings. He knew administration from the inside, and he knew me. I should have listened. Instead, I succumbed to the entreaties of my colleagues and went through the long, multi-phased interview process.

What led me on? Why not speak up for the things I thought important and let someone else deal with the nuts and bolts of administration? Because my ego was flattered by the urgings of my colleagues and by the prospect of being president. I allowed those to go to my head. Only later did I acknowledge this to myself.

I realized, of course, that I would have to give up my career as a full-time professional philosopher. I was determined, however, to continue writing semipopular, philosophically informed, essays. So I stated publicly that a condition of my accepting the presidency was that I not be expected to be in my office before 10:00 a.m.; I would spend the early hours of the day reading, reflecting, and writing. My ambivalence was evident. Members of the search committee should have taken me aside and said firmly, "Get serious. The presidency is a full-time position. Do you or do you not want to be president?"

I do think it is important for the heads of institutions of higher education to be educational leaders, not just technocrats, and that requires that they reserve time for reading, reflecting, and writing. But it's clear to me, in retrospect, that I was not proposing to reserve time for those activities because I judged them to be important for properly filling the role of president. I was proposing to reserve time in order to continue in my profession of philosopher, albeit in a very altered form.

Calvin College is owned and governed by the Christian Reformed Church. The synod of the denomination chooses the president from a slate of candidates presented to it by a presidential search committee. Anthony Diekema, who was at the time an administrator at the medical school of the University of Illinois, and I were the two candidates whom the search committee presented. We were both interviewed in public, and Diekema was chosen.

I felt deeply hurt. I had been imagining myself as president—making plans. One of my colleagues held a "wake" that evening. We commiserated over what might have been but was not to be. After a week or so, the hurt was gone and a feeling of great relief swept over me. Synod had made the right choice. I had the sense that God had intervened to put a halt to my folly. I wrote a letter to the faculty urging everybody to get behind Diekema. He proved to be an excellent president, and he and I had a fine personal relationship.

In September 1975, I attended a conference at the University of Potchefstroom in South Africa that changed my life. Potchefstroom is a medium-sized city located about an hour's drive from Johannesburg. At that time, the university explicitly located itself within the conservative Afrikaner tradition: so-called blacks and coloreds were not admitted as regular students. The topic of the conference was "Christian Higher Education in the Reformed Tradition." A large number of Afrikaners were in attendance, along with a few "black" and "colored" scholars from South Africa; there was a large contingent of Dutch scholars, and a few from North America, Asia, and other African countries. I was the official representative of Calvin College.

Apartheid was still in full force. I knew about apartheid: one could not be a member of a denomination belonging to the Reformed family of churches without knowing about apartheid. What I knew about it, I found reprehensible—an embarrassment to my tradition. Now I saw it in operation. *Blankes alleen* ("whites only") were allowed to live in this area or ride that bus, to shop in this store or patronize that restaurant, to use these toilets. The racial segregation that the civil rights movement was dismantling in the United States was thriving in South Africa.

Though apartheid was not the topic of the conference, it figured prominently in the informal discussions among delegates during coffee breaks and meals. And the Dutch, who were very well informed about apartheid and very angry, skillfully managed to insert apartheid into the conference itself, making statements and raising questions about apartheid in the question periods following lectures, even though none of the lectures had anything directly to do with apartheid. Finally, the South African organizers of the conference, thoroughly exasperated with the Dutch for hijacking their conference, consented to hold a late-evening session in which apartheid would be the topic of discussion.

It remains the most intense discussion I have ever experienced.

The Dutch vented their anger. Later I learned that Afrikaners typically fended off criticisms of apartheid by telling the critics that they were misinformed. They could not charge the Dutch with being misinformed, so they charged them instead with being self-righteously judgmental. After some forty-five minutes of this angry back and forth, neither party had anything new to say to the other. Then the "black" and "colored" delegates from South Africa began to speak up, describing in moving detail the indignities daily heaped upon them by the official and unofficial segregation that pervaded South African society. They spoke of being forcibly expelled from their homes and herded off into Bantustans. They cried out for justice.

I was moved by this cry for justice. But more than that, the conviction welled up in me that I was being called by God to put justice on my agenda and to speak up for these oppressed people in whatever ways proved appropriate. I would be religiously disobedient if I did not. I did not hear words in the air; rather, it was through the speech of the "black" and "colored" delegates that God addressed me. Never before had I had such an experience.

The response of the Afrikaner defenders of apartheid to the call for justice issued by the "blacks" and "coloreds" took me completely aback. Justice, they insisted, was not the issue. Benevolence was the issue. They, the Afrikaners, were a generous people; the goal of apartheid was the greater good of all South Africans. They explained that in South Africa there were ten or so different ethnic groups. The goal of apartheid was that each nationality would flourish in its own unique way: its own language, its own stories and poetry, its own style of basket-weaving, its own ways of eating and dressing. Separate development was the goal. For this to happen, these different nationalities had to be separated: they could not live mingled through each other, they had to be apart—hence *apartheid*. The means required for achieving the glorious future of separate development did, admittedly, entail some suffering. That could not be avoided; a great good never comes without some pain. Some of the Afrikaner speakers went on to describe acts of personal kindness on their part to "blacks" and "coloreds" of their acquaintance: Christmas trinkets they gave to the children of their "black" and "colored" workers, clothing their own children had outgrown, and so forth.

Then they pivoted from defense to offense. Addressing the "blacks" and "coloreds," they asked: "Why do you never express gratitude for what we have done for you? Why do you only criticize us?" With tears in her eyes, one of them pleaded, "Why can't we just love each other?" I saw, as never before, benevolence—more precisely, self-perceived benevolence—being used as an instrument of oppression.

I left South Africa a changed person. In my support of the American civil rights movement, I had spoken of the injustice of racial segregation. In my opposition to the Vietnam War I had argued that it was not a just war. But I had not put justice on my personal agenda; I had not thought about justice in any sustained way. Now it was on my agenda. I did not conclude that I was being called to leave philosophy and become an activist. My support of the anti-apartheid movement would take the form of giving talks and writing articles in which I tried to awaken my listeners and readers to the call for justice and to the rank injustice of apartheid.

Somewhere, on the long plane trip home, I had a panic attack of sorts. My life seemed to be falling into pieces. I was thinking, teaching, and writing about art. I was thinking and writing about liturgy. I was thinking, writing, and speaking about education. I was publishing essays on various topics in philosophy of religion. I had a family to support and nurture. Now God had added justice to my agenda: not only thinking about justice in general and why it is important, but getting myself informed about the concrete injustice of apartheid and speaking out against it. Was there anything uniting the various projects in which I was engaged? Or was I just flitting from one thing to another, in danger of becoming a jack of many trades and a master of none? What do justice, liturgy, art, and philosophy have to do with each other? Was fragmentation the price to be paid for not setting my own agenda, for responding instead to whatever dropped on my doorstep? Was it the price to be paid for not being an inner-directed philosopher? It would be several years before I would find an answer to those questions.

Upon returning home from South Africa, I bought yards of books about the situation there—and its historical origins—and read avidly. I began to think, speak, and write about justice in general, and about injustice in South Africa in particular. I returned to South Africa several times, twice with Claire, and became friends with a number of people active in the anti-apartheid movement, especially Allan Boesak. A trip to South Africa on behalf of Allan remains one of the most memorable experiences of my life. I described the experience at some length in the chapter entitled "Six Days in South Africa" in my book *Journey toward Justice* (Baker, 2013). Here I will be brief.

Claire and I had become friends of Allan in the course of the 1980–81 academic year, when he was the first Multi-Cultural Lecturer at Calvin. I found in him a soul mate. Early on the morning of Tuesday, October 15, 1985, I got a phone call from Allan asking me to come to Cape Town as soon as possible to testify on his behalf in a court hearing to get his bail conditions lifted. To a call for help from a soul mate, one does not say no. The following Saturday afternoon I was on a plane from Grand Rapids to Chicago, visa in hand; Sunday night I stepped off the plane in Cape Town and was greeted by Allan, surrounded by family and friends.

For twenty-six days in September, Allan had been imprisoned—held in solitary confinement—on the charge of sedition. He was allowed no book other than his Bible, and no paper. He was released on the condition that he be in his house every night from 9:00 p.m. to 6:00 a.m., and that he report to the local police station every day before 9:00 a.m. Those conditions, plus the fact that the authorities had confiscated his passport, made it impossible for him to do the work of pastor and anti-apartheid leader to which he had been called.

The hearing in magistrate court was in response to the request of Allan's lawyers that the court order his bail conditions lifted and his passport returned to him. Several witnesses testified that Allan's anti-apartheid activity did not constitute sedition, as that was defined in South Africa's security laws. And I was a character witness: I testified that Allan could be trusted not to flee the country. The courtroom was full to overflowing, mostly with people of color, victims of apartheid.

My testimony took place on Wednesday; the following Saturday, the Boesaks drove me to the airport for my return trip to the United States. Monday, a week later, the magistrate was to deliver his opinion. About 6:00 p.m. (Cape Town time) I called to find out the news. The background noise in the Boesak home told me: the magistrate had ordered all the contested provisions lifted and had gone out of his way to castigate the state for the incompetence of its case.

Of the many things that remain vivid in my memory about those six days in South Africa, what remains most vivid is my memory of what took place during the two recesses in that court hearing. Adjacent to the courtroom was a walled courtyard, open to the sky except for a shallow roof that ran around the four walls, protecting people from rain and sun. When recess was declared, the people in the courtroom poured out into the courtyard. Standing in the shade, under the protecting roof, were twenty or so policemen, rifles at the ready, looking grim. In the middle of the courtyard, in the sun, people were laughing, singing, and dancing. The oppressors, grim—the oppressed, joyous.

The concern for justice that the conference in Potchefstroom awakened in me soon expanded and deepened. In May 1978, I attended a conference in Chicago on Palestinian rights. I never learned why I was invited, nor have I ever understood why I felt impelled to attend. Along with most other Americans, I had celebrated Israel's victory in the 1967 war: tiny Israel triumphant over Arab neighbors trying to crush it. I knew no more about the plight of the Palestinians than was reported in the mainstream American press, which was very little.

The conference was sponsored by an organization called the Palestine Human Rights Campaign. There were about 150 Palestinians present, most of whom identified themselves as Christian. They spoke in flaming rhetoric, rhetoric too hot, I would later learn, for most Americans to handle. They told of how their ancestral lands and orchards were being confiscated for Jewish settlements, and of how they were evicted from their homes in the middle of the night and their homes bulldozed as collective punishment. They told of the many ways in which they were daily demeaned. They cried out for justice. Once again, the conviction seized hold of me that in their speech I was being issued a call from God to speak up for these oppressed people in whatever ways might prove appropriate.

The US State Department had allowed Ambassador Terzi, the representative of the Palestine Liberation Organization to the United Nations, to attend the conference on the condition that he see to it that, whenever he spoke, there be no more than five people within earshot. This infuriated me. If my country's policy in the Middle East was so fragile that it would be endangered by more than five people simultaneously hearing what Terzi was saying, there must be something terribly wrong with that policy. A former employee of the US State Department reported on torture in Israeli prisons. She had been assigned by the department to investigate reports of torture, had discovered that many of the reports were accurate, but was fired as soon as she filed her report.

When I returned home, I again bought yards of books about the situation in the Middle East and its historical origins and read avidly. I spoke and wrote about injustice in the Middle East. Never once did Calvin College urge me, as a member of its faculty, to back away from speaking on the issue, and I honor the college for that. I became the chair of the board of the Palestine Human Rights Campaign and helped organize conferences that the campaign sponsored. I spoke at many of those conferences. I traveled to the Middle East several times, and became friends with a number of those who were protesting the situation, both Palestinian and Israeli. When the Oslo Accord was signed on September 13, 1993, I concluded that our efforts, along with those of many others, had proved successful, and that a just peace was now at hand. How naïve that has proved to be!

The Palestine Human Rights Campaign advocated a two-state solution. The skeptical view, to which I have now reluctantly come, is that Prime Minister Netanyahu in particular and the Israeli public in general are determined that there will never be two states. They are also determined that there will never be one binational state, since, in such a state, Palestinians would become the majority in the not-too-distant future. They think it best to live with the present situation of occupation of the West Bank and simmering resistance by the Palestinians. Then, when the time seems right, annex the West Bank but refuse citizenship to its Palestinian inhabitants. To most Israelis, this is preferable to both a two-state solution and a binational-state solution.

When Palestinian resistance turns violent, Israel declares that it will never negotiate under threat. When resistance is quiescent, it sees no need to negotiate. If the choice is between land and peace, Israel will choose land. Opinion writers in the United States will excoriate the American president, whoever that happens to be, for not achieving peace in the Middle East. But the powers that be in Israel—and their supporters in the United States—will see to it that no American president ever succeeds in securing peace with justice in the Middle East.

When I began speaking about justice to groups of Christians in the late 1970s, the audiences were small: twenty or thirty people. In January 2011, I was one of the speakers at a conference in Bend, Oregon, sponsored by an organization that calls itself simply "The Justice Conference." Eleven hundred people were in the audience, most of them young. Two years later, I again spoke at a conference sponsored by The Justice Conference. This time there were two thousand people in the audience—again, mostly young. The change from then to now is deeply gratifying to me. There are some who play down the significance of this development by saying that justice has become a fad among young people. I personally know many for whom it is not a fad but a cause to which they are deeply committed. But if, for some, it is a fad, there are worse fads!

Why was I so affected by the testimony of the so-called blacks and coloreds in Potchefstroom and by the testimony of the Palestinians in Chicago? Why had I not been similarly affected by injustice in my own society? I was well aware of the injustice of racial segregation in America. Why had that awareness not led me to put social justice on my agenda? What was it about my experience in Potchefstroom and my experience in Chicago that awakened me? One thing that triggered my reaction in Potchefstroom was the fact that the oppressors were members of my own religious tradition, the Reformed tradition of Protestant Christianity—more specifically, the *Dutch* Reformed tradition. I was embarrassed to be associated with them in this way, and I was angry. They had hijacked my tradition. Or if they represented the authentic tradition, I would have to repudiate that tradition.

That goes some way toward explaining my personal awakening in Potchefstroom, but it does not explain my awakening in Chicago two and a half years later. I think what awakened me in Chicago—and also, before that, in Potchefstroom—was hearing the voices and seeing the faces of the oppressed. I had not gone to Alabama and Mississippi when the civil rights movement was taking place. I had not personally witnessed what was happening there. I read about it in the newspapers, but I did not hear the voices or see the faces.

Hearing the voices and seeing the faces evoked empathy in me. Not pity. *Empathy.* I felt *with* these oppressed people. I did not just gain knowledge of their situation, but I identified with them emotionally. No doubt some people are motivated to struggle against injustice out of a sense of duty. Others are motivated out of a sense of religious calling. The latter was true of me. But I doubt that I would have heard God's call had I not identified emotionally with these oppressed people. It's my impression that what was true for me is true for most people involved in the struggle against some form of injustice of which they are not themselves the direct victims. It is emotional engagement that motivates them, either in the form of empathy with the victims or in the form of anger at the victimizers— or both. Knowledge and conviction are not enough; most people have to be stirred emotionally.

To feel empathy with someone is to imagine and experience something of what it feels like to be that person in her or his situation. That's the effect of hearing the voices and seeing the faces: one imagines and feels something of what it's like. Documentary film can have the same effect, as can fiction, both in the form of film and in the form of written text. Seldom does journalism have that effect.

The first of several books that have resulted from my two justice awakenings was *Until Justice and Peace Embrace* (Eerdmans, 1983). I dedicated that book to Allan Boesak, whose courage, hope, and biblical insight have inspired me ever since we first met. I will have more to say about that book later.

It must have been about 1975 that the evangelical theologian-philosopher John Warwick Montgomery gave a lecture at Calvin in which he presented arguments for the existence of God and for the truth of Christianity. In the question period following his lecture, he made it clear that he thought it very important for Christians to have such arguments, but he did not explain why he thought it important.

The following Tuesday afternoon, as we in the philosophy department were settling down for our weekly seminar, we began talking about Montgomery's lecture. We agreed it was unlikely that the secular philosophers we knew would have found Montgomery's arguments persuasive. Then someone asked, "Why do we need arguments?" We grappled with that question for the remainder of the two hours, ignoring the paper that had been distributed for discussion. Probably the reason we did not just go along with the assumption that arguments are needed, but instead grappled with the question *whether* they are needed and for what, was that making arguments for the existence of God and for the truth of Christianity had played no role in the education of those of us who had been students at Calvin. Faith seeking understanding was what we were taught, not understanding in support of faith.

Montgomery was by no means an outlier in assuming that it is important for Christians to have good arguments for their religious beliefs. For several centuries it had been commonly assumed—by Christian and non-Christian thinkers alike—that religious belief needs good arguments to support it. Those who reject Christianity typically give as their reason for rejection that good arguments are lacking. Those who wish to remain Christian, but regard the arguments for orthodox Christianity as inadequate, either compose some stripped-down version of Christianity, for which they deem the arguments to be adequate, or declare that Christian faith, properly understood, does not consist of believing propositions for which arguments can be given but consists, rather, of embracing certain values or attitudes. And then there are those, like Montgomery, who spell out what they regard as good and adequate arguments for orthodox Christian belief.

The answer to the question "Why do we need arguments?"

eluded us that day. But we were gripped. Over and over, in hallway conversations and subsequent seminars, we returned to the question, gradually getting clear on the crucial issues. Developments that had recently taken place in the philosophical subdiscipline of epistemology proved helpful. Epistemology is customarily explained as theory of knowledge, knowledge typically understood, in the analytic tradition, as justified true belief—an understanding of the nature of knowledge that goes back to Plato. In recent years, the field has expanded to consider merits of beliefs in addition to truth and justification, merits such as rationality, entitlement, and so forth, and to consider propositional attitudes in addition to believing—hoping, for example. Nonetheless, theory of knowledge remains the core of epistemology.

Among the significant developments that took place in epistemology in the late 1960s and early 1970s, the most important was the emergence of *meta*-epistemology. Rather than just plunging ahead and developing their own theories of knowledge, philosophers took a step back in order to identify and distinguish the structurally different *types* of theories of justified belief that were proposed. This had an extraordinarily illuminating effect. Philosophers began to understand more clearly than ever before the assumptions made by theories of different types and to identify the central issues in the debates among them.

Rather soon in these discussions it became clear that most theories concerning the nature of justification were of one or the other of two types: *coherentist* or *foundationalist*. Coherentists hold that, for one to be justified in holding a certain belief, that belief must cohere in a certain way with one's other beliefs. At a minimum, it must be logically consistent with one's other beliefs. But that is only the minimum; it has to "fit" with one's other beliefs in other ways as well. Disagreements among coherentists are mainly over the nature of that fit, that is, over the nature of the requisite coherence.

Foundationalists, as the term suggests, hold that, for one to be justified in holding a certain belief, that belief must rest firmly on an adequate foundation. They begin by distinguishing between beliefs held on the basis of other beliefs and beliefs not held on the basis of others—those held *immediately*. Nowadays, these beliefs are typically called "basic" beliefs. It has been my experience that a good many people, when first presented with the idea of immediate or basic beliefs, are taken aback by the claim that there are such beliefs. Beliefs held on the basis of other beliefs? No problem. But beliefs held immediately? How can that be?

Foundationalists argue that that is how it has to be. If there are to be beliefs held on the basis of other beliefs, there have to be some not held in that way in order to get the whole process going. We may believe A on the basis of B, B on the basis of C, and so forth. Always, if we follow such a chain to its end, we find basic beliefs. Those are the "foundations" of the person's belief structure. Examples of basic beliefs are one's belief that $1 + 1 = 2$ and someone's belief that she or he is in pain. Nobody holds those beliefs on the basis of other beliefs; we believe them immediately. Having made this quasi-psychological distinction between basic and nonbasic beliefs, foundationalists go on to discuss what types of basic beliefs a person is justified in holding and what the *based-on* relationship must be like if we are to be justified in holding a certain belief on the basis of another. The debates among foundationalists are mainly over those two points.

When I first read the literature in meta-epistemology in which these matters were being discussed, I had the sense of scales falling from my eyes. My graduate-school education at Harvard included a course in epistemology taught by Roderick Firth, widely regarded as one of the country's best epistemologists. At the time, I found the course boring, and I steered clear of epistemology thereafter. Now I was seeing why it was boring. Like most other epistemologists at the time, Firth took for granted the truth of foundationalism and devoted the course he taught to discussing various problems and puzzles that arose for foundationalism of the particular type he favored.

We discussed the problem of "the speckled hen" at some length (I remember the name of the problem but not the problem itself). Double images also posed a problem; again, I don't remember the problem. One day, Firth had us press our eyeballs to get double images. I pressed my eyeballs, but to no effect. Evidently, I wasn't doing it correctly. I felt embarrassed at my inability to perform so simple an operation, and said nothing.

Montgomery did not explain why he thought it important for Christians to have good arguments for their religious beliefs. He did not identify what would be amiss if they did not have such arguments. But a plausible guess at what he was assuming was now at hand. Intuitively thinking along foundationalist lines, he was assuming that Christians' beliefs about God are not properly basic. If held immediately, they are lacking in some merit—for example, lacking in justification. To be justified in believing what they do about God, Christians must hold those beliefs on the basis of other beliefs that adequately support them.

Having thus identified and formulated what Montgomery was probably assuming, we could now state the question that we in the department had been grappling with thus: Is it true, in general, that for beliefs about God to be properly held, we must hold them on the basis of other beliefs that support them? Is it true that it is never proper for beliefs about God to be basic?

Whereas my Harvard course in foundationalist epistemology was boring, meta-epistemology was proving to be not only fascinating in its own right, but exciting for the way in which it clarified the issues that we in the philosophy department had been grappling with. The epistemology of religious belief was now on my agenda, joining the many other issues already there.

A l Plantinga and I spent the 1979–80 academic year as senior fellows of the Calvin Center for Christian Studies. The topic for the year was "Toward a Reformed View of Faith and Reason." We were joined for that year by the Calvin College historian George Marsden and by the Calvin College New Testament scholar David Holwerda. The philosophers William Alston, of Syracuse University, and George Mavrodes, of the University of Michigan, were part-time adjunct fellows.

The philosophers in the group headed straight for the question that we in the department had been asking: Is it true, in general, that for beliefs about God to be properly held, they must be held on the basis of other beliefs that support them? The affirmative answer to that question has come to be called *evidentialism*, the idea being that religious beliefs, to be properly held, must be held on the basis of *good evidence* consisting of other beliefs. Is evidentialism concerning religious beliefs true? For several centuries, it had been widely assumed that it is. But is it?

Al and I, along with Alston and Mavrodes, concluded that it is not. Obviously, some beliefs about God are based on evidence— complicated beliefs about the Trinity, for example. But a good many are evoked by experience of some kind, evoked directly, without the intrusion of arguments, just as perceptual beliefs about physical objects in one's environment are often evoked by sensory experience without the intrusion of arguments. And just as many of those perceptual beliefs are proper, so also, we concluded, are many of those religious beliefs proper.

Thus it was that so-called *Reformed epistemology* was born: the position that some basic beliefs about God are properly held. Reformed epistemology takes somewhat different forms in the hands of different thinkers, but what unites them—as versions of Reformed epistemology—is their adherence to the tenet that it is not true, in general, that to properly hold beliefs about God, one must hold them on the basis of other beliefs that constitute good evidence for them.

The fruit of our year's work appeared in three essays: Alston's "Christian Experience and Christian Belief," Plantinga's "Reason and Belief in God," and my essay "Can Belief in God Be Rational If It Has No Foundations?" The essays were published in a collection that Plantinga and I edited, *Faith and Rationality: Reason and Belief in God* (Notre Dame, 1983). The three of us subsequently developed and published far more detailed and sophisticated articulations of Reformed epistemology, especially Plantinga, and secondarily, Alston. But it was in those three essays that Reformed epistemology made its first public appearance. For several decades now, it has been a lively topic of discussion among philosophers of religion. It is now included in most introductions to the field.

Plantinga gave the position its name. He had been reading around in various Reformed theologians—among them, John Calvin and the turn-of-the-twentieth-century Dutch theologian Herman Bavinck—and was struck by the fact that they intuitively rejected the claim that religious beliefs are never properly basic. So he called the position "Reformed epistemology." As he knows, I never liked the term: it makes the position sound parochial, when it is not. Thinkers in other traditions, not just in the Reformed tradition, have rejected evidentialism concerning religious beliefs—the medieval philosopher Thomas Aquinas, to name just one. Odd to call Aquinas a Reformed epistemologist! But when Al asked me for an alternative designation, I couldn't think of any. So the term "Reformed epistemology" stuck.

In the heady enthusiasm of giving birth to Reformed epistemology, we were dismissive of the traditional theistic arguments and of any attempt to update and add to them. In subsequent years we came to see that, though such arguments are not, in general, necessary for beliefs about God to be justified, they might well serve other purposes—apologetic purposes, for example, or the purpose of bringing to light certain deep structures in reality.

~

During my year in the Calvin Center, I began to read the eighteenth-century Scots philosopher Thomas Reid—I don't remember why. None of my professors at Calvin or Harvard had ever mentioned Reid. They all went straight from Locke, Berkeley, and Hume, the trio of British empiricists, to Kant and Hegel, skipping right over Reid. Almost at once I sensed in Reid a philosophical soul mate. Reid had identified and rejected foundationalism several centuries before we arrived on the scene; it would not be a mistake to think of Reformed epistemology as Reidian in its basic orientation.[3] I resolved to write a book on Reid, both because I found in him a soul mate and because I wanted to do what I could to rescue him from what I regarded as undeserved oblivion.

Though Reid was a wonderfully lucid writer, it took me many years to identify, to my satisfaction, the fundamental questions he was addressing. Initially, my problem was that I assumed he was addressing the same questions as those being addressed by present-day analytic epistemologists. After several false starts, I concluded that he was instead addressing a quite different set of questions. Whereas present-day analytic epistemologists are centrally preoccupied with questions about the "epistemic status" of beliefs—which beliefs are justified, which are rational, which constitute knowledge, and so on—Reid, I eventually concluded, was mainly addressing two prior questions: How does it come about that we get items of reality, especially of extramental reality, well enough in mind to be able to form beliefs about those items? and what accounts for the fact that we do then form such beliefs? But even after I recognized the questions Reid was addressing, elements of his thought continued to elude me for some time—for reasons I have never understood.

Reid was a highly polemical writer. Almost always, in his epis-

---

3. Strictly speaking, it was not foundationalism in general but what is now called "classical" foundationalism that Reid rejected. It's not necessary for our purposes here for me to explain what constitutes classical foundationalism.

temology, he had John Locke and David Hume in his sights. He disagreed profoundly with both their account of how we get items of reality well enough in mind to be able to form beliefs about them, and with their account of how such beliefs get formed. Reluctantly, I came to the conclusion that I could not fully understand Reid without first understanding Locke better than I did. So I devoted several years to a careful study of Locke. As I had anticipated, my study of Locke helped me understand Reid. What I had not anticipated is that it would also help round out for me the project of Reformed epistemology.

Those of us who were giving birth to Reformed epistemology that year at the Calvin Center had left unanswered an important question: Where and why did the idea originate that religious beliefs, to be properly held, must be held on the basis of other beliefs that provide good evidence for them? My study of Locke led me to conclude that Locke was the originator of the idea. One can find adumbrations of the idea in earlier thinkers—that's how it always is—but Locke was the first to go beyond adumbrations to work out the idea.

The cultural situation in Locke's day was that the religious unity Europe had once enjoyed had been fractured. Religious factions were at war with each other. I wanted to give my book on Locke the title "When Tradition Fractures." The publisher, Cambridge University Press, firmly rejected that title on the ground that librarians wouldn't know what to do with a book bearing that title. They suggested the bland title *John Locke and the Ethics of Belief*, and that's the way it was published in 1996.

Locke was convinced that if each religious party continued to appeal to its own tradition and to its own authorities in its arguments with other parties, there could be no peace. The possibility of peace depended on each party appealing to something that united them. That something was *reason*, properly employed. We must all have good reasons for our religious beliefs—good evidence. I concluded the book with the following words:

Locke's proposal will not do. Our problems with traditions remain, however. Traditions are still a source of benightedness, chicanery, hostility, and oppression. And our moral, religious, and even theoretical traditions are even more fractured today than they were in Locke's day. [Locke and the thinkers of the Enlightenment who followed him] hoped to bring about a rational consensus in place of fractured tradition. That hope has failed. In my judgment it was bound to fail; it could not succeed.

Yet we must live together. It is to politics and not to epistemology that we shall have to look for an answer as to how to do that. "Liberal" politics has fallen on bad days recently. But to its animating vision of a society in which persons of diverse traditions live together in justice and friendship, conversing with each other and slowly altering their traditions in response to their conversation—to that, there is no viable alternative.

My book on Reid, *Thomas Reid and the Story of Epistemology*, appeared five years later (Cambridge University Press, 2001).

The children were growing up. Claire and I delighted in watching their abilities develop, their interests, their convictions, their hopes and longings—different in each case. We assisted them, as best we knew how, to become what they were meant to be. We invested ourselves in them: their happiness was our happiness; their pride, our pride; their tears, our tears. And each of them was, in turn, a joy and a blessing to us, a cherished gift from God. The inner character of each of them, their inscape, was developing and gradually becoming clear. Let me try to describe, in a few words, the inner character that we saw coming to expression when they were in their teens—though my words fall far short. They were all bright, and good at school work.

Amy, the eldest—and the only girl—was the steady one, always there, dependable, ready to help others, cheerful and loyal, interested in what others were doing, gifted at seeing humor in things. She made friends easily.

Eric was intensely loyal to family and friends. He grieved when he graduated from college and had to say good-bye to friends. He was also the most venturesome of our children. One summer, when he was in high school, he traveled on his own to Alfred University in New York State in order to take a course in ceramics. When he was in college, he traveled alone to Japan one summer. He was a risk-taker—risks of many kinds—physical risks, for example. When driving, it was characteristic of him to drive too close to the car ahead of him, or so I thought.

Robert was the dreamy one—or, better put, easily distracted. When he was in elementary school, he would arrive late to school every now and then because, on the way, he had become absorbed in observing some ants or earthworms. The world was full of things that called for attention: things beautiful, fascinating, striking, funny, quirky. He was also the emotionally intense one. In high school and college, he often delayed writing an assigned paper until the last minute, whereupon he would go into a panic. Claire would have to calm him down.

Klaas did whatever had to be done and did it extremely well—without fuss and without delay. When a paper was assigned in high school or college, he got right at it and worked steadily until it was finished. And he was a fine writer. On one of the papers he wrote for an English course in college, he received an A+, the only A+, the professor told him, he had ever given. But Klaas hated drawing attention to himself. Once, when he was in kindergarten, he arrived late at school for some reason; instead of going in, he turned around, walked back home, and spent the morning in the playhouse in our backyard until he saw his classmates coming home for lunch.

Christopher, I would say, was the most sensitive to those around him, the most empathic, especially to those who were impaired, sick, or in some kind of trouble, very much like Claire in that regard. He's a gentle soul.

Beginning in 1974, the children were leaving home for college. Though they all attended and graduated from Calvin, and could have lived at home, Claire and I thought it best that they not live at home during their college years. Students who live at home miss too much of the college experience. But we did get together as a family on most weekends, with much warmth and laughter and, now and then, some tears.

Claire's principal vocation was managing the household and rearing the children: counseling them, consoling them, reading to them, crying with them, laughing with them, settling their disagreements, encouraging them, aiding them with schoolwork, helping them identify their gifts and interests, feeding them, and clothing them. It was a full-time job—and more. As they began to leave the house and live on their own, she began to look for a new vocation. She considered elementary or secondary school teaching, and took some education courses at Calvin. But she soon concluded that that was not for her; it did not use her spiritual gifts and interests.

In the 1970s, she and I had both been strong advocates for the ordination of women in the church. Originally, this, for her, consisted of being an advocate for opening up ordination to other women, but gradually she began to feel that she herself was called to ordination. In May 1980, she joined the Episcopal Church, feeling more at home there than in churches of the Reformed tradition. When she was a student at Vassar, she had become acquainted with an Episcopal priest who was working in the arts rather than serving in a parish. That awakened her to the realization that ordination did not necessarily imply full-time church work. So she asked for—and was granted—permission from the Episcopal bishop of Western Michigan to train for the priesthood. The nearest Episcopal seminary was some distance from Grand Rapids: Seabury-Western Theological Seminary in Evanston, Illinois. So as not to disrupt the life of the family, she decided to enroll for a year in Western Seminary, a seminary of the Reformed Church in America, located in Holland, Michigan, a short commute from Grand Rapids. She greatly enjoyed her year at Western (1980–81).

The following year she interrupted her education to accompany me to Amsterdam. Then, after taking another year off, she enrolled in Seabury-Western in the fall of 1983, graduating in the spring of 1985. She was ordained a deacon in the Episcopal Church in June 1985, and a priest on November 16, 1986. Her ordination as priest took place at Saint Philips, a small inner-city African-American church in Grand Rapids, where she had become a much-loved and devoted member. Though she preaches rather often, she has never been a parish priest, sensing that her gifts lay elsewhere. Her calling, explicitly recognized by her bishop, has been to give spiritual counsel and guidance in whatever venue might present itself. It would be a serious breach of confidence for her to tell me, in anything but the most general terms, what transpires in her spiritual guidance sessions. But every now and then I pick up hints, from her and others, that lead me to conclude that she is superbly gifted at what she does. She has found her vocation.

In the fall of 1981, I delivered the Kuyper Lectures at the Free University of Amsterdam. The year before, at the centennial of its founding in 1880, the university had established this lecture series in honor of its principal founder, Abraham Kuyper. I was the inaugural lecturer. Claire and I, along with Christopher, lived in Amsterdam for the fall semester and for three months of the spring semester. It was not a good experience for Christopher, and though he came to love Amsterdam as much as we did, we did not succeed in finding a school that was right for him. So, after a few months of bad experiences, he studied on his own in our apartment. The other children remained back in the States: Robert and Klaas were both students at Calvin, Eric was in graduate school at Yale, and Amy, after doing international volunteer work in England, was now working at a variety of jobs.

I decided to use the opportunity of the lectures to articulate a socially progressive version of the Reformed tradition. I began my opening lecture by distinguishing between what I called *world-avertive* Christianity and *world-formative* Christianity. These two versions of Christianity are alike in acknowledging that there are things deeply amiss in our social order; but they differ in their response to that acknowledgment. The response of world-avertive Christianity is to put up with this fallen world and focus one's attention on getting to heaven. The response of world-formative Christianity is to hope for a new day while trying to change the social order so that it comes closer to how it ought to be.

I went on to argue that the Reformed tradition—from its beginnings and in most of its variants—has been a version of world-formative Christianity. In developing this thesis, I made ample use of *The Revolution of the Saints*, Michael Walzer's provocative study of the social posture of the late sixteenth- and early seventeenth-century English Puritans. "The saints," Walzer wrote, saw themselves as "responsible for their world—as medieval men were not—and responsible above all for its continual reformation. Their enthusiastic and purposive activity were part of their religious life, not something distinct and separate."

I then asked what Christians should set as the comprehensive goal of their social activity. The answer I proposed was *justice-in-shalom*. One day, when I was reading around in the Hebrew prophets, I was struck by how often they connected peace with justice. I began to suspect, however, that the English word "peace" was a poor translation of the Hebrew, which I knew to be the term *shalom*. So I looked for books and essays on shalom, but found none; now, as I write these words, there are dozens of books on shalom and hundreds of essays.

Finding no books or essays on shalom in the early 1980s, I consulted some theological wordbooks of the Old Testament to find out what they had to say on the subject. Though I found their discussions rather flat and superficial, I gleaned from them a list of most of the occurrences of *shalom* in the Old Testament. I looked up every one of those, in each case attending to the context in which the word occurred, in the hope that context would illuminate meaning. I was not disappointed. I came to the conclusion that the best English translation of *shalom* is not "peace" but "flourishing." Shalom is flourishing in all one's relationships: with God, with one's fellow human beings and their creations, with the natural world, with oneself. The reason the prophets so often connected justice with shalom is that shalom incorporates justice; injustice is the impairment of flourishing.

In the idea of shalom I found what I had been groping for on the flight home from that first conference trip to South Africa, when I had the acute sense that my life was breaking up into unrelated fragments. What unites justice, aesthetic delight, worship, and theoretical understanding is that they are all dimensions of shalom.

After introducing my subject in that first lecture, I spent several lectures identifying and analyzing two of the major causes of suffering and oppression in the modern world, namely, the capitalist world-system and nationalism. I argued that the capitalist world-system was the cause of much of the world's poverty, and that nationalism was the cause of much of the world's oppression. Specifically, I argued that Afrikaner nationalism was the root cause of apartheid and that Israeli nationalism was the root cause of the oppression of the Palestinians. To the annoyance of some listeners, I did not offer "solutions." Given my training and skills, I judged that what I could best contribute was a social analysis of the roots of these evils, coupled with the cry, "This should not be."

I concluded the series with a lecture on the aesthetic ugliness of the modern city and with a lecture in which I argued that Christian social action and Christian worship each requires the other for its integrity and sustenance. My audiences for the lectures were sizable and appreciative.

After revising and expanding the lectures, I published them under the title *Until Justice and Peace Embrace* (Eerdmans, 1983). A year or two after the book appeared, Jeff Stout, in the religion department at Princeton University, invited me to come and discuss it with the students in his class on Christian ethics. That was the beginning of a warm and enduring friendship. When Stout was president of the American Academy of Religion for the year 2006–07, he invited me to give a plenary address at the annual convention of the academy in November 2007, in one of the Academy's series of annual lectures. A stipulation of the series was that the addresses were to be partly autobiographical. As the title for my address, I chose "How Social Justice Got to Me and Why It Never Left." I received a standing ovation—the only time, I think, that has ever happened to me. Jeff came up to me afterward and said, "That was a great speech, even the false parts." I loved him for it. I knew, without asking, which parts he thought were false.

Over the course of our stay in Amsterdam, Claire and I formed a number of warm friendships, many of them lasting to this day: I think especially of Bernhard and Myra Scholz, of Sander and Dorien Griffioen, and of Johan and Joka van der Hoeven. And we loved living in Amsterdam. Of all the cities I know, Amsterdam is my favorite. The seventeenth-century city remains intact, an enduring architectural trace of what it was like to be human in that place in another day, brick and water lovingly engaging each other. Alone of the large cities of the world, Amsterdam has retained its human scale. There are no skyscrapers; church spires continue to punctuate the horizon. Even the civic architecture of Amsterdam is unpretentious, unlike the monumental civic architecture of London, Brussels, Paris, Rome, and Washington. One enters the Rijksmuseum, one of the world's great museums, not as one does the Metropolitan in New York, up a grand and imposing staircase, but at street level.

To my mind, there is nothing more delightful than sitting outside an Amsterdam bar on an early summer evening, along a canal, sipping Genever (Dutch gin) with friends, the just-sprung leaves on the trees still bright green, the canal silvery green in the fading light, the sounds of street music in the background.

My sabbatical from Calvin was for the entire academic year. Around the middle of March, I finished revising my Kuyper lectures for publication; what remained on my docket was reading and reviewing a few books, something I could do anywhere in the world. Somehow the idea arose: Why not spend a couple of months on the Greek island of Patmos? I went to the Greek Tourist Office in Amsterdam and asked how we could find an apartment on Patmos to rent for a few months. Their answer was, "Take the boat from Athens (Piraeus) to Patmos; at the dock you will find people offering apartments for rent." They were right. We found a very pleasant apartment on the road that winds up from the harbor to the monastery at the crest of the mountain overlooking the harbor village. From our balcony we could look down to the harbor, and from our kitchen window we could look up to the monastery. Along the road, about halfway between our apartment and the monastery, there was a small church that enclosed the cave in which, as legend has it, Saint John lived while receiving his visions. I neither believed nor disbelieved the legend. True or not, his spirit was there.

The three of us—Claire, Christopher, and I—had a wonderful time on Patmos, enjoying fish dinners in restaurants along the harbor, drinking thick black coffee in the village square, attending Orthodox services on Sunday, browsing in the museum of the monastery, riding the bus around the island. The hills were vivid green, with small domed churches, painted white, scattered among the hills. Idyllic.

Somebody told us that one of the beaches on Patmos, Lambi Beach, was famous for the beautiful ocean-washed stones lying around. They were right, and we loaded our backpacks with beautiful stones. When we went through customs and security in the Athens airport on our way back home, the officials acted extremely suspicious of our cache of stones. I wondered whether it could be illegal to take stones out of the country that one had found on a beach. After conferring for what seemed like a very long time, they allowed us through.

As I write these words, I am looking at some Patmos stones on my desk, a few of the hundred or so that we brought back with us. It was Claire and her family who taught me to see beauty in stones. For me, growing up in the farm country of Minnesota, a stone was a stone.

SEVEN

Living with Grief

On Sunday afternoon, June 12, 1983, I received a phone call that shattered my comfortable life and divided it into before and after. The call was from our son Eric's landlady in Munich, Germany, where Eric was doing research for his doctoral dissertation in architectural history, under Vincent Scully at Yale, on a German architect, Schultze-Naumburg, who worked between the two world wars.

Eric had been extraordinarily successful in his graduate career at Yale: he had supervised all the discussion sections for the seven hundred students in Scully's introductory history of art course, and, as a twenty-four-year-old without a graduate degree, he had curated a show at Yale's British Art Museum. Some years ago, one of his graduate school classmates and friend reported to me an episode that he remembered with great delight. The professor—in a class they were taking on ancient Greek art—was piling detail upon detail. Finally, Eric raised his hand and asked, very gently, "Professor, why is all this important?" whereupon the professor explained, as he had not bothered to explain previously, why it was important. I was proud of my son.

The call came when Claire and I had just returned from driving Klaas to the plane headed for Munich, where he planned to work for the summer and room with his older brother. The legs of the journey were Grand Rapids to Chicago O'Hare, from Chicago to Luxembourg, then by train from Luxembourg to Munich.

"Mr. Wolterstorff?" the landlady asked.

"Yes."

"Is this Eric's father?"

"Yes."

"Mr. Wolterstorff, I must give you some bad news."

"Yes."

"Eric has been climbing in the mountains and has had an accident."

"Yes."

"Eric has had a serious accident."

"Yes."

"Mr. Wolterstorff, I must tell you, Eric is dead. Mr. Wolterstorff, are you there? You must come at once! Mr. Wolterstorff, Eric is dead."

It took a couple of seconds for the reality of what I had heard to sink in.

Somehow—I do not remember how—I got to the airport in Chicago in time to find Klaas standing in line waiting to board the plane for the second leg of his journey, to Luxembourg. I got the agent at the desk to allow me to use his ticket. In retrospect, that was a serious mistake. I should have bought a ticket for myself, and Klaas and I should have gone to Munich together. But I wasn't thinking clearly, and Klaas returned to Grand Rapids. My flight to Luxembourg was one long black hole.

Claire called friends of ours in Amsterdam, the Scholzes, to tell them what had happened. Bernhard, who is a German native, said he would take the train from Amsterdam to Luxembourg, meet me in the airport there, and accompany me on the train to Munich. A few of Eric's close friends, who had been planning to visit Eric for a few days and had learned of his death, greeted us as we got off the train in Munich. I have no memory of how they knew I was on that train.

Eric had a good many years of mountain-climbing experience behind him; he loved it, loved it intensely. He died doing what he loved. On Saturday, the 11th of June, he had taken the train from Munich to Kufstein, Austria, for a day's climb in the mountains. As I mentioned earlier, he was the most venturesome of our children, often taking risks. I wondered: Had the climb been dangerous? Later, I had mountain-cimbing friends of his look over the description of the route he took to tell me whether or not it was dangerous. They said it was not. On the other hand, it was the time of year when the snow was melting at that altitude.

After Bernhard and I had gone to the morgue, identified Eric's body, and made arrangements for having his body flown back to Grand Rapids—and after we had packed up his belongings and arranged for shipment to the United States—we took the train back to Luxembourg, where Bernhard continued on home to Amsterdam, and I went to the airport. I had a long wait before the flight to Chicago took off, so I began to write, pouring out my feelings and trying to put into words who Eric was. That was the beginning of what became my book *Lament for a Son*. Very little of what I wrote there in the Luxembourg airport found its way into the final draft, but that's where it began.

Why did I write? Out of helplessness. I had brought along some reading material from home, but I could not read. I could only think of Eric's death. What else was there to do but write? I know now that expressing one's grief in words mysteriously aids in coping with the grief, but I don't think I knew that at the time. I wrote because I had several hours to spend and I was incapable of doing anything else.

It was late when I returned home, but I assembled the family. I remember only what I said first and last. "Our Eric is gone," I said. And, at the end, I said that we had to remember him, not put him out of mind, not forget him. And that's what we have done: remembered him. Photos of him are on display, and ceramics that he made when he was in high school. We talk about him, more at first than now, naturally, but his name still comes up rather often, along with memories. I don't recall that any of us talked very much about our feelings of grief; instead, we talked about Eric. I have learned that some families are torn apart by grief. Initially, shared grief unites, but then, later, members of the family grieve at different paces, and that tears them apart. Our family was not torn apart, perhaps because we were surrounded by a loving community of relatives, friends, and church members.

The boys looked up to Eric as their admired older brother; Robert had begun to ask him for advice about his future education. Now, suddenly, he was gone, and we all had to live around the gap in our lives—differently in each case, because in each case the gap was different. Klaas had to live around the gap of not living with his brother in Munich for the summer. I think Christopher was the most affected. Several months after Eric's death, Claire happened to notice that the day-by-day calendar on Christopher's desk was still at June 12, the day we heard of Eric's death. She asked him why that was. He answered, "Because that's when my life stopped."

I had composed a funeral liturgy at the request of a friend of ours who was dying of brain cancer. She had wanted to put her stamp of approval on the liturgy that would be used at her funeral. As it turned out, we used that liturgy for the first time at Eric's funeral, and the friend for whom I had composed it was present. The musicians were several of Eric's friends. We had not planned a eulogy, but as the service progressed, I felt I had to say something. So, as the final hymn was concluding, I got up, went to the front, and spoke. I don't remember what I said; all I remember is finding it extremely difficult to get words out, choking up several times, and seeing people in the audience wiping away their tears. Recently, someone who was present at the funeral remarked to me that it was both the most beautiful and the most painful service he had ever attended.

I composed *Lament for a Son* over the course of the following year. It consists of fragments—with lots of space between the fragments. Rather early in the process of writing I tried to join the fragments into a continuous flow, but it didn't work. My life had been fragmented, so my lament would have to be fragmented as well. I think of the white space between the fragments as silence. In the face of death, we should not talk much.

It occurred to me that it might be helpful to read some books about grief, so I went to the library and took out a few books by theologians about grief and a few books by psychologists about the grief process. I could not read them. I found it impossible to read and think about an abstract thing called Grief. Not only impossible, but repellent, a distraction from what I so urgently needed to do, namely, shape a way of life from which Eric was absent and I was in grief. *Lament for a Son* is not a book *about* Grief—it's a *cry of grief*. I took the books back to the library, unread.

Lament for a Son is in a style completely different from anything I had written previously, and from anything I have written since. Not only is it fragmentary, it is also highly metaphorical. At one point I wrote, for example: "Sorrow is no longer the islands but the sea." I had the sense that the words were given to me: I did not search for words to express my grief; words came and I took them in. I could not write the book today.

Of course, it was not automatic writing: I had intentions and resolutions. In particular, I resolved not to say anything that I did not truly feel and believe, not to say the things that a person in grief is expected to say. Many readers who have experienced grief have told me that the book gave them permission to think and say what they, too, felt and believed, rather than what they were expected to feel and believe. The book is thus ruthlessly honest, raw at some points. I learned from some readers that it took them some time, after the death of someone they loved, before they could read it. I understand.

A friend called attention to the fact that the book asks lots of questions, dozens and dozens of them. He quoted a passage that he interpreted as explaining why all the questions: "I am not angry [at God] but baffled and hurt. My wound is an unanswered question. The wounds of all humanity are an unanswered question."

I gave the manuscript to Claire to read before I sent it off for publication, but I did not give it to our children to read. I don't know why I didn't give it to them, and I very much regret not doing so. It is, after all, as much a lament for their brother as it is for my son.

The book was published in 1987 by Eerdmans. By a strange quirk of timing, I first saw copies when I went to the Eerdmans printing plant on some unrelated business one day and happened upon a stack of copies of the book on a wooden pallet. I froze. I had the vivid image of lying on my back on a hospital gurney, with my gut exposed, people filing by, gaping and gawking. "What have I done?" I asked myself. "What *have* I done?"

I have received hundreds of responses to the book, initially by post, nowadays by email. To the best of my knowledge, I have replied to all but a very few. Shortly after publication, a review in a religious periodical sharply criticized the book for what the reviewer regarded as its heretical theology. Five or six readers of the review wrote to me in stern tones, taking it upon themselves to chastise me for my heretical theology. From what they said, it was clear to me that they had not themselves read the book, only that review. When I sat down to reply to those letters, I found myself paralyzed. There is, to be sure, theology in the book—implicit in my expression of grief. I am willing to defend that theology, even though much of it was blurted out rather than thought out at the time I wrote it. But I found myself incapable of arguing theology with these critics—my grief got in the way. I did not reply.

After reflecting for some time on what kind of memorial we could establish for Eric, Claire and I decided to commission a requiem in his honor. I had been listening to my recordings of requiems, in the hope of finding music that fitted my grief, but found them impossible to listen to. I had always loved Brahms's *Requiem*. Now I had to turn it off; the music was too lovely, too soaring, too confident. Though the words are about brokenness, the music is not itself broken. A friend brought over a record of Fauré's *Requiem*, confident that this would prove to be what I was looking for. My reaction was similar. It was too smooth, too lush, too lovely—again, the music was not broken music. The only broken music I found was the Renaissance lowlands composer Heinrich Isaac's "Lament upon the Death of Lorenzo the Magnificent" and Henry Purcell's music for the funeral of Queen Mary.

When I mentioned to various musician friends that we were thinking of commissioning a requiem in Eric's honor, they named a number of composers they thought we should consider. While we were going through the process of settling on a composer, I set about looking for a text. I looked first at the text of the traditional Catholic requiem. This too I found impossible: none of the words gave voice to my brokenness. And as for the *Dies Irae* section, the words stuck in my throat:

> The day of wrath, that day,
> > will consume the world to glowing ashes,
> > as David and the Sibyl bear witness....
> Full of tears that day will be,
> > when from the ashes shall arise
> > guilty mankind, to be judged.
> Spare them therefore, O God.

The Orthodox requiem was better. Though I could not use it in its entirety, there were passages in it that did give voice to my brokenness:

> Truly terrible is the mystery of death.
> I lament at the sight of the beauty
> created for us in the image of God
> which lies now in the grave
> without shape, without glory, without consideration.
> What is this mystery that surrounds us?
> Why are we delivered up to decay?
> Why are we bound to death?

In the end, I composed a text of my own, using that passage from the Orthodox liturgy along with passages from Scripture, especially from the book of Psalms.

The composer we eventually settled on was Cary Ratcliffe, a young composer from Rochester, New York. When we met with

Cary, I remarked that we were asking him to compose broken mu-sic—not just music *about* brokenness, but broken music. He suc-ceeded wonderfully, especially in Part II, which begins with these words from Psalm 102:

> Like a bird alone in the desert
>> or an owl in a ruined house
> I lie awake and I groan,
>> like a sparrow lost on a roof.
> Ashes are the bread that I eat,
>> I mingle my tears with my drink.

Requiem: Eric Wolterstorff in Memoriam was first performed in Grand Rapids on May 18, 1986, by the Calvin College Alumni Choir under the direction of Anton Armstrong, currently the conductor of the St. Olaf College Choir. It's a wonderful composition. To my surprise and disappointment, the composer has not succeeded in getting the music published. The text can be found in the appendix to *Lament for a Son*.

When I was writing *Lament for a Son*, I understood nothing about grief, other than that I would not be grieving over Eric's death had I not loved him. Grief was the price I was paying for love. More than that, I did not understand—nor did I try to understand. Now I understand more.

Love comes in different forms. There is the love that consists of seeking to promote or sustain the good of some person or living thing: call it *love as beneficence*. There is the love that consists of being drawn to someone or something because of their excellence: call it *love as attraction*. It is love as attraction that one expresses when one says, for example, "I love Beethoven's late string quartets" or "I loved last night's display of the northern lights." There is the love that consists of finding enjoyment in some activity, for example, loving to play the piano, loving gardening, loving woodworking, and so on: call such love *activity-love*. And there is the love that consists of being attached to someone or something: to one's children, one's spouse, one's pet, one's house: call this *love as attachment*. These different forms of love are often combined, for example, in friendship.

Love as attachment is mysterious. I may acknowledge that your cat is finer than ours, but ours is the one I found huddled on our doorstep one cold winter morning, meowing piteously. I took it in and became attached—bonded. Of course, when we become attached to someone or something, we begin to discern good and excellent things that we had previously overlooked. Attachment opens our eyes to what is praiseworthy.

It is love as attachment that makes us vulnerable to grief. When our attempts at beneficence fail for some reason, we feel frustration, disappointment, regret—not grief. When the object of our love as attraction changes, so that we are no longer attracted, we feel regret and disappointment—not grief. Grief comes when the object of our attachment dies or is destroyed, or is no longer accessible.

Attachment manifests itself in desires and commitments with respect to the one loved. Some of those are desires for some benefit that comes to the lover; we delight, for instance, in the company of a child. Many are desires and commitments for the well-being of the beloved. We want our *children* to flourish; we don't just prize their contributions to *our* flourishing. So we invest ourselves in them, doing what we can to promote their flourishing, rejoicing with them over their attainments and the good things that come their way, sorrowing with them over their failures, their disappointments, their broken bones. These desires and endeavors change as our children mature.

When Eric died, a big part of my own self was ripped out. My desires with respect to him, my commitments, my hopes, my expectations—they were no more. My expectation that he would be home for the summer was no more; my plan to attend his graduation was no more. For a month or so I caught myself still planning to do things with him, still expecting him to call. Eventually, the realization sunk in, all the way down, that he was dead. I had to learn to live around that gaping wound and with that grief. Grief was not just an additional component in my life. I had to live a new kind of life, one for which I had no practice.

When someone to whom we are attached dies or is destroyed, we are cast into grief. That tells us when grief befalls us, not what the thing itself is. Grief, I have come to think, is *wanting the death or destruction of the loved one to be undone, while at the same time knowing it cannot be undone.* Grief is wanting the loved one back when one knows he can't come back. Tears and agitation are typical expressions of grief, but they are not the thing itself. My grief was wanting intensely for Eric to be alive when I knew that could not be.

It has to be *wanting*, not wishing. When I was a teenager, I wished to become a major-league baseball pitcher—one of the very best, a twenty-game winner. I fantasized about it. But the fact that I have not become a baseball pitcher has caused me no grief whatsoever, since it wasn't something I really *wanted*. I had no talent for baseball, and I took no steps toward becoming a pitcher. I wished, but I did not want. And one has to know, or be convinced, that what one wants is impossible. Otherwise, it is hope rather than grief that one experiences—perhaps worried, anxious hope, perhaps hope against hope, but hope. Grief is wanting with all your heart what you know or believe is impossible. The more intense the wanting, the more intense the grief.

In grief, wanting collides with knowing. I desperately wanted Eric to be alive, but I knew he was dead and could not be brought back to life. Grief is banging your head against the wall. If you are frightened, you can run away or hide; if you are angry, you can vent your rage. When you are in grief, there is nothing you can do, other than altering yourself by getting rid of the frustrated want or by repressing your awareness of it.

By virtue of wanting what you know or believe to be impossible, grief is irrational: it makes no sense to want what you know cannot be. In this way, too, grief is different from fear and anger. Some fear is irrational, as is some anger; but fear and anger are not inherently irrational. It makes good sense to be fearful when you are in danger; it makes good sense to be angry when you are insulted. Grief, by contrast, is inherently irrational.

It is this irrationality at the heart of grief that leads people who are not personally acquainted with grief to say to the person in grief such things as, "No use crying over spilt milk." "You can't bring him back." It is this same irrationality at the heart of grief that leads many in our society to regard the person in grief as needing therapy or counseling. Some grieving persons do need therapy because their grief is pathological. But grief is not pathological as such. If you are attached to your child, you will feel grief upon learning of his or her death. This is not pathology; this is human nature.

How was I to live with this strange and painful intruder—grief? I was well aware that a common way of dealing with grief in our society, perhaps the most common way, is to try to *disown* one's grief. Note the language we use: "putting it behind you," "getting over it," "getting on with things," "getting on with your life." This is the language of disowning. The aim is to get to the point where one doesn't think of mentioning it when asked to identify the significant events in one's life.

"But I think I remember hearing that you lost a 6-year-old son."
"Oh yes, that's true. I had forgotten."

That is disowned grief.

I felt intuitively that to disown my grief would be to live a lie. It would be to declare, implicitly, that Eric's death was not an evil, or that my love of him was not a good. But his death *was* an evil, a great evil, and my love for him *was* a good, a great good. My grief spoke the truth. It was an existential shout of "No" to the evil of Eric's death and an existential shout of "Yes" to the good of my love for him.

I would own my grief. When tears came, I would let them flow. When telling about significant events in my life, I would tell about my love for Eric, and about his death, and about my grief over his death. I would preserve the memories, and I would live with the disturbances and disruptions in my life that those memories created. Setting out some of the truly beautiful ceramic pieces that Eric created when he was in high school, where we see them daily, is a way of keeping alive our memory of him and a way of honoring him. They are memorials, as are the photographs we keep out.

Not only would I own my grief rather than disown it. I would seek to own my grief redemptively—to own it in such a way that it would bring about some good that would otherwise not have come about. In writing *Lament for a Son*, I was owning my grief redemptively, as I was when, on occasion, I gave a talk on "living with grief."

People often ask me how my grief has changed over the years. Usually, those who ask have just recently been cast into grief, and they are wondering whether the dark cloud will ever lift. At first, my grief was always there, if not in the forefront of my thoughts, then in the felt background. Gradually, it was no longer always there. But it's always ready to return. Anything in my experience, no matter how innocuous—a chance remark, a piece of clothing, a work of art—bears the potential of trigging a chain of associations that culminates in renewed grief. Initially, whenever something reminded me of Eric and of his death, wanting him back surged through me. Now that happens less often. What happens now is a feeling of deep regret for all the promise that never came to be. My lament now is more sorrow over the good lost than grief over the evil of Eric's absence.

After Eric's funeral and burial, friends came by the house to express their condolences. One of them mentioned that he had placed a basket of strawberries under the boxwood at the front door. The memory of eating strawberries after my mother's funeral came immediately to mind.

Arabbi friend, Phillip Sigal, who participated in Eric's funeral by reading a passage from the Hebrew Bible/Old Testament, remarked afterward that what he had witnessed was the endurance of faith. He was right: my faith endured. But it would become a different kind of faith, a faith that incorporated Eric's death and my grief. And that would reveal to me a different kind of God, more mysterious. My relationship with my fellow human beings also changed: I felt an emotional affinity, often unspoken, with those whom I knew were also in grief.

Faith involves cognition of some sort, be it belief or something else; but faith, at its core, is not belief but trust. After Eric's death, my trust in God became more wary, more cautious, more guarded, more qualified. I pray that God will protect the members of my family. But I had prayed that for Eric. I still trust God; but I no longer trust God to protect me and my family from harm and grief.

Lament had been a minor part of my religious life; praise and thanksgiving dominated. Now, in this dark place, I found myself drawn to the psalms of lament. They spoke to me. Or rather, they spoke *for* me. Their words became my words.

> As a deer longs for flowing streams,
>> so my soul longs for you, O God. . . .
>
> My tears have been my food day and night,
>> while people say to me, "Where is your God?"
>
> Why are you cast down, O my soul,
>> and why are you disquieted within me?
> Hope in God; for I shall again praise him,
>> my help and my God. (Psalm 42)

Some who have lost a child are angry with God. "God, how could you do this to me? I have loved and served you faithfully these many years." It was not anger I felt but hurt—hurt and bafflement. How could I fit together my son's untimely death with the God I worshiped? I knew the traditional strategies for doing so, but I found I could not accept them.

God did it, some say: it's part of God's plan. That made no sense to me. Scripture speaks of God overcoming death, bringing about a new day when death shall be no more. Saint Paul calls death the last great enemy to be overcome. If death is God's enemy, how could Eric's death be something God did? God may have permitted Eric's foot to slip, but God did not make it slip.

Some say that tragedy is part of God's strategy for soul-making—part of God's strategy for bringing about moral and religious improvement in people. This view, which goes far back in Christian history, is the "solution" C. S. Lewis proposed in *The Problem of Pain*. But Eric was dead. The tragedy of his untimely death did nothing for his soul. And as for the souls of those who loved him: I found the very idea repulsive, that God would use Eric's death as a device for making me, and the others who knew and loved him, better persons.

Others echo Job's friends, arguing that tragedy is God's way of punishing us for our wrongdoing. John Calvin was inclined toward that view, adding that we must patiently accept the punishment and not rail against it. I joined Job in rejecting the idea that God used Eric's early death as a way of punishing me—or anyone else. Jesus healed the infirm and raised the dead. He did not declare that infirmity and untimely death are God's just punishment for sin, and then walk on. I shall continue to rail against Eric's untimely death. This should not be.

Then there are those who argue that God is as pained by tragedy as you and I are, but that there is nothing God can do about it. This is the position defended by Harold Kushner in *When Bad Things Happen to Good People*. I found this position nonsensical. Was the God who created this vast and intricate cosmos not capable of forestalling Eric's death?

Finally, there are those who hold that the untimely death of a child is a price to be paid for some greater good that God is bringing about for human beings in general. All such views seemed to me oblivious to the each-and-every theme sounded in Scripture: God desires that each and every human being flourish until she or he is full of years. I could not accept that Eric's death was a tradeoff for some greater good God was bringing about for humanity at large.

I did not think long and hard about these proposals for making sense of it all. Neither, after rejecting them, did I try to think up a new and better theodicy. God has not told us why there is natural and moral evil in the world, has not explained to us why we do not all flourish until full of years. I live with that. What we are told is that God is engaged in a battle with evil and will eventually win the battle. Rather than embracing some traditional theodicy, or trying to construct a new one, I have argued in some essays that if God is indeed engaged in a battle with evil, we should reject the traditional doctrine of divine impassibility, which says that God surveys what transpires in the world with undisturbed bliss. Our suffering disturbs God.

Something else in me was steering me away from the so-called problem of evil. I think I might have been interested in the problem of evil had Eric not died. His death, and my grief over his death, held me back. I would begin reading some new treatment of the problem of evil, and find I had to put it down. I did not understand then—nor do I understand now—why that was, nor why it remains the case to this day. Why did Eric's death, and my grief over his death, not intensify my desire to make sense of it all?

I did not shy away from taking note of the gaping void in me that his death caused. I did not shy away from voicing my lament over his death. But I could not bring myself to try to figure out what God was up to in Eric's death. I joined the psalmist in lamenting without explaining. Things have gone awry in God's world. I do not understand why, nor do I understand why God puts up with it for so long. Rather than Eric's death evoking in me an interest in theodicy, it had the effect of making God more mysterious. I live with the mystery.

If I cannot make sense of it, why not give up on God? I cannot. When I consider the stupendous immensity and astonishing intricacy of the cosmos, and the miracle of human consciousness and intelligence, I find that I cannot believe it all just happened. A being of incomprehensible wisdom, imagination, and power must have brought it about—or rather, is *bringing* it about. I have come to think of God as performing the cosmos. I look out the window of my study on this autumn day in western Michigan, at the deep blue sky and the gorgeous colors of the leaves. This is a brief but glorious passage in God's performance of the cosmos.

The words "wisdom," "imagination," and "power" do not describe; they point. They're the best we can do. Something like our wisdom, something like our imagination, something like our power—yet infinitely beyond. The God who became more mysterious to me has also become more awesome, awesome beyond comprehension. And that has magnified my astonishment that God would care about human beings. The words of the psalmist speak for me:

> When I look at your heavens, the work of your fingers,
>> the moon and the stars that you have established,
> what are human beings that you are mindful of them,
>> mortals, that you care for them? (Psalm 8)

Or, rather than being astonished that God would care about human beings, might Marilynne Robinson be onto something when she suggests that the Creator always had human beings in mind?

Christ as Creator implies to me that his role as Christ is intrinsic to Creation—that in that first moment creatures were foreseen whose nature and course of life he could take on altogether without in any way diminishing his high holiness.... Then in this profounder sense we are not aliens in the universe, taking the word in the largest sense, but are singularly rooted in it.[1]

In recent years, there has been renewed interest among philosophers in arguments for the existence of God. Traditional arguments have been reformulated in the light of developments in philosophy generally, and new arguments have emerged. Among the new arguments is the so-called fine-tuning argument. Scientists have noted that, if certain physical constants were ever so slightly different from what they are, there could be no life. The sheer unlikelihood of the fact that, from the infinite number of alternative possibilities, the cosmos that does exist is one that supports life, calls for explanation. The most plausible explanation is that it was created by a being who wanted such a cosmos and accordingly selected those physical constants. It is also extremely unlikely that, among living things, there would be creatures who could develop mathematics and discover that the fundamental physical laws of nature can be formulated in terms of the mathematics they have developed. I cannot shake the conviction that God wanted creatures of just our kind.

And when I read the New Testament Gospels, I find myself believing that the Jesus of whom they speak was raised from the dead, thereby vindicating his proclamation of the coming of the kingdom of God. Saint Paul speaks for me when he says that, if Christ was not raised, our faith is in vain. I live in the hope of a new day coming.

1. Marilynne Robinson, *The Givenness of Things* (New York: Picador, 2015), 213.

EIGHT

Amsterdam, Church, Garden

L ate in the fall of 1984, I received a letter from the philosophy department of the Free University of Amsterdam asking whether I would consider being appointed to the position, in their department, of professor of epistemology (*Kennis- en Wetenschapsleer*). The professor who was then holding that position, Cornelius van Peursen, would be retiring at the end of the academic year. They were willing to consider a half-time rather than a full-time professorship. (In the Dutch university system, a good many professors teach part-time at one Dutch university and part time at some other university, either in the Netherlands or elsewhere.) I talked it over with Claire and the children, and with my colleagues at Calvin. The more I thought about it, the more intrigued I was by the prospect. After a month or so of deliberation, I replied that I would consider a half-time professorship. The offer came forthwith, and I accepted.

Spring in the Netherlands is much more beautiful than fall. I would teach at Calvin in the fall and at the Free University in the spring. My first stint of teaching at the Free was the spring of 1986, the first of what would prove to be five wonderful years. Claire and I loved living in Amsterdam again, this time in the old city (previously we had lived in the southern suburb of Amstelveen), and renewing our acquaintance with old friends and making new ones. Of the new friends we made, I think especially of Nico ter Linden and his wife, Annette. Nico was the pastor of the prominent Westerkerk (West Church) in Amsterdam, preacher extraordinaire, and writer of an immensely popular series of what he called "Bible stories for adults."[1]

Until World War II, the Free University had remained small, housed in canal houses in old Amsterdam, and had continued to be staunchly Reformed in its religious orientation. After the war, it became part of the Dutch university system, and that changed everything. The university constructed a large new building in southern Amsterdam (poured concrete, in a style known in architectural cir-

---

1. Nico ter Linden died in January 2018.

cles as Brutalism), the student population surged, and the dynamics unleashed by being part of the national university system resulted in the gradual erosion of the religious orientation of the university, to the point where it is now a secular university with vestiges, here and there, of its religious origins.

I taught in English. Though I could understand written and spoken Dutch, I was not fluent at speaking Dutch, especially not academic Dutch. And in any case, the students wanted me to teach in English so that they could gain fluency in the language. Dutch law requires that foreigners appointed to full-time positions in Dutch universities teach in Dutch after two years, but since my position was half-time, the law did not apply in my case. The courses I taught were small seminars rather than lecture courses, and the students were bright, enthusiastic, and receptive.

The ethos of the philosophy department at the Free, still under the influence of Dooyeweerd and Vollenhoven's philosophy, was rather closed and insular. Faculty and students were aware of currents in French and German philosophy, but they were almost entirely ignorant of what was going on in analytic philosophy in the United States and England. My students were excited by the opening I was giving them into the analytic tradition, as were several of the younger instructors, and I found it gratifying to play a role in opening up the department to the Anglo-American philosophical world.

As I write these words, in the spring of 2017, the philosophers at the Free University are thoroughly immersed in the analytic tradition while remaining conversant with developments in continental philosophy. And whereas the philosophers there, when I joined the department, were in the habit of simply commenting on the work of other philosophers, the philosophers who now hold positions there are making significant systematic contributions of their own. I think especially of René van Woudenberg in this regard. René was well along on his doctoral dissertation (on the thought of the contemporary German philosopher Karl Otto Apel) when his supervisor became ill and René asked me to take over. I read what René had written, and saw that it was a paradigmatic example of a Dutch philosophy dissertation of the time: a careful analysis of Apel's thought, now and then timidly posing a critical question. I told René that I would be happy to supervise his dissertation on the condition that he not just summarize Apel's thought but think for himself on the issues Apel raised. In a long final chapter, René did exactly that, and did it superbly. I found it fascinating that, in the public examination, all the questions directed at him were about that final chapter. René has gone on to a prolific career as a systematic philosopher and to training a number of others in that line. Claire and I are warm friends with him and his wife, Annamiek.

From the time I first attended college, the basic structure of American colleges and universities seemed to me sensible and transparent. Each institution does, of course, have idiosyncrasies that can be mysterious to newcomers; but the basic structure is the same across the land. I found the structure of the Dutch university system to be opaque at many points. When I mentioned this to my Dutch colleagues, they said they often found the American system opaque. The familiar seems transparent—the unfamiliar, opaque.

Begin with the title "professor." I soon learned that being a professor in the Dutch system is very different from being a professor in the American system. In the American system, professor is the topmost of the four traditional ranks: instructor, assistant professor, associate professor, and professor (the last often called "full professor"). Being promoted to full professor does not change what one does. The rank does not, for example, automatically come with supervisory responsibilities. It's just a rank. Most people begin as instructor or assistant professor, and move up the ranks to full professor if their work is judged satisfactory. It's possible for all the members of a department to be full professors, though most departments try to prevent that from happening.

When a department in the United States invites applicants for an opening, it specifies some area of expertise that it is looking for—expertise, say, in the area of ancient philosophy. But the candidate whom it chooses is usually not appointed as professor of ancient philosophy. The candidate is appointed as professor of philosophy, with the expectation that she will teach the department's courses in ancient philosophy. She might also have interests in other philosophical fields, for instance in ethics, and might publish in that area, perhaps even do some teaching in that area. In most American philosophy departments, the boundaries among the various philosophical subdisciplines are porous in that way.

In the Dutch system, each department has an allotted number of professorships, those typically constituting a rather small proportion of the faculty, and most faculty members never become professors. Each professor is appointed to a particular subdiscipline: mine was epistemology. Being appointed as the professor of a particular subdiscipline comes with the responsibility of supervising all those working in that subdiscipline, both those who are teaching and those who are graduate students working on dissertations. In earlier days, these members were all regarded as assistants to the professor. I was told that it was not unheard of, in former days, for a professor to call up one of his "assistants" in the evening and ask the assistant to go to the library to get a book for him. If that were to happen today, there would be an insurgency.

Those who are working in a certain subdiscipline, both teachers and graduate students, are organized into a *vakgroep*, with the professor appointed to that subdiscipline serving as supervisor of the *vakgroep*. (The Dutch word *groep* is synonymous with the English word "group"; the Dutch word *vak*, when combined with the word *groep*, means something like "subject area" or "subdiscipline.") All teachers and graduate students in a department (*faculty*, in Dutch terminology) are assigned to a *vakgroep*. Teachers who are members of a particular *vakgroep* do all their teaching within that subdiscipline, and all members of the *vakgroep* are expected to devote a substantial proportion of their research to topics within that subdiscipline. When I was teaching at the Free, the members of most of the philosophy *vakgroepen* had gotten together with other members of their *vakgroep* to formulate a common research project, for which they were receiving support from the government. To what extent this was expected or required of them, I do not know.

This was all quite unlike anything I had experienced in the United States. The faculty and graduate students at Harvard and Yale, and the faculty at Calvin, were not divided up into subdisciplinary groups, with the instructors in the group expected to do all their teaching within that subdiscipline, and with all the members of the group expected to devote a substantial part of their research to some topic within that subdiscipline. In my own case, I wrote extensively in the areas of philosophy of education and philosophy of religion while I was at Calvin, though I never taught courses in those areas; and the courses on liturgy that I taught were outside philosophy entirely. The Dutch system, as I experienced it, was considerably more communitarian than was the American system, modeled in good measure—so it appeared to me—on the natural sciences. In the United States it's unusual for members of a philosophy department to be working together on a common research project.

My colleagues at the Free University were exceedingly kind and patient in explaining to me the role of professor in the Dutch system and assisting me in carrying out my duties. But I never felt entirely comfortable in the role. Every now and then I would be surprised by someone's response to something I had done, or I would be informed of something I should have done but had failed to do. There were unwritten rules of decorum and protocol that eluded me. Looking back, I think this contributed, paradoxically, to the sense of excitement I felt. Teaching in the American system—and particularly, teaching at Calvin—had become too comfortable.

What contributed significantly to my bewilderment at certain points was the extreme centralization of the Dutch university system. The universities are all under the authority of the national minister of education and, with the exception of theological schools and departments, are almost completely funded by the national government. To me, the resulting bureaucracy was astonishing, as was the number of rules and regulations issued by the bureaucracy and the quantity of paperwork required to deal with these. What also struck me, during my time there, was the restlessness of the system. Each time a new minister of education came into office—which was rather often—he seemed to think he had to show he was in charge by issuing a new set of regulations. The same was often true when a new administrative head of a university came into office.

When I mentioned to friends and colleagues how different I found the Dutch system of higher education from the American, the response I often got was surprise. The traditional Dutch system was being Americanized, they said. My response was that, though that was true in certain respects—for example, in the push toward devising quantitative criteria for the evaluation of teaching and research—the American system as a whole was fundamentally different from the Dutch system.

The most important difference is the radical decentralization of the American system, compared to the Dutch. There is no national university system in the United States, nor is there any minister of education issuing directives to all the universities of the land. Unlike the Dutch system, the American system includes a vast array of private colleges and universities independent of government control and supported, for the most part, by tuition and private philanthropy rather than government funds. There are state universities, of course, but I know of no state in which some government official has the kind of authority over the state universities that the Dutch minister of education has over the Dutch universities.

Second, American colleges and universities differ vastly in terms of quality. Some are among the best in the world, others are dismal. The Dutch, by contrast, try to see to it that their universities are roughly equal in quality, and by and large, they are successful at that.

And third, competition is everywhere in the American system—among colleges and universities, among students seeking to gain admittance, among students seeking financial support, among faculty members striving for advancement. The administrative head of the Free University, Harry Brinkman, became a good friend of ours. On one occasion, he signed up for an extended tour of American universities. Upon his return, he told me that what he found most striking about the American system, and also most troubling, was the extent and depth of competition.

On October 19, 2007, two decades after I first taught at the Free University, I was awarded an honorary doctorate by the university. The *laudatio* (praise) of the work I had done, for which I was being honored, was delivered by Henk Woldring, a member of the philosophy department and a longtime friend. Rather than giving the usual kind of acceptance speech, I decided to respond to Woldring's *laudatio* of my work with my own *laudatio* of the Free University. This is what I said:

> To the Free University, to its rector and other officials, I express my deepest gratitude for the honor you have bestowed on me with this honorary doctorate; and to my promoter, Professor Woldring, my gratitude for the words of your *laudatio*.
>
> When a university bestows an honorary doctorate on someone, it thereby says something about the person it honors. At the same time, it implicitly says something about itself. You have heard, in the *laudatio*, what the Free University wishes to be understood as saying about me. May I be so bold as to put into words what I understand the Free University to be implicitly saying about itself?
>
> You have honored a philosopher. Thereby you have declared that the Free University is not simply a cog in the machinery of the technocratic society. You have declared that you are committed

to providing an arena for the deepest questions of our human existence, questions that underlie all we think and do, yet never receive final answers: What is justice? What is beauty? What is truth? What is consciousness? What is it to speak? What is time? Is there only matter? Can we know God? And why is it so difficult to answer these questions? Why is reality, deep down, so elusive, so profoundly mysterious?

You have also honored someone who has not shied away from speaking with a religious voice in the academy and society when that has seemed relevant. Mine has been a particular kind of religious voice: not angry, not abusive of those who disagree, yet not silenced by the acids of skepticism, committed to the flourishing of all God's children, willing to be corrected, concerned to promote the modern university as a place where genuine dialogue can take place among persons of different visions of life and reality. In granting me this honor, you have declared that you are committed to the legitimacy and worth of such a voice in academy and society.

And in honoring me, you have honored someone who, throughout his career, has spoken up for both the wronged of the world and for the importance of the arts in our human existence. Thereby you have declared your support of both those who struggle for justice and those who create beauty—and of those who long for the day when these two come together. For justice without beauty is unjust; beauty without justice is ugly.

This is my *laudatio* of the Free University. I am honored to be honored by such a university. I thank you.

Perhaps I was whistling in the dark. I am told by friends that disturbing changes in Dutch higher education that were noticeable already in the late 1980s have picked up speed in recent years. Whereas universities were once the place where the intellectual life of the nation was nourished and handed on, the Dutch universities are now increasingly becoming the place where students are trained for the job market. Humanities departments are being severely contracted. This seems to me the almost inevitable result of an educational system in a capitalist economy that is government controlled and financed.

This same reconceptualization of the mission of the university is taking place in the United States, of course, but not, it appears to me, to the same extent as in the Netherlands. I think this is partly because of the prominence of liberal-arts education in American colleges and universities—Dutch students focus on one particular discipline from the start of their university career—and partly because of the prevalence of private colleges and universities in the United States. No government official is telling Calvin College or Yale University, or any other private college or university, that they have to eliminate philosophy and ancient languages because those subjects are useless for growing the economy.

Simultaneous with the reconceptualization of the university as servant to the economy, a passion for bureaucratic efficiency is sweeping through the Dutch universities. New structures are constantly being devised and instituted. Small departments are eliminated or grouped together into larger units—then, a few years later, grouped together into yet different units. To me, a foreigner, it appears that considerations of bureaucratic efficiency are shaping the character of instruction and scholarship, rather than bureaucracy being in the service of instruction and scholarship. It's true of bureaucracies in general that rules and regulations are often devised and applied on the assumption that people cannot be trusted to do their assigned job well, those rules and regulations then typically being supplemented by strategies for measuring how well people are doing what the rules and regulations say they are supposed to do. This is happening relentlessly in the Dutch system.

Claire and I received many dinner invitations while I was teaching at the Free. One of the most memorable dinners was at the home of a colleague who taught in the theology department, Anton Wessels, and his wife, Toka. A number of other guests were present, including a professor at the Free who taught nurses in the medical faculty. Somehow, the conversation got around to the instructions he gave prospective nurses concerning how to engage mothers whose babies were stillborn or died shortly after birth. "I tell them," he said, "that you need two eyes. With one eye, you have to check the IV; with the other eye, you have to cry. I tell them that one eye is not enough. You need two eyes."

I have used this moving and profound statement as the theme for some college commencement speeches I have given. You, college graduates, need two eyes, the eye of competence and the eye of empathy. One eye is not enough. You need two eyes.

Included in the idealistic and overly grand mission statement adopted by those of us who founded Church of the Servant in the early 1970s was the declaration that we would never own property. We had observed the money that churches poured into their buildings, money that could better be spent, we thought, on social concerns, and we resolved not to do likewise. We would rent. Initially we rented the facility of a small Presbyterian church, sharing the building with their congregation. Upon outgrowing it after a couple of years, and looking around for another facility to rent, we soon learned that the only ones available that would serve our purposes were schools: the gymnasium for worship services, the classrooms for church school. So we rented a school.

By the mid-1980s, renting was wearing us down. Fewer and fewer volunteers made themselves available to set up and take down chairs in the gymnasium, and we regularly got complaints from teachers in the school that, when they arrived on Monday morning, they found the chairs not lined up properly, the wastebasket moved from its designated place, and so forth. Some of us began talking about buying a

224

building and remodeling it to serve our purposes. Given our founding declaration, this proved controversial: one party emphasized that to buy a building would be a repudiation of one of our founding principles, while the other party argued that we had to be realistic. The latter group was in the majority, and I was among them.

I was appointed as a member of the search committee commissioned to find a building to buy and remodel. We looked at many buildings, but something was wrong with each of them: a warehouse for sale had no insulation and no windows; a movie theatre for sale had seats sloping down to a stage, violating our commitment to a participatory form of worship; a church for sale was dark inside and all wrong for our style of worship. So it went.

After about a year of fruitless searching, our committee reported to the church council that we had found nothing that seemed worth considering, which faced the congregation with the issue of whether we should build. This proved much more controversial than the proposal to buy and remodel. One party argued that to construct a new building would be to repudiate not only the letter but the spirit of our founding documents; remodeling would, at least, be putting to good use a building that might otherwise stand empty or be torn down. The other party argued that we had to be realistic: the search committee had looked diligently for a year and found nothing. Those who argued that we had to be realistic were again in the majority, and again I was one of them. We would build.

A property search committee charged with finding a suitable piece of land located an empty tract in the city that was for sale. Some members of the congregation expressed misgivings: the property seemed rather small, parking was likely to be a problem, and it was located in a residential neighborhood at the end of a narrow cul de sac. The neighbors were not likely to take kindly to a church, with heavy traffic on Sundays, in their quiet neighborhood.

In spite of these misgivings, the congregation voted to buy the property. But shortly after we bought it, the city declared eminent domain on the property and bought it from us for use as a holding pond for water runoff. In retrospect, that was providential; the space would have been much too small, parking would indeed have been a problem, and conflict with the neighbors would have been inevitable.

Rather soon after this deflating development, the property search committee located a very sizable piece of land for sale on the south-eastern edge of the city. It was easily large enough—so that parking would be no problem—and neighbors were at some distance. A new point of controversy now arose. It was wrong, some said, for us to participate in the flight of the middle class to the suburbs; we should be in the city. Nevertheless, the congregation voted to buy the property. What none of us knew at the time was that the property was just a short distance from a housing development populated largely by low-income families and immigrants. Our social mission proved to be on our doorstep!

After buying the property, the church council appointed a committee to formulate an architectural program, to choose an architect, and to work with the architect during the design process. They gave the committee, of which I was a member, a construction budget that they acknowledged was low. Two members of the committee were young architects who had received their architectural training at the University of Michigan. The instructor who had impressed them most was Gunnar Birkerts, a practicing architect who taught a course or two each year at the university. So those two were assigned to ask Birkerts whether he was interested in the job. He replied that he could not possibly design the space we needed for such a low budget. Eventually, we settled on a Grand Rapids architect who had designed some rather handsome buildings around the city. After presenting to him the architectural program we had formulated, we asked whether he thought he could design the space we needed within our budget. It would be difficult, but not, he thought, impossible.

He opened our first meeting by saying that we had to talk budget. I sensed what was coming. He and his partners had concluded that they could not design the space we needed for the budget the council had given us; the budget had to be doubled. Crestfallen, we told the architects that we would discuss the matter with our church council and get back to them. The response of the council was astounding. The congregation had voted to build, and we owned the property, they said. If the budget had to be doubled, so be it. Let's go forward, trusting that the money will come in. We notified the architect of the council's decision.

Within a month or so, he called to say that he had some tentative designs to show us. The designs turned out to be conventional, uninspired. So we offered suggestions. A month or so later, we received a call saying that a new set of designs was ready; but these, too, were uninspired. It was evident what was going on: though our budget had been doubled, it was still low, and the low budget, rather than challenging him to think outside the box, had stifled his imagination. After a few more meetings, it was clear to us that this was going nowhere, so we paid him for the work he had done and reluctantly parted ways.

The two young architects on our committee were assigned to go back to Gunnar Birkerts, to tell him that we were now wiser about the budget, that it had been doubled, and to ask whether he was now interested. He said he was. Thus began one of the most fascinating episodes of my life—watching a highly creative architect design a building.

Birkerts's offices were in Birmingham, Michigan, just outside Detroit. Our committee met with him in his offices, riding from Grand Rapids together in a minivan and having great fun on the way. I knew that Birkerts had designed important high-budget buildings in the United States and abroad, so in one of our early meetings I asked him why he had accepted this low-budget commission. "Because it's a challenge" was his answer. Whereas our low budget had stifled the imagination of the Grand Rapids architect, it challenged and stimulated Birkerts's imagination.

Our first meeting was devoted to discussing the architectural program we had drawn up. The program was a blend of functional and expressive considerations. Let me mention two of the expressive considerations. In preparation for drawing up the architectural program, our committee spent considerable time discussing what we understood ourselves to be doing when we assembled for the liturgy. Our conclusion, in brief, was that we understood ourselves as the family of God—brothers and sisters of Christ—assembling around word and sacrament to address God in song, prayer, and acclamation, to listen to what God had to say to us, and to celebrate the Lord's Supper as a memorial of Jesus. We specified in the architectural program that the building had to be expressive of this self-understanding.

To express the family aspect of this understanding, the seating would have to be in a semicircle around pulpit and table, rather than straight rows facing forward, and the building itself would have to have a strong horizontal axis. To express the fact that we were not an ordinary family assembled for a picnic or potluck, but the family of God assembled for worship, the building would have to have a strong vertical axis. We acknowledged that most architects would probably throw up their hands and say, "I can give you horizontal and I can give you vertical, but I cannot give you both." We were challenging Birkerts to give us both.

In preparation for drawing up the architectural program, our committee had also visited a number of churches that had recently been built in the Grand Rapids area. Almost all of them were dark inside, with big swooping roofs coming down low, some with a light-scoop sending a shaft of light onto the front wall, some with low stained glass windows along the sides, some with almost no light at all coming in from outdoors. We felt intuitively that this was all wrong. As for me, I had the Epistle of 1 John ringing in my ears: "God is light, and in God there is no darkness at all." In our architectural program we specified that, when entering the building, one had to have the sense of coming into the light.

The issue of materials came up in our second meeting with Birkerts. There was some talk about the obvious point: since our budget was low, the materials had to be basic; no laminated wood beams, no stained glass windows, no marble. "Mr. Birkerts," I said, "you can use exposed concrete, provided you use it in such a way that people will say, 'I had no idea concrete could be so beautiful,' and you can use exposed steel, provided you use it in such a way that people will say, 'I had no idea exposed steel could be so beautiful.'" I added: "What we are asking you to do, Mr. Birkerts, is to dignify the ordinary." (What was in my mind was the dignifying of the ordinary by the Dutch painters of the seventeenth century: cows, milkmaids, apples, barns, etc.)

Birkerts looked down for what seemed a very long time, saying nothing. I began to worry that I had annoyed or insulted him. Finally he looked up and said: "I think I understand. A dumpy woman can wear silk and still look dumpy. An elegant woman can wear burlap and look elegant. What you want, if I understand you, is an elegant burlap building. Is that correct?" We burst into laughter. He had caught the point exactly. And that's what the building is, "elegant burlap": exposed steel trusses, sealed concrete floor, cement block, drywall, and KalWal, what was then a rather new translucent building material—all used with great elegance.

In the next meeting, Birkerts raised another point about materials and budget. "Nowadays," he said, "we can build long spans with steel. But the longer the span, the more expensive. Will you permit me to use a post to reduce the length of the spans?" Someone replied, "Sure, provided that, when people see it, they don't say, 'Too bad he put that big post there.'"

Eventually, it became clear that Birkerts was being somewhat coy. There is indeed a post, but its principal function is not to reduce the length of any span. The post is a steel column, with branches off the column, and branches off those branches—it's a tree. The branches support a translucent peak rising a considerable height above the flat ceiling; the base of the peak is an irregular octagon. The trunk of the tree goes through the point of the peak and is topped by a cross outside the building. The tree of life becomes a cross.

The tree is the architectural focus of the building: the people sit facing it, and in front of it are the pulpit, the communion table, and the baptismal font. Communion is celebrated by people coming forward in successive groups and, while standing around the tree, passing the bread and wine to each other.

The peak is made of the translucent KalWal, and the entire sanctuary is surrounded at the top by a clerestory made of KalWal. Mysteriously, even in bright daylight, there are no shadows in the sanctuary, not even under the translucent peak. The tree is a strong vertical element within the space of the sanctuary; the clerestory running around the sanctuary beneath the flat roof is a strong horizontal element. Daylight streaming through the translucent KalWal gives one the sense of coming into the light as one enters the sanctuary. Birkerts had brilliantly achieved the expressive components of our architectural program.

It's a feat of great architectural imagination, and it has won a number of architectural awards.[2] The ordinary is dignified: the steel trusses are beautiful, the sealed concrete floor is beautiful, and the cement blocks are beautiful. Some of those who had opposed building our own church remarked, when they saw the completed structure, that if they had known that this was the kind of structure we would build, they would not have been opposed to building.

The first service in the new building was held on January 15, 1994.

2. Gunnar Birkerts died on August 15, 2017. He was the recipient of a number of awards by architecture organizations, including the Twenty-Five Year Award by the Institute of American Architects in 2006.

amily and friends tease me about the large number of hostas in our garden: about a hundred varieties, with multiple plants of most of the varieties. "Aren't ten enough?" they ask. "A hosta is a hosta." They don't understand! Though I very much admire individual species and varieties of hostas, that's not why I have so many. I grow them because they are indispensable to the composition of my garden. It's the *garden* I love—and the gardening.

There are different kinds of gardens: vegetable gardens, for example, and botanical gardens. Mine is neither of those kinds. My garden is for aesthetic delight: visual delight primarily, but also olfactory delight, from the fragrance of flowers, and auditory delight, from the sound of running water and of wind rustling the leaves. Such gardens have no standard name, so let me call them *delight gardens*. Delight gardens are works of art.

Such gardens go back into the mists of history. The Garden of Eden was a delight garden, and Adam and Eve were the gardeners. Evidently such gardens answer to something deep in human nature. Some writers, noting that the arc of Christian Scripture is from the garden of the opening chapters of Genesis to the holy city of the concluding chapters of Revelation, suggest that gardens will be left behind. I am confident that in the holy city there will be delight gardens.

What is nowadays called "landscape architecture" consists of plantings whose purpose is to enhance the appearance of the building that the plantings surround. When such plantings are successful, they give delight; but they are not delight gardens. One admires them for the contribution they make to the appearance of the building, not for their own sake. Delight gardens are for their own sake.

Our garden surrounds our house. But the garden is not for the sake of the house; rather, the house is a central component in the composition of the garden. It's true, of course, that we did not build the house for the sake of the contribution it makes to the composition of the garden. But once the house was built, and I set about designing a garden, the house became a component within the composition. After about ten years of trying to design a garden, I became extremely frustrated. Developing a satisfactory design defied me, for reasons I did not understand and still do not understand. I had designed a few houses to my satisfaction, including the one we were living in, and I had a good knowledge of plants. So why couldn't I design a garden? I gave up, looked in the yellow pages for garden designers, and called one, Terry Horrigan, whose office happened to be near us. Terry proved to be a genius. I have worked with his design ever since he composed it, adapting it here and there when some plants he recommended didn't work out, but always retaining his overall composition.

Gardens resemble architecture in that they shape space, determine the play of light and shadow within that space, and create paths through space. What makes them fundamentally different from architecture is that they are composed of living things: plants that sprout, grow, flourish, struggle, die prematurely, go underground in the fall in temperate climates and reappear in the spring, lose their leaves, grow new leaves, age, and die. Typically, gardens also contain benches, stones, walkways, sculptures, and expanses of gravel; but plants are almost always the main compositional components, certain Japanese gardens being the exception. Delight gardens are works of art composed of living things.

A work of architecture is finished at a certain point; so is a sculpture and a painting. Because the plants of which a garden is composed are always changing, a garden is never, in the same sense, finished. One may finish installing plants in accord with the design; but in the garden itself, there is never a still-point. This plant here is finally maturing as I hoped it would, anchoring this part of the composition; that one there is outgrowing the bounds set for it; that one over there is struggling, evidently in need of more light. And as for this one: I'm going to replace it with a better variety that I noticed in a nursery. I, the gardener, am engaged in an ongoing, never-finished process of artistic creation.

There is another way in which gardening is a most unusual form of artistic creation. Just as painters are dependent on the properties of paint and canvas, and sculptors on the properties of wood, stone, and metal, gardeners are dependent on the properties of plants. But unlike painters and sculptors, they are dependent on the *flourishing* of their material. The success of the garden depends on the flourishing of the plants. This form of dependence has no close analogue in painting and sculpture. One can encourage the flourishing of the plants in one's garden, but one cannot *make* them flourish; the plants themselves have to do that. It's like bringing up children.

I'm making it sound too ruthless. I do indeed have an overall composition in mind that determines which plants I select, where I place them, how I trim them, and so forth. But I also want them to come into their own, to flourish for their own sake and not just for the sake of contributing to the work of art that is my garden. I act in the best interests of my plants. When they flourish, I am delighted; when they do not, I am disappointed. Gardening engages the emotions.

When tramping in a Michigan woods or wandering through a plant nursery, I am entranced by the diverse habitats and the varied beauty of the genera, species, and varieties I see. I love plants. It's a love I have to discipline when composing and tending my garden. A delight garden is not a collection of the plants one loves. Much as one might love some species or variety of plant, if it doesn't fit within the overall composition, it has to be rejected. My gardener-self has to restrain my plant-lover-self, and it's not always easy. I have plant-loving friends who are plant collectors rather than gardeners. I understand.

Not all who garden love gardens; some do it for the pay. And not all who love gardens love gardening; some prefer not to get their hands dirty. I love not only gardens but gardening, and I have no problem with getting my hands dirty. Is this the residue of working as a teenager on Uncle Chuck's farm? Perhaps. It goes without saying that delight-gardening is very different from crop-farming. But is the delight that I experience in seeing my hostas flourish, my ferns and

233

my astilbes, perhaps the residue of sharing Uncle Chuck's delight at seeing his crops of corn, oats, and soybeans flourish? And is the indescribable delight I feel in the spring, when the plants in my garden rise up out of their winter sleep, a residue of the delight I remember feeling when sprouting corn and oats plants turned the gray-black of the Minnesota fields into expanses of green? The fecundity of God's good earth!

All gardeners work within constraints, the most obvious of these being climate and soil. Much as I love bougainvillea, I cannot grow it in Michigan. For me, the most important constraint, apart from climate, was the fact that the lot on which we built our house was then, and remains now, heavily wooded. Along the south side of the lot there is a strip, approximately thirty feet wide by three hundred feet long, that is, essentially, a Michigan woods: ash, maple, and black walnut. The ground there is in full shade. The rest of the lot, while not a woods, nonetheless has a good many trees on it: oak, willow, ash, dogwood, redbud. No area is in full sun; everything is in partial or full shade. The implication for me as a gardener was obvious: I would have to be a shade gardener—no lilies, no zinnias, no daisies, no phlox.

Most shade plants bloom in the spring. The flowers of the summer bloomers tend to be either inconspicuous or unattractive, so the shade gardener has to work mainly with the leaves of plants, creating a composition of different shades of green, from black-green to chartreuse, a composition of different textures, from feathery to broad and flat, and a composition of different growth habits, from ground covers to shrubs and trees. It is here that hostas enter the picture. Hostas thrive in partial shade and thus are indispensable to the shade garden. Their native habitat is Japan, Korea, and China.[3] A few have attractive flowers, and a few have flowers that are fra-

3. Those who are interested should consult W. George Schmid, *The Genus Hosta* (Portland, OR: The Timber Press, 1991).

grant. The flowers of *hosta plantaginea*, for example, are a beautiful lily-shaped white and intensely fragrant. But mainly it's the leaves of hostas that contribute to the composition of a garden, leaves ranging in size from a few inches to a foot and a half—some flat, some cupped, some crinkled, some straplike, some round, some glossy, some mat, some with veins forming an elegant design, some uniform in color, many variegated, ranging in color from blue-green to yellow-green to near-white. The plants themselves vary in height from just a few inches to four feet.

The genus has a large number of species, varying in the ways I've mentioned. But what makes the genus a true godsend for the shade gardener is that it is easy to produce hybrids by crossing species, and that it is not uncommon for a plant to throw up a variegated sport. The number of varieties available commercially is amazing.

The numerous hostas in my garden are interspersed with a great many ferns of various species, and with ground covers of moss, myrtle, ivy, and native ginger; they are shades and textures of green, laid out in swooping curves. When we built our house, almost nothing grew in the woods: the soil under the trees was hard clay. Now, in the spring, before the leaves on the trees come out, a riot of wildflowers native to the Michigan woods bloom: trillium, bloodroot, trout lily, geranium, spring beauty, jack-in-the-pulpit, may-apple, Dutchman's breeches, squirrel corn, bishop's cap, hepatica, and more.

I must relate the story told me by Claire's father of some ferns he was growing. He was a plant-lover, more a collector than a gardener. He did have a garden design in mind, but his love of plants and of growing them always thrust the implementation of the design into the indefinite future. He made a point of knowing the Latin botanical name of every plant he grew.

When the family was living in Philadelphia, he became friends with the gardener on a large nearby estate, an African-American man named Pettiford (Claire's father always called him Mr. Pettiford). A shipment of plants from Japan included some unlabeled ferns that

Claire's father very much admired, so Mr. Pettiford gave him a clump or two. Claire's father put a good deal of time and effort into identifying the species and discovering its botanical name, but he was unsuccessful. He and the family called it simply "the Pettiford fern." The fern multiplied. When the family moved from Philadelphia to Grand Rapids, the Pettiford ferns came along. Somewhere along the line, Claire's father gave me a clump; so it's now in my garden, where it has multiplied nicely. Late in his life, Claire's father finally succeeded in identifying the species. It is *Polystichum standishii* (also classified as *Arachniodes standishii*), commonly called the "upside down fern"—for reasons obscure to me. Those who are curious about what it looks like should Google it: type in the name of the species, and note especially the tiny bracts that parallel the main stems of the leaves. Most unusual!

NINE

Return to Yale

On a Sunday afternoon in the summer of 1988, I got a call from Harry ("Skip") Stout, a Calvin graduate who was teaching American religious history in the religious studies department at Yale. Skip mentioned that he was a member of the search committee for the position in philosophy of religion and philosophical theology at Yale Divinity School that was about to be vacated by the retirement of Paul Holmer, and asked whether I would be willing to come for an interview for that position. He added that he had been prodded to call me by Hans Frei, Yale's senior theologian and also a member of the search committee, who, according to Skip, had remarked that he feared that, if the committee just waited for applications to come in and did not itself take some initiative, "some damn process theologian" would wind up in the position.

I told Skip I was not interested, explaining that the seminaries and divinity schools I was acquainted with seemed to me either oppressive or flaky—the conservative ones, oppressive, the liberal ones, flaky. "Well, okay," he said, "but how about coming by and letting us talk with you informally the next time you're on the East Coast?" "Sure," I said. That fall I was on the East Coast for something and took a detour to Yale. I talked informally with members of the search committee, but also with other faculty members and with students, a few of them Calvin grads. I was impressed. This divinity school was different, neither oppressive nor flaky. If they were considering me for the position, I would have to take it seriously. A few weeks later I got a letter from the chair of the search committee inviting me to come for a formal interview. Claire and I agreed I should take this first step, and she came along.

I was interviewed at length by the committee, gave a public lecture—on Reformed epistemology, as I recall—and visited a few classes. Everything went well, with the exception of one of the classes I visited. John Cook, a senior faculty member at the Divinity School and head of Yale's Institute for Sacred Music, was teaching a course in theological aesthetics. The previous week the students had read and discussed some chapters from my book *Art in Action*. Cook invited me to come to his class, say what I wanted to say about the book, and then answer whatever questions the class might have.

Immediately after he opened it up for discussion, a number of women in the class began berating me for the sexist language in the book: in the book I refer to God as "he" and to human beings as "men." I explained that when I wrote the book, I had not yet been sensitized to the issue of sexist language; now, ten years after its publication, I was thoroughly embarrassed and chagrined by how much of it there was in the book. They were not mollified and continued to press the issue. Nobody had much to say about the philosophy of art that I presented in the book.

A dinner that I had asked to be arranged with the women on the faculty proved to be one of the highlights of the visit—both for Claire and for me. We ate at Mory's, the venerable old Yalie eating club, where the atmosphere is better than the food. The women were wonderfully welcoming, especially, as I recall, Letty Russell and Margaret Farley.

Early in the spring of 1989, I received a letter from the dean of the divinity school offering me the position, salary to be negotiated. Our children were all out of the house and did not express any firm views one way or the other. Claire was eager to go. She had read some of the books by the women theologians at Yale and looked forward to interacting with them. Also, as an ordained woman in the Grand Rapids area, she felt rather lonely, and she anticipated that she would feel less so around Yale.

An additional consideration for her was what had happened to Elisabeth House, an ecumenical place of prayer that she had opened—and of which she was the director—in a large old house in the inner city of Grand Rapids in January 1986. Elisabeth House had flourished for several years, with sizable numbers of people coming for prayer and meditation. Claire felt that she had found her calling. But then, truly spooky things began to happen. Without any signs of break-in, things were stolen, flowerpots were smashed, sugar and flour were strewn across the kitchen floor, pillows were pulled off the sofas and thrown on the floor, and so on. The police investigated and staked out the house, but turned up nothing. Our best guess as to what had happened was that a member of the board whom Claire knew to be quite angry with her—because she, the board member, thought she was not being given enough recognition—had chosen to vent her anger by trashing the house rather than trying to talk it out with Claire. Elisabeth House closed in January 1989. Claire was grieving that loss and was ready to move on to something new.

I talked the Yale offer over with my colleagues in the Calvin philosophy department. Calvin College as a whole—and the philosophy department in particular—had been ideal venues for me: nowhere else could I have flourished as I had flourished there. I was deeply attached to the institution, and to my colleagues. But the department was changing, and the old gang was breaking up. Al Plantinga had accepted an offer to teach at Notre Dame; Rich Mouw had accepted an offer from Fuller Seminary; and Pete De Vos, a gifted young philosopher and a former student of mine, had died a tragically early death from a heart attack. The younger members of the department were fine philosophers, and eminently collegial, but it wasn't the same. I was on the fence about going to Yale.

What tipped me to accept the offer was a call from the dean of the divinity school. In the course of our conversation he said that one of the reasons they wanted me was that I was, in his words, a "committed churchman." He did not elaborate, but I took him to mean they wanted me because my interest in philosophy of religion was not just as a matter of intellectual curiosity but as a person of faith committed to the church. I felt called, and I accepted Yale's offer.

From remarks people made, I inferred that many thought I went to Yale for prestige, for money, and for more time to "work on my own things." Not so. Prestige meant little to me. My pay at Calvin was adequate. And as for more time to "work on my own things," had I gone to Yale with that in mind, I would have been sorely disappointed. It turned out that, at Yale, I spent at least as much time *not* "working on my own things" as I did at Calvin. At Calvin, the standard teaching load was three courses per semester; at Yale, the standard load was two courses per semester. But one of the courses at Yale was always, in my case, a graduate seminar, typically requiring a good deal more work than an undergraduate course. In addition to teaching, there was directing doctoral theses and serving on committees. In the case of search committees for senior positions, this proved to be unbelievably time-consuming. I went to Yale because I felt called.

A year before we left for Yale, in September 1988, Claire's mother died at the age of eighty-five. For several years she had been living near us in Grand Rapids, in an apartment that was part of a retirement complex. We saw her often. She was a striking woman, beautiful in a handsome sort of way, with the appearance of having some Spanish ancestry mixed in with her Dutch ancestry. I mentioned earlier the wonderfully beautiful embroideries that she made. She also painted—lovely floral paintings. She painted and did embroideries until she could no longer see well.

I mentioned above that the "old gang" was breaking up. Since that time, both Al Plantinga and Rich Mouw have had distinguished careers. Rich, after teaching at Fuller Seminary for several years, became provost of the seminary, and then, for twenty years, president of the seminary. He retired from the presidency in 2013, but he remains at Fuller as president emeritus and Professor of Faith and Public Life. In his various roles at Fuller he was not only a leader of that institution but also, from his position there, a leading Kuyperian voice in the broader worlds of evangelical and mainline Christianity, and, beyond those, in the public square. He is regularly consulted by the media on religious issues of the day.

Al's career has more closely paralleled mine, in that he has remained more strictly within the field of philosophy. Like me, he has not devoted himself to building a system but has, in good measure, responded philosophically to what presented itself to him from outside, especially to the widespread and multifaceted charge that theism in general—and Christian belief in particular—is intellectually deficient in one way or another. As one of my Yale colleagues put it, religious people "suffer from a rationality deficit." Al has made important contributions to other areas of philosophy as well: to the metaphysics of modality; to our understanding of God's nature; to an updated formulation of the ontological argument; to a general account of knowledge as grounded in the proper functioning of our faculties. But I would say that the scarlet thread running throughout his work is his response to the charge that Christian belief suffers from a "rationality deficit."

That charge takes a number of different forms. Al has addressed several of those forms with tenacity, rigor, and extraordinary brilliance. A form of the charge of nonrationality that we have already come across is that religious people do not hold their beliefs on the basis of arguments that provide good evidence for them. This was the charge to which Reformed epistemology responded. From his earliest work, *God and Other Minds* (1967), to his latest, *Knowledge and Christian Belief* (2015), Al has repeatedly addressed this charge by questioning the assumption that arguments are necessary for holding one's religious beliefs rationally. Though the core of his response has remained the same, each time he has addressed the charge, he has done so with yet greater power and subtlety. I think one can safely say that no one who has carefully read Al's latest writings on the matter would make that charge any longer.

Another ground commonly given for charging Christian belief with being deficient in rationality is that the Christian understanding of God as omnipotent, omniscient, and all-good is incompatible with the nature and extent of evil in the world. Al addressed this charge in a number of writings published in the first decades of his career, the definitive statement of his position being his book *God, Freedom, and Evil* (Eerdmans, 1974). The core of his argument there is that, since God cannot determine how a human being will freely act, even an omnipotent God might not be able to create a world in which all creatures who are capable of free action will always freely choose to do good. It is now almost universally recognized that Al's argument laid to rest the claim that the nature and extent of evil in the world is incompatible with the Christian understanding of God.

Over the last couple of decades, Al has focused his attention on the claim that contemporary natural science, particularly discoveries concerning human evolution, render Christian belief nonrational. His argument, presented most fully in *Where the Conflict Really Lies: Science, Religion, and Naturalism* (Eerdmans, 2011), is that while there is certainly conflict between Christianity and the worldview commonly known as *naturalism*, there is no conflict between Christianity and contemporary natural science as such. From there he goes on the offensive, arguing that whereas theism supports science, naturalism undermines it. I will forgo an attempt to lay out his argument on this last point.

I was invited to give a talk at the conference held in honor of Al's retirement from Notre Dame in the spring of 2010. I anticipated discussing one or another aspect of Al's thought, but when I sat down to compose my talk, I found myself immobilized. I could not discuss Al's thought as though he were just another philosopher. He was my friend of many years, and a coworker in the project of Christian philosophy. Tacitly, without ever making an explicit agreement, we had parceled out the field: he would defend Christianity against the multifaceted irrationality objection, and I, on the *assumption* that Christian belief does not suffer from a rationality deficit, would look at art, at justice, at political authority, and so on—"through the eyes of faith." *Credo ut intelligam.* We overlapped only at the point where he and I both participated in the project of Reformed epistemology.

I asked the organizers of Al's retirement conference whether, instead of my giving the usual academic lecture, they would allow me to speak personally about my relationship with Al, and about his contribution to philosophy in general and to Christian philosophy in particular. They consented. I gave my talk the title "Then, Now, and Al," and I closed it with these words:

> Philosophy in general, and Christian philosophy in particular, is very different now from what it was then. And you, Al, good friend of a good many years, have played a leading role in making it so. It's my view that philosophy is in a much better state now than it was then, and that Christian philosophy in particular is in a much better state. So when I say that you have played a leading role in making the field what it is today, I mean those words as an expression of gratitude. I speak for everyone here when I say that we are grateful for the extraordinary contribution you have made to our field. And as for me personally, I am deeply grateful for the personal and philosophical friendship that you and I have enjoyed over these sixty years. It's been a fascinating journey, much of it over terrain hitherto unknown, never before explored, but now, thanks to your work, familiar.

On April 25, 2017, the Templeton Foundation announced that it was awarding the 2017 Templeton Prize for Religion to Alvin Plantinga. A few of the preceding recipients of the prize are Mother Teresa, Brother Roger of Taizé, Desmond Tutu, and Rabbi Jonathan Sacks. In its statement announcing the award, the Foundation quoted one of the philosophers who nominated Al for the award: "Alvin Plantinga's intellectual discoveries have initiated novel inquiry into spiritual dimensions. His precise and carefully developed insights have opened up intellectual spiritual space. In the 1950s there was not a single published defense of religious belief by a prominent philosopher; by the 1990's there were literally hundreds of books and articles

...defending and developing the spiritual dimension. The difference between 1950 and 1990 is, quite simply, Alvin Plantinga."

"Salary to be negotiated," said the letter from the dean of Yale Divinity School. I had never negotiated my salary. None of the faculty at Calvin College negotiated their salary. If you knew a faculty member's highest degree, how long that person had been teaching, and a few other factors, you knew where she or he was on the salary scale. It was completely egalitarian.

How to negotiate? Claire and I decided to keep our house in Grand Rapids, live there in the summers and over the holidays, and buy a condo in New Haven. Yale would have to pay me enough to make that possible. How much would that be? I didn't know; I could only guess. I asked a colleague and friend at Yale, Joe Stevens, what he was being paid. Joe was more senior than I was, and he was the director of a research institute. I decided to ask for about fifteen thousand dollars less than Joe made. The dean's immediate response was, "Fine, let's make it that." I had the sense that, had I asked for five thousand more than Joe made, rather than fifteen thousand less, his response would have been the same: "Fine, let's make it that."

In the fall of 1989, I began as a professor in Yale Divinity School and as an adjunct professor in both the philosophy department and the religious studies department of the university. Yale requires that its faculty members in arts and sciences not hold regular positions in any other university. I would have to resign my half-time professorship at the Free University.

It was a return to Yale after thirty years of teaching at Calvin. Two things especially struck me as having changed in the interim. The university had become a gated community. The undergraduate component of Yale consists of twelve "colleges," each college having its own set of elaborate buildings surrounding a quad, with entrances to the quads controlled by large gates. When I taught at Yale in the late 1950s, I had never seen the gates closed; I assume that they were closed at night, but I never saw them closed. Now they were always closed. The city of New Haven had become unsafe.

The other difference that struck me was that there were no longer dinner parties of the kind we used to have, where faculty members from different departments and of different academic ranks got together. Now it was just friends getting together for dinner, and these were usually from one's own department and of one's own rank. The same thing had happened at Calvin over my years there: the old kind of intergenerational and interdepartmental dinner party had all but disappeared. The cause has to be the increasing specialization of higher education, along with the weakening of institutional bonds and loyalty. The regnant attitude has come to be: "I don't understand what people in other departments are doing, nor do I care. All I ask of the university is that it enable and permit me to do my own thing. I will dine with friends." The disappearance of the old-fashioned faculty dinner party represents the loss of something precious.

The children were getting married—three of them in a two-and-a-half-year span. We have come to love their spouses dearly, all of them. Robert married Mari Jones in Rockport, Maine, Mari's hometown, on June 25, 1988, in a cold, driving rain that made the tents set up for the celebration useless. They had met in the Philadelphia art museum, where Mari was working in the administration and Robert was serving as an intern after getting a master's degree in art history from Williams College. They lived in Philadelphia for a few years and then moved to Portland, Maine, where Mari worked in an organization that supported the arts and Robert served as the director of the Victoria Mansion, an over-the-top Victorian house that had been opened up to visitors.

Klaas married Tracey Gebbia in Grand Rapids on December 30, 1989, this time in a freezing rain that made driving and walking treacherous. They met as students at Calvin, where Tracey majored in art and Klaas in German and Latin. Klaas began working at Eerdmans Publishing immediately after graduating from Calvin, and Tracey did freelance work as a graphic artist.

Amy married Thomas J. Ryckbost in Grand Rapids on December 22, 1990, a cold but mercifully bright day. They also met as students at Calvin. For a few years after graduating from Calvin, T.J.—as we call him—served as an appraiser of mobile homes. But that was clearly not his calling; so, after a few years, he established his own business as a renovation contractor, work that he is very good at and that he loves. Amy established herself as a freelance writer, writing news stories for a neighborhood newspaper, revising manuscripts, and so forth.

Somebody asked me recently whether I got nervous before teaching a class or giving a public lecture. I used to get quite nervous before giving a public lecture—not much anymore. But throughout my teaching career, from beginning to end, I was always nervous on the first day of a course. Each time that day rolled around again, I was conscious of the fact that, for the next three months, we were in this together, that how it went was not just up to me but also up to the students, and that they were not in my control. We were setting out on an adventure whose success I could not guarantee. I was taking a risk. I imagine this is how an orchestra conductor feels when he or she lowers the baton: nervous excitement. My nervousness always disappeared after a few class sessions.

Before the first session of my first graduate seminar at Yale, in the fall of 1989, my nervousness was intense—for reasons I didn't understand. I had, after all, taught graduate seminars when visiting at various universities: Princeton, Notre Dame, the Free University. The building in which the class was to meet, the philosophy department building, was just off the New Haven Green. I left our apartment well before class time and sat by myself on a bench in the Green for about forty-five minutes—doing my best to calm my nerves. It worked. The class went beautifully.

People often speak of Yale as a "secular" university. My experience was that it was, instead, a pluralist university in which many distinct voices, including religious voices, could be heard. In the law school there was a course entitled "Theology and Law"; the course listings for the English department included a course entitled "Jewish Hermeneutics"; Robert Adams regularly taught a seminar in the philosophy department on the philosophical theology of the nineteenth-century German theologian Friedrich Schleiermacher.

Every spring I offered a seminar on some aspect of the classical Western understanding of God: immutability, eternity, impassibility, and so on. I taught these seminars in the philosophy department building, and no one ever questioned the propriety of my doing so. After I had been teaching at Yale for a few years, about forty students would typically show up for the first class session—too many for a seminar. So I would ask each of them to write out their case for being allowed into the seminar, and then select about twenty on the basis of the cases they made.

The Divinity School was distinctly Christian, centrist in its theological orientation—neither liberal nor conservative. It was my impression that the university officials were proud of the Divinity School; I never heard anyone propose eliminating it on the ground that it belonged to a bygone era, or that it was incompatible with the mission of the university. This was not a secular university. I could be myself here.

I have often been asked how teaching at Yale differed from teaching at Calvin. My standard answer has been that the main difference was in the "you" of the classroom. I could teach the same things at Yale that I taught at Calvin, but, whereas at Calvin I could assume that most of the students—not all—were Christians, this was not true at Yale. There *were* Christians of all stripes in my Yale classes—

evangelical and liberal, Protestant and Catholic, Pentecostal and Orthodox—but also Jews, Muslims, and skeptics. At Calvin there was a higher proportion of average students than at Yale, but the best of my Calvin students were on a par with the best of my Yale students.

In the fall of each year at Yale I taught a lecture course in philosophy of religion. Though there were discussion sessions led by teaching assistants, I also entertained questions in the lecture sessions. Now and then a small group of male students would come up after class and ask me not to allow questions in the lecture sessions. Why not? Because, they said, their parents were paying forty or fifty thousand dollars a year for them to attend Yale, and their parents were not paying that money for them to listen to their fellow students shoot off their mouths. My response was that questions are often an occasion for learning.

Every other year or so a student would raise his hand and say something to this effect: "But as Jesus says in John 5 …" I knew at once that the student was an evangelical, speaking as if he were at an evangelical campfire. Students in the class would cringe, look down at their hands, roll their eyes. I would take such a student aside afterwards and say that he could make approximately the same point he was trying to make, but that he had to learn to make it in a voice appropriate to a Yale philosophy classroom rather than in a voice appropriate to an evangelical campfire. Evangelicals often interpret the hostility they experience in academic settings as hostility to Christianity, or more specifically, as hostility to evangelical Christianity. Sometimes it is that, but not always. Sometimes it's a reaction to the fact that the voice in which the evangelical is speaking is inappropriate to the situation.

I n 1993, Robert and Marilyn Adams, both superb philosophers, came to Yale from UCLA, Bob as chair of the Yale philosophy department, Marilyn as professor of theology in the Divinity School and in the religious studies department of the university. We had been good friends for many years. Both Bob and Marilyn had participated in the founding of the Society of Christian Philosophers, and both were former presidents of the society.

Marilyn was interested in systematic theology, including philosophical theology; but her specialty was medieval theology and philosophy. Not only was she among the very best scholars in the field, but she had an extraordinarily winsome and engaging way of presenting the thought of the medieval theologians and philosophers so that it would capture the attention of students and make that thought accessible. Students adored her. She was also an ordained Episcopal priest and a gifted preacher. Bob, ordained in the Presbyterian Church USA, specialized in metaphysics, philosophy of religion, and ethics. His book *Finite and Infinite Goods*, published while he was at Yale, is a magisterial treatment of Christian ethics. The three of us participated together in seminars, read drafts of essays and book chapters that we were working on, plotted strategy, and greatly enjoyed each other's company.

Excellent students began to show up, many of whom now hold positions at prominent universities. Three with whom I have remained in close contact are Andrew Chignell, presently at Princeton, Terence Cuneo, at the University of Vermont, and Eric Gregory, also at Princeton. But these are just three of the many students whom it was a great joy to teach and mentor. There was a buzz in the air about philosophy of religion and philosophical theology. I miss it.

Shortly after writing this section, in the late fall of 2016, I received the distressing news that Marilyn Adams had been diagnosed with pancreatic cancer. The cancer proved to be extremely aggressive; she died on March 22, 2017. Two weeks before her death I visited her. It was both joyful and painful: she was alert, but extremely weak, and getting words out was an effort. I told her, once again, what a grace she had been in my life, and I remarked on the golden years we had enjoyed together. Then, after the many hellos and good-byes we had spoken to each other over the years, we said the final good-bye.

To a person, my Yale colleagues were congenial and supportive. I have singled out Bob and Marilyn Adams for special mention because we had long been good friends and because they worked in the same area that I did, namely, philosophy of religion. But there were other colleagues who also proved to be stimulating conversation partners and with whom I became good friends. I think especially of David Kelsey and Miroslav Volf, both fine theologians and both very knowledgeable in philosophy, of Martin Jean, a highly gifted musician (organist) and head of the Yale Institute for Sacred Music, and of Skip Stout, whose inquiry on that summer afternoon led eventually to my appointment.

It wasn't long before Claire found her new calling, namely, spiritual direction. Affiliated with Yale Divinity School is the Episcopal seminary, Berkeley Divinity School. Berkeley had just begun a program of spiritual direction for its own students and for the students at Yale Divinity School, and the director, who had come to know Claire informally, invited her to join the program and to offer spiritual direction on a regular basis. She loved it—and from all reports, excelled at it.

Our early collecting of art prints had slowed down, and in its place we were collecting ceramics. Already in the 1960s we had acquired a few pieces of American folk pottery by anonymous potters, mostly jugs whose shape, glaze, and wisps of decoration we admired. Our collecting of ceramics picked up the year we lived in London (1970–71). During the day, when the children were in school, Claire and I, along with Christopher in a stroller, would often take the train into central London to explore the architecture, especially the churches, to explore byways that our guidebooks said were interesting, and to visit print and craft shops. Of the several craft shops we visited, the one we returned to most often was the Craftsmen Potters Shop on Marshall Street. We bought a number of works by prominent British potters, including Richard Batterham, Svend Bayer, Joanna Constantinidis, David Leach, Alan Wallwork, and Sarah Walton.

What drew me to ceramics was much the same as what drew me to graphic art prints, namely, the transgression of the sacrosanct boundary between so-called fine art and so-called craft. In his well-known book *The Principles of Art*, the British writer R. G. Collingwood almost never refers to the crafts without adding the adjective "mere"—"mere craft." Take almost any ceramic item by any of the six British potters I mentioned above, and ask yourself this question: Is this "mere craft"? Is it "mere" anything? Preposterous! Yet none of the items we purchased had turned its back on craft to become a work of art sculpture made of clay. They were all plates or vessels; they could all hold water.

Sometime in the early 1990s, when we were living in New Haven, we noticed an advertisement in the *New York Times* by a gallery in central Manhattan, Gallery Zero, which announced that it specialized in contemporary Japanese ceramics. The black-and-white photographs in the ad were difficult to make out, but clearly these were ceramics of a kind we had never seen before. So Claire and I took the train from New Haven into Manhattan and located the gallery. I was mesmerized. These, too, were plates and vessels that were capable of holding water—that is, not "fine art." But they were of a different order altogether from the ceramics we had been collecting: rough, only partly glazed, some lopsided, some with cracks in them. It was as if they had only partly emerged from the earth. For me, they were reminiscent of the way in which the figures of slaves in four of Michelangelo's late works only partly emerge from the stone—with this all-important difference: in Michelangelo, what the partial emergence means is that the slave is not free, whereas in these ceramic works, the partial emergence means that clay has acquired a voice of its own. Rather than the artist imposing his will on the clay, the clay and the artist (along with the fire) have together brought forth this new creation. The ordinary has been dignified, but not in such a way as to conceal its ordinariness—in this case, its earthiness. The display in the gallery was entitled *The Artists' Skill in Harmony with the Forces of Nature*.

Over the years we bought a good many pieces from Gallery Zero (which later changed its name to Dai Ichi Arts), works by, among others, Kai Tanimoto, Abe Anjin, Kiyotsugu Sawa, and Yasuhiro Kohara, and we became good friends with the gallery's owner, Beatrice Chang.

As with our collecting of graphic art prints, the question arises: Why collect? Why not take the train into Manhattan, seek out the Dai Ichi Arts gallery, allow yourself to be mesmerized, take the train back to New Haven, and do the same thing over again when a new installation is ready for viewing? My answer is the same: I want to live with these pieces, not to go on a journey to see them; I want them as companions in my house, where I can daily study them, touch them, move them around, show them to friends. I want to live in the presence of these extraordinary co-creations of clay, artist, and fire, this inseparable blend of mud and imagination.

One of the Dai Ichi Arts ceramicists whose work we much admired was Abe Anjin, especially some extraordinary cups for drinking sakê and some for the Japanese tea ceremony. But their prices were out of reach for us. As we were discussing the vessels with Beatrice, she mentioned that Anjin was in New York for a couple of weeks, and she asked whether we would like to meet him. We said we would, and a lunch was arranged. After we had talked for a while with Anjin about his ceramics, his work habits, his kiln, and so forth, he said he wanted to ask our advice on something. He had a daughter who wanted to attend college in the States, and he wondered whether we could give him some advice on which colleges and universities she should apply to, how to apply, and so forth. He wrote down our suggestions. Two weeks later, a parcel from Dai Ichi Arts was left at the door of our apartment in New Haven. Inside the parcel, in a small, beautifully crafted wooden box, was one of Abe Anjin's sakê cups that we had admired at the gallery, and a card that said, "With compliments from Abe Anjin and Gallery Dai Ichi Arts."

In the spring of 2015, our Japanese ceramics, along with some items from our collection of British ceramics, were included in a show at the Calvin College art gallery of three southwest Michigan ceramics collections. The show was entitled *Earthwork*, and the pieces were all beautifully displayed and lighted. I found myself conceding that there was something to be said for not just living with the works we owned but, on occasion, seeing them beautifully displayed under ideal lighting.

In the fall of 1993, I gave the Wilde Lectures at Oxford University. The full title of this venerable and well-known lectureship is The Wilde Lectures in Natural and Comparative Religion. The invitation to give the lectures did not specify that they had to be about natural and comparative religion—just something to do with philosophy of religion. I was to give eight lectures, one a week.

Early in my teaching career at Calvin I had immersed myself in so-called speech-act theory, originated by the Oxford philosopher J. L. Austin, who had visited Harvard during my time there as a graduate student. The basic idea of speech-act theory is that, by performing the act of uttering or writing a sentence with a certain meaning in mind, one also performs another act of quite a different sort, such as making an assertion, asking a question, or issuing a command. Austin called acts of the former kind—uttering or writing a sentence with a certain meaning in mind—*locutionary* acts. He called acts of the latter kind—asserting, asking, commanding, and so on—*illocutionary* acts. By performing the locutionary act of uttering the sentence "It's raining again" with a certain meaning in mind, one can perform the illocutionary act of *asserting* that it is raining again.

The reason for thinking that these acts are indeed distinct is that one can perform each without performing the other. One can utter those words without making that assertion—by offering them as an example of a well-formed English sentence, for instance, and one can make that assertion in ways other than by uttering those words—by making the assertion in another language, for instance. One day, while I was immersed in speech-act theory, it occurred to me that the idea of one act counting as another might open up a way of thinking about how God speaks. To use the jargon of speech-act theory: Might it be that God performs illocutionary acts by way of human beings performing locutionary acts?

To work out this idea, I would have to develop the idea of *double-agent* discourse, that is, the idea of one person's performing some illocutionary act by way of another person's performing some locutionary act, or by way of another person's performing some distinct illocutionary act. So far as I knew, the topic of double-agent discourse had been completely neglected in the speech-act literature; the literature took for granted that the person who performed some locutionary act was identical with the person who thereby performed some illocutionary act. Yet the phenomenon of double-agent discourse is common: guardians sign documents on behalf of their wards; lawyers sign documents and speak on behalf of their clients; ambassadors speak on behalf of their heads of state, and so forth.

After entertaining the idea for a while, of God's performing an illocutionary act by way of a human being's performing a locutionary act, I dropped the idea because there were other things on my agenda. But I never forgot it. The invitation to deliver the Wilde Lectures prodded me to drop everything else and work out this understanding of how God speaks.

I sat down to begin composing the lectures a year or so before I was scheduled to deliver them, but found that I couldn't get going. I would finish a draft of the first lecture in the early evening, the next morning I would read what I had written, and I would say to myself, "This is boring. The content is okay, but it's boring." This happened perhaps fifteen times. Finally, the thought occurred to me, "How about starting with a story?" At once, I knew which story: the story Augustine tells in his *Confessions* of hearing a child saying in a singsong voice, *Tolle lege, tolle lege* ("take and read, take and read"), and interpreting that as God telling him (Augustine) to pick up his copy of Paul's Epistles and read whatever passage his eye fell on. I used this story in the first lecture to locate my topic; the remaining seven lectures more or less wrote themselves, and the delivery of the lectures went well. My book *Divine Discourse* (Cambridge University Press, 1995) is an expansion of my Wilde Lectures.

Our host for the term we spent in Oxford was Professor Richard Swinburne, whom I had known for quite some time. He was a wonderful host. He secured for us a fine ground-floor apartment on High Street in Oxford, and he arranged to have me appointed as a visiting fellow of Oriel College, of which he was a fellow. One of the perks of this appointment was that, in the evenings, Claire and I could dine with the faculty in the college dining hall at high table (so called because the table is elevated a bit above where the students sit).

The provost of Oriel at the time was Ernest Nicholson. Over lunch a few days before my first lecture, Nicholson and Swinburne got into a disagreement as to whether I should wear an Oxford gown when delivering the lectures. Swinburne insisted that I should not, because the rules clearly stated that only those holding an Oxford MA were permitted to wear the gown. Nicholson conceded that that was the stated rule, but he argued that those who wrote the rules surely intended that someone who delivered an official series of named lectures, such as the Wilde Lectures, should wear a gown. The matter was left unresolved.

The day before I was to deliver the first lecture, Nicholson took me aside after lunch, said that I should definitely wear a gown, and added that he had a number of spare gowns hanging in the entry to his quarters. No need for me to go out and rent one. I went with him to his quarters, we found a gown that fit, and I wore it for my first lecture.

At the postlecture reception, when only a few people remained, Swinburne came up and observed that some people had found my Midwest American accent somewhat difficult to understand. Then he asked why I had worn the gown. Wasn't I aware of the rule that only those holding an Oxford MA were permitted to wear a gown? I explained that Nicholson had told me, the day before, that I should definitely wear a gown. The gown I was wearing was a spare that he had hanging in his quarters. Swinburne responded, "Oh, that's our problem with Ernest. He's always going by the spirit instead of the letter."

One of the two most unsettling teaching experiences of my career occurred about five years into my time at Yale. (The other was the course I taught, many years earlier when I was a young instructor, at the Yale Psychiatric Institute.) Shortly after I arrived at Yale in 1989, John Cook resigned his position as a member of the faculty of Yale Divinity School and head of the Yale Institute of Sacred Music to take a position with the Luce Foundation in New York City. He invited me to take over his course in theological aesthetics. The courses in aesthetics that I had taught were all in philosophical aesthetics—not theological—but I said I would try my hand at it. I asked Cook to let me see his syllabus and reading list. I noticed that he devoted several weeks to readings from Hans Urs von Balthasar's *The Glory of the Lord: A Theological Aesthetics*. Though I had not myself read any of von Balthasar's writings, I knew of his reputation as one of the finest Catholic theologians of the first half of the twentieth century, so, without reading Cook's selections, I put them on the syllabus.

We were now up to the von Balthasar segment of the course. The day before the class was to meet, I read and took notes on the pages assigned for the next day. I had come to my reading of von Balthasar with high expectations, given his reputation, but I was disappointed. Not only did I find the writing turgid, but this was not theological aesthetics; instead, it was aesthetic theology—all about the beauty of the crucifixion and so forth. But there was now no going back; I would have to do my best. The class went okay, rather sleepy and listless, but no problems—except that one of the students remarked to me after class that she had understood von Balthasar better *before* I explained him than after.

In the assigned reading for the next session I found myself confronted with a twenty-page paean of praise to the sheer passivity of the Virgin Mary. "Blessed receptivity," von Balthasar called it, if I remember. "Oh, oh, I thought, I've got problems." A number of the women enrolled in the course were taking courses in feminist studies in the central university, and they were sure to be upset by this encomium to womanly passivity. What to do? I made the decision, cowardly in retrospect, to say nothing at all about the passage. If some students called attention to it, I would deal with what they said.

We were about fifteen minutes into the class when, sure enough, one of the women whom I knew to be taking courses in feminist studies downtown raised her hand, called attention to the passage, and delivered an impassioned speech that ended with the words, enunciated loudly and slowly, with emphasis on each word, "I—FELT—RAPED." Thereupon another woman snapped back, "You have no RIGHT to say that." The latter woman had explained to me, after our first session on von Balthasar, that she was glad we were reading von Balthasar because, after a traditional Catholic upbringing, she was barely Catholic anymore, and von Balthasar was her only remaining Catholic hero.

"What do you mean, I have no RIGHT to say that?" said the first woman. "I'm a woman, and I—FELT—RAPED."

"You have no RIGHT to say that," said her antagonist. "You are showing no respect." Chaos broke out. Students began shouting at each other, some got out of their seats and walked around, waving their arms, stabbing fingers at each other. One pushed another. It must have been fifteen minutes before I could restore order. We had two more sessions on von Balthasar, but they were subdued; in fact, I had difficulty getting the students to speak up. I have never again taught von Balthasar.

Some years later I was at a conference with someone who had been in that class. I described to him my memory of what had happened, and I asked him whether my memory was accurate. He said it was. The moral for young professors: Never assign readings that you yourself have not read in advance.

I was invited to give the Gifford Lectures in the spring of 1995 at the University of St Andrews in Scotland. The Giffords are a famous lectureship that began in the late nineteenth century with a sizable bequest from Lord Gifford, a Scottish judge with a strong personal interest in religion and philosophy, to each of the four ancient Scottish universities: St Andrews, Aberdeen, Edinburgh, and Glasgow. The full title of the lectureship is: "The Gifford Lectures in Natural Theology." Karl Barth is famous for having said, in the introduction to his Gifford Lectures, that he judged the best service he could render natural theology would be to attack it as vigorously as possible, which he then proceeded to do.

The topic for my Wilde Lectures had been clear to me immediately after I received the invitation; not so for the Giffords. I fumbled around, finally deciding that the philosophy of Thomas Reid, on which I had been working episodically ever since my year in the Calvin Center for Christian Studies (1979–80), would be my topic. I entitled the series "Thomas Reid Returns to Scotland," the idea being that Reid had become virtually unknown in his native land of Scotland. It was agreed that I would give the ten lectures late in the term.

Just before Christmas 1994, I received a letter from the organizing committee informing me that they had decided to move the dates of the lectures forward by three months: instead of beginning in mid-April, the lectures would begin in the last week of January 1995. The months I had planned to devote to preparing final drafts of the lectures were now to be the months in which I was to give the lectures. I was terrified. The lectures were far from finished, but there was nothing to do. Claire and I arrived in St Andrews around the middle of January, and I gave the first lecture in the last week of the month. I have never worked so hard in my life as I did preparing the subsequent lectures.

The lore around St Andrews was that, when Alfred North Whitehead gave the Gifford Lectures, on which his magnum opus *Process and Reality* was based, there were just three people in the room when he delivered his final lecture—Whitehead, his wife, and the person who introduced him! The audience for mine remained, mercifully, more or less constant, around eighty people.

But I did not feel satisfied with the lectures. Though I had been studying Reid for fifteen years, I felt that I had still not fully grasped what he was up to. I no longer interpreted him as addressing the questions of twentieth-century epistemologists: What is justified belief? What is entitled belief? What is rational belief? What is knowledge? And so forth. As I mentioned earlier, I discerned that he was instead asking these two deep questions: How do we manage to get a cognitive grip on elements of reality sufficient for being able to form beliefs about them? And what accounts for the formation of those beliefs? But though I saw that these were Reid's fundamental questions, I felt that I did not yet have a firm grasp of his answers, only adumbrations. A few years later, when I felt that I did finally understand both Reid's questions and his answers, I wrote *Thomas Reid and the Story of Epistemology* (Cambridge, 2001). I wrote it quickly and easily.

Once the lectures were over, Claire and I enjoyed our stay in St Andrews immensely. It's a wonderful old city, and the Scots were extraordinarily hospitable to Claire and me. The college chaplain invited Claire to preach on a Sunday in the college chapel. Claire's ancestors, on her mother's side, were Stewarts from Scotland: in the seventeenth century, one of her ancestors left Scotland for the Netherlands to serve as a mercenary in the Dutch army in its war against the Spaniards. Claire reported that, when she ascended the pulpit, she had the sense that her Scots forebears were feeling mighty proud of her, but, at the same time, disapproving of a woman in the pulpit— even if she was one of their descendants.

The vice chancellor of the university at the time was Struther Arnott. (In the British system, the vice chancellor is the executive head of the university, whereas the position of chancellor is purely honorary.) Struther had worked for some years in university administration in the United States and saw himself as bringing American practices of university administration to St Andrews. He and his wife took Claire and me out for dinner several times. We got to know them rather well and liked them both very much, though, given Struther's top-down style of administration, it was clear to me that I would not like being a faculty member in a university of which he was the head.

Shortly after he became vice chancellor, a few years earlier, Struther concluded that there was not sufficient interaction among members of the different schools and departments in the university, so he inaugurated an annual Dead Poet's Dinner, to which the entire faculty would be invited, a fine meal would be served, single-malt scotch would be offered after dinner, and passages from the poet chosen for that year would be read aloud. As it happened, the poet chosen for the year I was giving the Gifford Lectures was Henry Wadsworth Longfellow. Struther invited me to be one of the readers, and told me that a committee would inform me which passage I was to read.

I was delighted. Longfellow's *Song of Hiawatha* was part of my Minnesota childhood. The poem is set in Minnesota, though there is no evidence that Longfellow ever set foot in the state. Over the years I had delighted in teasing my children and grandchildren by reciting, until they screamed, "Stop," the lines:

By the shores of Gitche Gumee,
By the shining Big-Sea Water,
Stood the wigwam of Nokomis,
Daughter of the Moon, Nokomis.
Dark behind it rose the forest,
Rose the black and gloomy pine-trees,
Rose the firs with cones upon them.
Bright before it beat the water,
Beat the clear and sunny water,
Beat the shining Big-Sea Water.

Nokomis was the mother of Hiawatha.

The committee asked me to read the passage about the death of Minnehaha, Hiawatha's wife. My principal challenge was to subdue the rollicking rhythm, which I delighted in exaggerating for my children and grandchildren but which would not be appropriate for a lament. I practiced at home.

And he [Hiawatha] rushed into the wigwam,
Saw the old Nokomis slowly
Rocking to and fro and moaning,
Saw his lovely Minnehaha
Lying dead and cold before him,
And his bursting heart within him
Uttered such a cry of anguish....
Then they buried Minnehaha;
In the snow a grave they made her,
In the forest deep and darksome,
Underneath the moaning hemlocks....
"Farewell," said he, "Minnehaha!
Farewell, O my Laughing Water!
All my heart is buried with you."

The passage continues at some length. Several people came up to me afterward and remarked how moving they had found the passage. After much practice at home, I had succeeded at subduing the rollicking rhythm.

At one of our dinners with Struther and his wife, he remarked that, whereas it was the practice at St Andrews to commission a portrait of the vice chancellor upon his or her retirement, he had decided to commission a portrait of himself before he retired. He told us that the portrait would be unveiled at the Dead Poet's Dinner. But the evening ended without any unveiling. As the guests left, Struther was at the exit shaking hands. I asked him why the portrait had not been unveiled. "Ah yes," he said, "the portrait. It proved to be too large to get through the door."

It's good to have an experience every now and then that keeps one humble. Though I was not pleased with the lectures I had given, I was pleased—proud even—to be among those who had given the Gifford Lectures, many of them illustrious. In the summer of the year I gave the lectures, I taught a three-week summer course at Regent College, in Vancouver. Claire accompanied me. Regent invited me, in addition to teaching the course, to deliver an evening public lecture on a topic of my choosing. I decided to give a talk entitled "Christianity Engages Postmodernism." The audience was large and enthusiastic, and the questions posed in the question period afterward were excellent. I was exhilarated.

There was a bar on the way to our lodging, a short walk away, so I suggested to Claire that we get a drink before we turned in. As I was standing at the bar, ordering our drinks, a woman, elegantly dressed in white, with gold bracelets on both wrists, came up, said that she had been at the lecture, and asked whether she could join us and talk about it. Anticipating that she wanted to tell me how wonderful she had found the lecture and to pose some questions that had occurred to her, I said, "Of course, please join us."

We settled into a booth, Claire and I across from our new acquaintance. I opened the conversation by asking her to tell us a bit about herself. She narrated that, after her conversion to Christianity in her mid-twenties, she had spent the subsequent twenty years or so wandering from one Christian group to another, trying to find one that fitted her convictions and sensibilities. Finally she had discovered a group in Vancouver that preached and practiced the simple life. Tolstoy was their inspiration. This, at last, was what she had been looking for all those years.

Then she said, "I must tell you how repulsive I found your lecture. The Christian gospel is simple. You made it complicated."

A slap in my self-satisfied face.

"I agree that it's simple. But it's also rich. I was trying to present some of the richness."

"But why did you make it so complicated? It's simple."

"I agree. It is simple. But it's not only simple. Beneath the simplicity there are depths and riches. I was exploring some of those."

"But why did you make it so complicated? It's simple."

"I wasn't making it complicated. I was exploring some of the depth and richness of the gospel."

"Then why did you make it so complicated?"

"I did not make it complicated."

"You did."

I lost my cool. "We're leaving. There's no point in talking with you. You just keep saying the same thing over and over. You don't listen to anything I say."

I got up, gestured to Claire to follow me, and headed for the exit. I was about halfway there when I began to feel terribly guilty. I spun around, returned to the booth where she was still sitting, leaned over, embraced her, awkwardly, and said, "You are my sister in Christ, but

I'm not going to talk with you anymore"—and strode out into the balmy Vancouver night, wife in tow.

I noticed a small ad in the Sunday edition of the *New York Times* for used mid-twentieth-century Danish furniture. I had been in love with midcentury Danish furniture ever since I saw some chairs by the Danish designer Hans Wegner—in my view, the greatest chair designer of the twentieth century—in a store in Manhattan in the late 1950s. The prices were out of reach for us. On our European tour of 1971, I had made a point of stopping for a few days in Copenhagen, both to see the city and to see more midcentury Danish furniture than could be seen in the United States. Den Permanente, a store that specialized in modern design, had a large selection of Wegner's furniture. I was enthralled. I felt as if I had been on a pilgrimage and had finally arrived at the holy site. Though our financial condition was considerably better than it was when I was a young instructor at Yale, the prices were still out of reach.

Eleven years later, in January 1982, when we were living in Amsterdam, Claire, our sons Christopher and Klaas (who was visiting us for a few weeks), and I had driven from Amsterdam to Copenhagen, through icy fog between Amsterdam and Lübeck. Den Permanente had closed, but a number of other stores were displaying and selling Wegner's furniture. I was again smitten. I turned fifty while we were in Copenhagen, and Claire urged me to buy a Wegner chair as a birthday gift to myself. I readily agreed, and we bought Wegner's spectacular "Peacock Chair." I love it. It joined another Wegner chair that Claire had bought a few years earlier, at an affordable price, in Santa Barbara, when she was visiting her parents.

I rang the phone number in the aforementioned *Times* ad. A man with a gruff voice and a Danish accent answered. I told him I had seen his ad in the *Times*, and asked him whether he had any Hans Wegner furniture for sale.

"That's all you Americans know," he growled back. "All you know is Wegner. There are dozens of great Danish designers."

"Yes," I said, "I'm aware of that, but I am especially interested in Wegner."

"There you go again. All you people know is Wegner."

I tried once more and got the same gruff response. Our conversation was going nowhere. I thanked him and hung up. To find out whether he had any Wegner furniture for sale, we would have to drive to his store—in Patterson, New York, just across the western border of Connecticut—and see for ourselves. He was not going to tell me over the phone.

We located his store, a nondescript cement-block building on the edge of the small village of Patterson, and walked in. We found ourselves in a large room filled with broken-down midcentury Danish furniture—the caning on this chair broken, a leg on that table missing, and so on. I said to Claire, "This is a scam. Let's get out of here." But before we could leave, a man appeared from a room in the distance and beckoned to us to come further in.

This proved to be the man I had talked to on the phone, Haakon Boldsen, a crusty old Dane. In courtly fashion, he took Claire's hand and kissed it, but no matter what I said, he disagreed with me. I happened to glance at a corkboard on which were pinned a few cartoons. One caught my eye. Two women are standing at a gravesite, and one says to the other, "I always told him it wouldn't kill him to be nice, but I seem to have been mistaken."

The crusty exterior slowly melted, and we began to talk seriously. There were many great Danish designers, but yes, he conceded, Wegner was perhaps the greatest of them all. He explained that once a year he returned to Denmark, bought up a quantity of used mid-century Danish furniture, and had it shipped in a container to his store, where he repaired it. We were now standing in a back room, a much larger room than the one we had entered, surrounded by beautifully repaired furniture. Why would he greet customers with a room full of broken-down furniture and put the repaired furniture in the back?

There were lots of Wegner chairs, the prices between a third and a quarter of what they would cost new—still considerably more expensive than ordinary chairs in ordinary furniture stores, but affordable. Thus began our collection of Hans Wegner furniture. I have counted: we now have twenty-four Wegner chairs in sixteen different designs, two end tables, a sewing table, a coffee table, and a lounge. We purchased a few items in Copenhagen—some new, some used—but most of them came from Haakon, a few items at a time, as we could afford them. Claire and I have made gifts of Wegner chairs to all of our children.

Why collect chairs? Collecting graphic art prints or ceramics, that's understandable. But why chairs? Let me explain. In the eighteenth century, our familiar dichotomies between *art* and *craft*—and *artist* and *craftsman*—emerged. Before that time, when writers talked about painters, poets, and so on, they blended language we use about craftsmen with language we use about artists. As everyone knows, the *art/craft* dichotomy and the *artist/craftsman* dichotomy carry within them a pecking order: art is superior, craft is inferior; artists are superior, craftspeople are inferior.

After being demoted to the position of poor sister of the arts, the so-called crafts were dealt a second blow by the industrialization that took place in Europe during the nineteenth century. All kinds of things that had once been produced by craftsmen now poured out of factories: chairs, tables, wallpaper, fabric, dishes, cutlery, glass—you name it. The Arts and Crafts movement in England in the late nineteenth century, led by William Morris—and the counterparts of that movement in Scotland and various places on the continent—were a pushback against industrialization, a pushback aimed at a renewal of the crafts.

Producing things by hand is, in general, a good deal more costly than producing those same things by machine, so the clientele for the products of the Arts and Crafts movement proved to be exclusively people of the upper-middle and upper classes. And to persuade even those who could afford it to buy handmade work, the members of the Arts and Crafts movement had to point to something distinctive about things made by hand that made it worth paying more for them: things made by hand have imperfections and irregularities; they can be customized; they can be one-of-a-kind; due account can be taken of aesthetic considerations, and so forth. Things made by machine were charged with being uniformly bland and/or ugly.

In the twentieth century there was, in turn, a pushback by the managers of industrial production to the charge that their products were bland and ugly. The so-called *good-design* movement emerged: the core of the movement was the insistence that more should go into the design of industrial products than just pragmatic considerations. Yes, a chair should hold up under people of somewhat more than average weight, should be comfortable, and should be reasonable in price. But good design requires something more, namely, aesthetic excellence. The Herman Miller Company, which I discussed above, has been a prominent member of the good-design movement ever since the mid-1930s.

I come now to chairs. I mentioned that, in my judgment, Hans Wegner was the greatest chair designer of the twentieth century; just behind him was an American, Charles Eames. Both Wegner and Eames were inheritors and members of the good-design movement. Eames's chairs are industrially produced, many of them by Herman Miller; the handwork that goes into them consists of nothing more than assembling components that come off the assembly line. Though some components of Wegner's chairs are also industrially produced, considerably more handwork goes into his chairs than just assembling components, which is why they are expensive and why quite a few of his designs are no longer in production. Wegner's chairs are an interesting blend of industrial production and craft production.

Almost all of Eames's chairs are what might be called "leg-attachment" chairs; almost all of Wegner's chairs are what might be called "leg-integrated" chairs. Let me explain. The development in the twentieth century of fiberglass, plastics, mesh-steel, and bent plywood made it possible to form in one piece the part of the chair that you sit on, that you lean back against, and that you rest your arms on (if it has armrests)—and then to attach legs to that component. Eames's classic Lounge Chair is a paradigmatic example of a leg-attachment chair, as are his various "shell" chairs. For almost all of Wegner's chairs, the idea of attaching the legs is inapplicable. Legs, seat, backrest, and armrest are an integrated composition.

Eames's leg-attachment chairs and Wegner's leg-integrated chairs are both superb products of the good-design movement. I see no reason to think that one of these styles is intrinsically better than the other. My reason for thinking that Wegner was, nonetheless, the greater designer overall, is that Wegner's chairs are generally more comfortable than Eames's chairs—the big exception being Eames's Lounge Chair. And second, while both Eames and Wegner had great sculptural imagination, Wegner's was an imagination that did not *impose* itself on the wood but *capitalized* on its woodiness. Wegner often handles the wood in surprising ways, and sometimes it takes a long time to figure out how the chair was made. But a Wegner chair is never a tour-de-force in wood; it honors the wood. I know of no Eames chair about which I would say that it honors the wood. Can one honor fiberglass? I doubt it.

The question remains: What's the point of a good-design chair? Rather than paying a considerable amount of money for either a Wegner chair or an Eames chair, why not go to the nearest furniture store and buy the first chair that catches your eye?

Good design ennobles the humble act of sitting—elevates it, dignifies it. The function of a great deal of art is to ennoble some humble act that we could perform without the artistic enhancement. Work songs, when sung to accompany work, do that. Hymns do that: we can praise God in spoken prose, but hymns ennoble, enhance, and enrich our praise. Wegner's chairs ennoble the humble act of sitting. They dignify the ordinary, joining beauty with comfort. It's a joy to look at them—and a pleasure to sit on them.

Haakkon Boldsen never changed. Each time, he would bow before Claire, take her hand and kiss it, and disagree with whatever I said. But during each of our visits, after a while, the crusty exterior would soften.

Though I had long been interested in issues of political philosophy, my interest was casual and episodic. That changed when I accepted an invitation from Paul Weithman, political philosopher at Notre Dame, and one of the best in the field, to participate in a conference he was organizing for February 1996, entitled "Religion and Contemporary Liberalism." Paul had read my book *Until Justice and Peace Embrace*, and what I said there led him to suggest that I give a talk on "the political implications of Dutch Calvinism, on how believers are to act on those implications, and on how this strengthens both their religious and political communities." I decided to place my discussion of the topics Paul suggested in the context of engaging the Harvard philosopher John Rawls's recently published *Political Liberalism* (Columbia University Press, 1993).

The prose of *Political Liberalism* is dense—the details of its thought, elusive. But the main thesis is clear: when debating fundamental political issues, citizens of liberal democracies should not appeal to their own "comprehensive doctrines," be those Christian, Jewish, secular utilitarian, or whatever, but should appeal instead to what Rawls called "public reason," which, he said, comprises those core principles of justice and equality implicit in the "idea" of liberal democracy. It was the first edition of *Political Liberalism* (1993) that I engaged at Weithman's conference. In a second edition, Rawls qualified his position slightly: it is acceptable to appeal to one's own particular comprehensive doctrines when debating fundamental political issues *provided that* one stands ready to defend the same position on the basis of public reason.

Though I didn't say so at the conference, Rawls's position rubbed against my Kuyperian convictions. It was Kuyper's contention that, in our highly pluralistic societies, the attempt to find some shared set of principles sufficiently thick to settle fundamental political issues was futile. In politics, as in other areas of life, we approach the issues from our own particular worldview. We cannot shed our worldviews, nor can we put them in cold storage for a time; they unavoidably shape how we see the issues. We should, indeed, aim at securing agreement on political matters, not just declare, "Here I stand." But if the issues are fundamental, it is to be expected that, in a pluralistic society such as ours, we will find ourselves disagreeing at the end of the day. Then we take a vote. The endurance of democracy depends on the vote being fair and on losers being willing to live with losing the vote. It does not depend on everyone's having appealed to a shared public reason.

My talk for the conference was published in a collection of conference talks that Weithman edited under the same title as the conference, *Religion and Contemporary Liberalism* (University of Notre Dame Press, 1997). The published talk was soon followed by a small point/counterpoint book that I wrote with Robert Audi, *Religion in the Public Square* (Rowman and Littlefield, 1997). Audi's position on the place of religious convictions in political debate was similar to that of Rawls. In the book we each state our contrasting positions, and then reply to the other person's contribution.

That debate between Audi and me spurred the religion department at the University of Richmond (Virginia) to organize a public debate a few years later between Richard Rorty and me on the subject of the place of religion in public political debate. Rorty's position on the subject was essentially the same as that of Rawls and Audi:

he had recently published an article entitled "Religion as a Conversation Stopper."

Rorty and I had been friends since graduate school days. At the time of our debate, he was one of America's most prominent philosophers. Though he was a sharp critic of religion, he regularly asked me for offprints of articles I had published, and every now and then he mentioned to me that he had assigned one of my books for reading in one of his classes. As we were chatting before our debate, he said that he tried to keep up with discussions in philosophy of religion.[1]

Rorty stated his position, I stated mine, and then we engaged in a friendly back-and-forth dialogue. In the course of our back-and-forth, I remarked that religion did not seem to be a stopper in our conversation. He conceded the point and, toward the end of the session, said that he found himself coming around to my position. He told me afterward that he regretted having written "Religion as a Conversation Stopper," and he remarked that, in his response to some of the students who had accused him of being ignorant of religion, he had barely restrained himself from revealing that Walter Rauschenbusch, the great "social gospel" theologian active in the first third of the twentieth century, was his grandfather on his mother's side.

A few years after our debate, he accepted an invitation to give a talk in a summer seminar at Calvin College on the topic of religion in the public square. I was invited to attend for the day. In the question period after his talk, someone asked him why he had changed his mind from what he had written earlier about religion as a conversation stopper. He graciously remarked that it was our Richmond debate that led him to change his mind. At the dinner afterwards, I asked him why he had interrupted his summer to give a talk to a small seminar at Calvin. He answered that he had long wanted to see this college from which so many prominent philosophers had graduated.

My participation in Weithman's conference was the beginning of

1. Richard Rorty died in 2007.

more than fifteen years of thinking and writing in the area of political philosophy. Would I have turned to political philosophy even if I had not received Weithman's invitation? I don't know. His invitation was another of those many occasions in my life when something I had not anticipated provoked me into pursuing a line of thought. Of course, had his invitation not tapped into an underlying interest, I would not have accepted.

The issue of the role of the religious voice in political debate continued to hold my attention for a good many years, and I wrote a number of essays on the topic. Another lecture invitation provoked me to turn my attention to a different topic in the area of political philosophy. I was invited to give the Stone Lectures at Princeton Theological Seminary in 1998, the hundredth anniversary of Abraham Kuyper's now-famous Stone Lectures at Princeton under the title *Calvinism*. The thought of giving the Stone Lectures on the centenary of Kuyper's giving them pleased me greatly.

No topic suggested itself immediately upon my receiving the invitation. I wanted my lectures to have something to do with Kuyper's lectures. But what? The project Kuyper had set for himself in his lectures was to articulate the "essence" of Calvinism, and then to point to the contribution of Calvinism to various aspects of the modern world. In his third lecture, "Calvinism and Politics," he offered an imaginative and provocative theological account of political authority. I decided to honor the centenary by reflecting anew on the relationship between divine and political authority, incorporating into my discussion some reflections on what Kuyper had said on the subject.

Apart from the fact that I found the topic intrinsically interesting and important, I had a reason for choosing the topic that I did not state explicitly. I was disturbed by the critical attitude of John Howard Yoder, Stanley Hauerwas, Alasdair MacIntyre, and their many followers, toward government in general and toward American liberal democracy in particular. I regard liberal democracy as a pearl of great price. And whereas Hauerwas often says things to the effect that Christians have no responsibility for what their government does, I hold that we have deep responsibility. The popularity of the Yoder-Hauerwas-MacIntyre line of thought seemed to me to contribute to the muffling of a robust Christian voice in American political discourse. My unstated aim was to offer an alternative perspective.

In this case, too, I was not happy with the lectures in the form in which I delivered them. So, rather than preparing them for publication, I set them aside. Every once in a while in subsequent years I returned to them, reorganized them, revised some passages, developed some points more fully, and so forth. But each time I found myself once again unhappy with the result, until, finally, in 2010, I achieved a version that satisfied me. It was published under the title *The Mighty and the Almighty* (Cambridge University Press, 2011).

After finishing the final draft of *The Mighty and the Almighty*, I decided to collect in one volume the essays I had written on various topics in political philosophy that were scattered about in journals and anthologies. When I had the pile in front of me, I realized that they would not make a good book. Overall, they were too negative, too much focused on attacking one or another version of public reason, on disagreeing with one or another understanding of the core principles of liberal democracy, and so on. I needed to compose a number of new essays in which I would develop my own positive views more fully. When I had done so, the collection was published under the title *Understanding Liberal Democracy* (Oxford, 2012). Almost half of the chapters had not previously been published as essays.[2]

---

2. In preparing the volume for publication, I had the invaluable editorial assistance of my former student Terence Cuneo.

Looking back over what I have written in this memoir thus far, I am struck by how often the word "love" occurs. I have written of loving the village of Bigelow, of loving Claire and the children, of loving philosophy, gardening, our land, Hans Wegner chairs, living in Amsterdam. Sometimes, when I could have used the word "love," I did not: I loved seeing Hagia Sophia in Istanbul, I loved teaching at Calvin and at Yale, I love our graphic art prints and our ceramics. And then there are the things I love that I haven't even mentioned: my deep love of music, of Claire's cooking, of the farmers' market in Grand Rapids, of the Russian *matryoshka* (nesting dolls) that we have collected. My life has been laced through with what I have found lovable. More than that, my life has in good measure been *shaped* by what I have found lovable. I have followed the loves of my life: practicing and teaching philosophy, being with family and friends, worshiping God, gardening, collecting prints, attending concerts—on and on.

Many people find almost nothing lovable in their lives: they are alienated from relatives and have no friends; they live in squalor and on subsistence food; their lives are shaped by sheer necessity rather than love. Following their loves is not, for them, an option. I have been fortunate, and I am deeply grateful, to have lived a life rich with what I found lovable. Let me not overstate: there have been things in my life that were not lovable, happenings that gave me grief or regret, things done or said that hurt or angered me, tasks to be done that I found distasteful or boring. What stands out among these is the death of our son Eric.

When reflecting on the fact that it was my love for Eric that was the source of my grief, I distinguished four kinds of love: *beneficence-love, attraction-love, attachment-love,* and *activity-love.* Whereas love as beneficence seeks to bring about some good in someone's life, the other three forms of love are distinct ways of relishing and delighting in some extant good. My attraction-love for Beethoven's late string quartets consists of relishing and delighting in their excellence. My attachment-love for Eric consisted of relishing and delighting in the great good of my interactions with him. My activity-love for doing philosophy consists of relishing and delighting in the good of thinking, reading, writing, teaching, and discussing philosophy. The fact that my life has been shot through with love indicates that it has been shot through with goodness and excellence. Wonders! And running throughout has been my abiding conviction that these are a reflection and manifestation of God's excellence.

On October 2, 1999, my stepmother, Jen Hanenburg, died in Edgerton at the age of ninety-eight. (Teaching responsibilities made it impossible for me to get to the funeral.) For some years she had suffered either from severe depression or from Alzheimer's, it was hard to tell which. She was, perhaps, the most giving person I have ever known, constantly spending herself for others. Though my siblings and I were stepchildren, we were never made to feel like stepchildren. We were her children. I have a vivid memory of her at Eric's funeral. Eric was her grandson and, like her, had red hair—though his came from Claire's family. For many years she suffered physically, never complaining: from ulcers, from dentures that did not fit, from loss of hearing. The loss of hearing isolated her. Always so generous with her time and efforts, she now withdrew. It was painful to watch.

TEN

Still Vistas

I retired from my position at Yale at the end of 2001, a few weeks short of turning seventy. Though I still enjoyed teaching, the routine was beginning to wear on me: delivering lectures and leading seminars every week, preparing syllabi, turning in book lists, grading student papers, holding office hours, going to committee meetings. I had done these things for forty-five years. We kept our condo in New Haven for a few years after my retirement and continued to live there for much of the academic year. In the spring of 2005 we sold it and moved everything into our house in Grand Rapids.

After retirement, I taught a seminar on justice in the fall at Notre Dame for a couple of years. I had agreed to do so a third year, but in April of the second year I received a peremptory request from the Notre Dame bookstore to turn in, as soon as possible, the list of books I would be requiring my students to buy for the seminar I was to teach in the fall, and that made something inside me snap. I don't want to turn in book lists, I don't want to prepare syllabi, I don't want to lead a seminar every week at the appointed time. I've been in the harness long enough—I want to be in the saddle.

I called Paul Weithman, chair at the time of the Notre Dame philosophy department, and explained, with some embarrassment, that getting the request from the bookstore for my book list six months in advance had made something inside me snap, and I asked to be released from my agreement to teach a seminar that fall. Paul laughed, and said there was no problem, he understood. Since then, I have not taught a regular course anywhere.

I did have a worry about retirement. When I talked to Yale colleagues in the natural sciences who were my age, I discovered that many of them were very reluctant to retire. Quite soon I learned why. Except for those whose work was entirely theoretical, their lab work was the center of their lives; when they retired, they had to give that up and find something entirely different to do. No problem if they had hobbies; but many did not. They were apprehensive.

In my case, I would continue doing much of what I had always done—namely, think and write philosophy. Still more vistas to contemplate, now in greater tranquility. But it had been my experience, over the years, that teaching and practicing philosophy worked to the benefit of each other: practicing philosophy gave depth to my teaching, and teaching philosophy brought to light unnoticed gaps and obscurities in my thinking. Now my practicing of philosophy would have to make do without the benefit of teaching.

Early in 2005, Galen Byker, president of Calvin College, invited me to give the college commencement address in May of that year. I gladly accepted, and the announcement went out. But about six weeks before the event, Byker called to say that he was withdrawing the invitation. He explained that he had invited President George W. Bush to speak at Calvin's commencement, and Bush had accepted. He invited me to speak to the seniors at their breakfast on the morning of graduation, and to give the commencement address the following year.

Later I learned what had happened. President Bush had informed members of his staff that he wanted to give a commencement address that year at an evangelical college, and he asked them to secure an invitation. A presidential staff member contacted the US congressman from western Michigan, Vern Ehlers, a former member of the Calvin physics department, and asked him to inquire whether Calvin would be willing to invite the president. Ehlers obliged. No doubt Bush was looking for a quiet evangelical college that would applaud his work, a respite from the controversies swirling around him. Calvin was not that kind of college. When the news was out that Bush would be the speaker, an uproar ensued.

A few days before the event, a half-page ad appeared in *The Grand Rapids Press*, signed by over half of the Calvin faculty, expressing strong opposition to a number of policies of the Bush administration.

On the day of the event, the streets leading to the college were lined with hundreds of protesters, as were the sidewalks on the campus leading to the gymnasium where the graduation ceremony was to be held. Police and reporters were everywhere.

I had been invited to take a front seat, but I declined and stayed home. I could not face the prospect of people coming up to me afterward and asking, "What did you think?" A reporter from *The Washington Post* asked me what I was doing during Bush's address. I told him that I was working in my garden, cleaning up the debris of the winter, which was the truth. Later in the day I joined a group of friends who had been among the protesters.

That same spring (2005), James Davison Hunter, head of the Institute for Advanced Studies in Culture at the University of Virginia, asked me whether I would consider being appointed a senior research fellow in the institute.

"What would my duties be?" I asked.

"Not many," he replied. "No teaching. Participation in our biweekly seminars and in whatever conferences we hold. For the rest, do your own thing. We like what you've been writing lately, and we think it fits perfectly with the program of the institute." He offered to pay me nicely. I talked it over with Claire, and we decided to do it. I would be in residence at the institute from early September to mid-May, and we would continue spending our summers in Grand Rapids. Thus began eight wonderful years.

Hunter, whom I had known for some time, is a sociologist on the faculty of the University of Virginia. A recent book of his, *To Change the World*, has received a good deal of attention. The project of the Institute for Advanced Studies in Culture, which Hunter founded, is to identify the normative dimensions of contemporary culture; to contrast those with the normative dimensions of earlier American culture; to ask what accounts for the changes; to uncover the ways in which the normative dimensions of present-day culture stifle human flourishing; to ask how that might be changed; and to contribute, in whatever way it can, to bringing about the change. Hunter was right: the work I was doing on justice fitted perfectly with the overall project of the institute. I found the cross-disciplinary conversation at the institute fascinating and stimulating, and both the junior and senior fellows were, to a person, wonderful human beings.

Claire and I found a funky apartment to rent in downtown Charlottesville, just two blocks off what had been Main Street but was now a bustling pedestrian mall. The apartment was on the ground floor of a refurbished warehouse, but with all the features of a loft: ceilings fifteen feet high, exposed wooden beams, exposed pipes, brick walls. The typical response of anyone under twenty-five who saw it was, "Cool. This is really cool." We loved it, as did our children and grandchildren when they came to visit.

When I wrote *Until Justice and Peace Embrace* (1983), I said a good deal about justice without having in mind a theory of justice; I relied on my intuitions. But I was uneasy with that. There are a number of different ways of understanding justice. If I was to write more in the area, it was incumbent on me to stand back and ask what justice is. I postponed doing so, however, giving priority instead to my work on the epistemology of John Locke and Thomas Reid. In my final year at Yale Divinity School I took up, at last, the long-postponed topic of justice, continuing that in the two seminars I taught at Notre Dame after I retired. My position as a fellow of the Institute for Advanced Studies in Culture provided me with a welcome opportunity to advance that work.

A number of philosophers and theologians at the University of Virginia expressed interest in discussing drafts of chapters of the book when I felt the drafts were sufficiently developed to make discussion worthwhile. The first chapter was on the work of John Rawls. My readers didn't like it. What I said was correct, they thought, but boring. One said emphatically that he would never begin a book this way. I took their criticism to heart, scrapped the chapter, and began anew. The book has the distinction—*dubious* distinction, some would say—of being one of the few books on justice written in the past forty years by a philosopher in the analytic tradition that says almost nothing about John Rawls.

Two competing accounts of justice have come down to us from antiquity, one from Aristotle, the other from the Roman jurist Ulpian (c. 170–223 CE). Aristotle's view was that justice consists of the equitable distribution of benefits and burdens. Ulpian's view was that justice consists of rendering to each person what is his or her *ius*— that is, his or her right, or due. I was drawn to Ulpian's view. Aristotle's view seemed to me untenable for a number of reasons, one of them being that it seems to me grotesque to suggest that what makes rape, for example, a violation of justice is that benefits and burdens are distributed inequitably.

Having embraced Ulpian's view, I now had to work out an account of rights, especially an account of natural rights, that is, rights not conferred on us by society. Rape is a serious violation of justice whether or not the laws of the land declare it to be a crime; the right not to be raped is a natural right. But before I could set about developing an account of natural rights, I had to face the fact that rights in general—and natural rights in particular—have acquired a bad name in many quarters.

The story most commonly told about the origin of the idea of natural rights is that the idea was devised by secular eighteenth-century Enlightenment philosophers, and that it cannot be detached from the secular individualism of those who devised it. Communitarians such as Alasdair MacIntyre rejected the idea on that account, as did a good many Christian ethicists, including Oliver O'Donovan and

Stanley Hauerwas, to name just two. Some writers went further and rejected rights-talk in general, not just talk about natural rights. We should be talking about responsibilities, they insisted, not about rights. Rights-talk, they said, is an expression of the malignant modern attitude of *possessive individualism*: "I, an autonomous individual, demand my rights from the rest of you." No matter what account of rights I developed, it would get no hearing if I did not address these out-of-hand dismissals.

Just as I was beginning to think about these matters, John Witte, a legal historian in the law school of Emory University (and a Calvin graduate), called my attention to the recent publication by the medieval intellectual historian Brian Tierney, *The Idea of Natural Rights* (Scholars Press, 1997). In his book, Tierney argues persuasively that the canon lawyers of the twelfth century were explicitly using the idea of natural rights. They spoke, for example, of the rights of the poor, the rights of aliens, the rights of spouses. Rather than being an invention of the (supposedly) secular Enlightenment, the idea of natural rights emerged from the seedbed of medieval Christianity. This was a godsend for my project. My book *Justice: Rights and Wrongs* (Princeton University Press, 2008) opens with a presentation of Tierney's alternative narrative concerning the origin of the idea of natural rights.

Whereas Tierney limited himself to discussing the explicit use of the idea by the twelfth-century canon lawyers and their successors, I wondered whether the idea had perhaps been implicitly used earlier. In the course of doing some reading I discovered that some of the church fathers had used the idea, especially when they were discussing the moral condition of the poor. In one of his sermons on the parable of Lazarus, preached in Antioch in 388 or 389, John Chrysostom, the "golden-tongued" preacher, declared that the extra shoes in the closet of the wealthy person "belong" to the person who has no shoes. Though Chrysostom used no word synonymous with our word "right," he was clearly invoking the idea of a right. The poor person has a *right* to the extra shoes of the wealthy person. It's likely that Chrysostom also believed that the wealthy person has an *obligation* to bestow his extra shoes on the poor person. But that's not what he said; what he said was that the extra shoes *belong to* the poor person. Chrysostom declared that he was delivering to his hearers "testimony from the divine Scriptures."

On the theory of rights that I developed in the book, natural rights are grounded in dignity or worth: you have a right to someone's treating you a certain way if treating you that way is required for treating you as befits your dignity, your worth. You have a right, for example, to the receptionist's treating you courteously if her treating you courteously is required for treating you as befits your dignity or worth. You have a right to be awarded an A for my course if that's required for treating you as befits the worth you have of doing top-notch work in the course.

Rights are social relationships, with the exception of those rights that we have with respect to ourselves. (The idea that we have rights with respect to ourselves may take some readers aback. But to be deprived of what one has a right to, is to be wronged. And it seems clear that we can wrong ourselves—for example, by allowing ourselves to become drug addicts.) With the exception of those rights, it takes two or more for there to be a right. And just as I have rights with respect to you, you also have rights with respect to me. The situation is symmetrical. The possessive individualist who talks only of his own rights with respect to others—and ignores the rights of others with respect to him—is abusing rights-talk.

I wanted to convey the idea that rights pervade the fine texture of our existence. For that reason, I saved my discussion of those special rights that are human rights for the last part of the book. Human rights are those we have just by virtue of being human, not by virtue of being some particular kind of human being. I noted that, when thinking about human rights, it's important to keep in mind that the circle of human beings includes those who are incapable of functioning as persons, for example, those in a permanent coma, those in an advanced stage of dementia, and those born severely impaired. As I was reflecting on what it is about even such human beings that gives them certain rights—the right, for example, not to be poisoned and have their bodies tossed into a dumpster—I found myself led to the conclusion that none of the secular accounts of human rights that were being offered could explain what it is about such human beings that gives them rights. Secular accounts can explain what it is about human beings who can function as persons that gives them rights, but they cannot explain what it is about those who *cannot* function as persons that gives *them* rights.

Secular accounts of human rights typically ground the dignity that accounts for human rights in some capacity—for example, the capacity for rational agency. But human beings who are incapable of functioning as persons don't have the relevant capacities. So far as I could see, only a theistic account that appeals to God's love for every creature who bears the image of God can account for the rights of all human beings whatsoever, including those not capable of functioning as persons. I emphasized that not having a satisfactory account of why even such human beings have rights does not mean that secularists should give up the idea that such human beings do have rights, any more than not having a satisfactory account of obligation, say, means that one should give up the idea that there are obligations. Nonetheless, my claim that only a theistic account of human rights is successful has proved not only controversial but, to some readers, offensive.

When planning the book, I projected a chapter on the relationship between justice and love. As it turned out, that would have made the book too long. But in any case, when I began thinking about the topic, it became clear to me almost immediately that an adequate treatment would require a book of its own, and that's how *Justice in Love* came about (Eerdmans, 2011). I noted in the preface to the book that we are the recipients of two comprehensive imperatives issued by the writers of antiquity: one, coming to us from both the Athens-Rome strand of our heritage and the Jerusalem strand, is the imperative to do justice; the other, coming to us only from the Jerusalem strand, is to love one's neighbor as oneself, even if that neighbor is an enemy. These two imperatives do not reveal on their face how they are related to each other, which is why writers, through the centuries, have repeatedly addressed the question of their relationship.

I noted that the theme of tension or conflict between justice and love is prominent in the literature. Sometimes this theme takes the form of a writer arguing that one cannot follow the two imperatives simultaneously: to act out of love is perforce not to act as one does because justice requires it, and to act as one does because justice requires it is perforce not to act out of love. At other times, the theme takes the form of a writer arguing that, in following the love-imperative, one will sometimes wreak injustice, or that, in following the justice-imperative, one will sometimes act unlovingly.

I felt intuitively that this was mistaken. The thesis that shapes the discussion in the book is that between justice, rightly understood, and love, rightly understood, there is no tension. Love, so I argued, incorporates justice. In loving the neighbor, one sometimes goes beyond doing what justice requires, but one never does *less than* what justice requires. One of the challenges I took upon myself when writing the book was to conduct the discussion in such a way that it would seem as natural to bring Jesus, Paul, and the Old Testament prophets into the philosophical discussion as to bring Aristotle and Kant into the discussion. I think I succeeded.[1]

1. I owe the Institute for Advanced Studies in Culture a debt of gratitude for providing me with an ideal setting for working on my two books on justice: *Justice: Rights and Wrongs* and *Justice in Love*.

In March 2010, I flew to Tegucigalpa, Honduras, to observe the work of La Asociación para una Sociedad má Justa (Association for a More Just Society, abbreviated ASJ). For several years Kurt Ver Beek, cofounder of the organization, had been urging me to observe firsthand what ASJ was doing because he knew how deeply I cared about justice. Each time, something had stood in the way. Finally, the opportunity opened up. Another awakening to injustice awaited me, but a different kind of injustice from what the Palestinians and the people of color in South Africa experienced.

ASJ is self-consciously not a relief or development organization but a justice organization, focusing on what it sees as the most egregious of the injustices present in Honduran society, and it is explicitly Christian in its orientation. Its staff consists almost entirely of native Hondurans. Carlos Hernandez, the head of the organization, remarked to me that the deepest cause of injustice in Honduran society is that the laws are often not enforced. Though the laws, in general, are quite good, public officials often do not enforce them, especially in cases of crimes against the poor. The common explanation for this is corruption: graft and bribery. It was the analysis of ASJ, however, that though there are indeed corrupt officials, the more basic problem is a pervasive fear and lack of trust. Poor people do not trust the police, the judicial system, or the bureaucracy; the police do not trust the prosecutors; and the prosecutors do not trust the police. The result is that victims of crime and of wrongdoing by public officials are afraid to take action. They fear that if they file a report with the police or with some government official, the person or persons who wronged them will learn about this and retaliate. The police and prosecutors likewise fear that they will be the victims of retaliation if they take action. What I saw, more clearly than ever before, is that social justice is impossible without a well-functioning police and judicial system, and that this, in turn, is impossible in the midst of pervasive fear and distrust.

The aim of ASJ in this situation is not to do an end run around government by, for example, establishing private security forces or independent schools, but to get government officials to do what they are assigned to do and to assist them in doing that. I learned about the many ingenious strategies ASJ has devised for coping with the pervasive fear and distrust. The work is dangerous. The previous year, their head lawyer, Dionisio Diaz Garcia, had been shot at point-blank range on a main street in Tegucigalpa as he was on his way to court. On the very day I wrote these words, December 16, 2016, I received word that, the night before, there had been an attempt on the life of Pastor Jorge Machado, a board member of ASJ. Though the pastor and his wife escaped unharmed, one of his bodyguards was killed and the other was severely wounded.

On one of my afternoons in Tegucigalpa, some other visitors and I were driven up into one of the areas of the city where ASJ is concentrating its work, and invited into a small, tidy living room. The walls were cinder block—the floor, packed earth. A number of brightly colored posters were attached to the walls. Humble beauty! Two women spoke of the rape of their daughters and told of how the police refused to do anything until ASJ intervened. The perpetrators were eventually identified, apprehended, and convicted. A young man reported being shot and told of how, in his case, too, the police refused to do anything until ASJ intervened. Again, the perpetrators were identified, apprehended, and convicted.

Once again, I had been accosted by the faces and voices of the victims. I described my experience in an article I wrote for *Christian Century* entitled "Just Demands." The article, in slightly revised form, is included in *Hearing the Call: Liturgy, Justice, Church, and World* (Eerdmans, 2011), a collection of my semipopular writings.

A few years later I returned to Tegucigalpa to give some talks on justice under the sponsorship of ASJ. At the reception after one of the talks, a person from Nigeria who had read a good deal of what I had written about justice remarked that he would like to see me write an autobiographical "take" on my thinking about justice. How did I come to think about justice as I did? That, he said, would give a humanizing touch to my thinking. The idea had never occurred to me, but I liked it. That's how *Journey toward Justice* came about (Baker, 2013). There are some new things in the book, particularly the chapters on the structure of social justice movements and the chapters on how beauty, hope, and justice are related. But mainly it is what he suggested: an autobiographical "take" on my thinking about justice.

I am sometimes asked, usually by someone just beginning an academic career, how I go about writing. Much about it defies my attempt to put it into words, but let me do my best to explain. I will focus on writing philosophy. (Writing semipopular essays is somewhat different.)

It begins with a process as mysterious and awesome as anything in our human existence: I sit down to think about some topic, whereupon thoughts on that topic come to mind. How can this be? I understand, in a general way, how perception works: we are so constituted that, upon receiving sensory input of a certain kind, we perceive objects. But how can it be that, upon deciding to think about some topic, thoughts on that topic come to mind—new thoughts, thoughts one never had before? This is truly mysterious. We would find it awesome if it were not so familiar. It's one of the reasons I cannot accept purely naturalistic theories of evolution.

Sometimes my aim is to survey some terrain and describe how it looks to me as a philosopher, but usually my aim is not to describe but to understand. Something baffles me. I want to understand it, but I don't. What, for example, is the nature and basis of moral obligation? I want to understand, but I don't. I am frustrated. It's the frustration of wanting to understand what I don't understand that motivates most of my philosophical thinking. What keeps me going is that, most of the time, I do eventually achieve understanding—or at least I think I do. For me, thinking philosophically is a seesaw emotional experience between frustration and gratification, energized by the desire to achieve understanding.

What achieving understanding presupposes, of course, is that, between reality and our capacities as human beings, there is a distinct sort of fit. That fit is another reason why I cannot accept naturalistic theories of evolution. It's amazing that there are creatures who have the faculties required for understanding reality, reality deep down. It cries out for explanation.

Seldom is philosophical understanding achieved immediately; patience and persistence are required. It may take years before understanding is achieved. Sometimes I set a project aside for a time and come back to it later. Sometimes I happen to read something that triggers some ideas. Sometimes nothing works: understanding never comes. With regret, I give up the attempt, put the matter behind me, and get on with other things. In a couple of cases, this has happened when I had committed myself to contributing an essay on a certain topic to a collection of essays or to a special issue of a journal without having any clear idea, when I made the commitment, of what I would say. Then, with some embarrassment, I had to ask to be released from my commitment.

When I begin thinking about some topic, I write my thoughts down in longhand. I don't first have the thoughts and then write them down; I think while writing—or better, I think *in* writing. Perhaps there are some people who can develop a train of thought in their mind without writing anything down. I cannot. I think with fingers and pen—and with my eyes. I must have my thoughts in front of me where I can inspect them. I don't worry about rhetorical niceties at this point; much of what I write down consists of poorly composed sentences or sentence fragments. Nor do I worry about how I will put it all together. I write the thoughts as they occur to me, in whatever form and order they come. Worrying about niceties of rhetoric or style and about matters of order inhibits my brainstorming. I let the thoughts come as they may.

There comes a point when I sense that nothing more is to be gained by brainstorming. Up to this point, I have been alone with my thoughts. Now it's time to bring an intended audience into the picture by composing an essay or chapter with readers in mind. I do this at my computer. I don't prepare an outline in advance (I am incapable of doing that). I settle on a beginning and, with a vague idea in mind of how it should go from there, I let it happen.

How do I determine when the time has come to stop writing down thoughts and to begin composing? That's hard to say; one gets a feel for it. Composition can be delayed too long. A former student wrote to say that he was having writer's block and asked whether he could talk about it over the phone. When he called, I asked him how he prepared for writing an essay or a chapter. It became evident to me that he was trying to have everything thought out in precise detail before he began writing. I described how I went about writing and suggested that he try that. He did, and it worked.

Ideally, when I compose, I formulate the thoughts I have had into well-formed sentences and organize them into a sequence that will carry the reader along. But seldom does it go that smoothly. I cannot come up with a sentence that says what I want to say, a sure indication that I haven't reached clarity about what I want to say. Or the sentence is accurate but awkward. Or the writing becomes clotted and convoluted at a point, another sign that I have not achieved full understanding. Gaps in the argument appear. Or the whole thing is boring—and for me, being boring is an unforgivable sin. All this time, I am thinking with the computer.

Writing philosophy, like thinking philosophically, is an emotional seesaw of frustration and gratification. It requires patience and persistence. But when, after the frustration, it finally comes together, the experience is truly gratifying—otherwise, I wouldn't keep doing it. Claire says that when it's going well, I tell her that I don't want to stop because it's going well, and when it's not going well, that I don't want to stop because it's not going well!

When I stop writing down thoughts and begin to compose, I feel anxious. The image sometimes comes to mind of trying to whip a recalcitrant mule into doing what I want it to do. On occasion, the mule refuses to budge, and I throw away what I have written. The "delete" button on one's computer is indispensable.

I cannot write efflorescent prose, prose that calls attention to itself for its sheer splendor. Fortunately, philosophy doesn't call for such prose. I aim instead for clarity of thought and presentation. But I don't want my writing to be dry in the way that much analytic philosophy is dry, lacking in rhetorical imagination; thus, I freely use metaphors, similes, and all the other rhetorical tropes. And I do my best to carry the reader along, to give a dramatic quality to the essay, chapter, or book, not just one thing after another but the sense of heading somewhere and finally getting there.

After my youthful excursions into metaphysics, most of what I have written flies rather close to the ground. What I mean is that my goal has been to illuminate the specific and the concrete: to illuminate the fine texture of justice; to illuminate the many ways in which we engage works of the arts; to illuminate what we are doing when we act liturgically, and so forth. It's typical of philosophers in the analytic tradition to preoccupy themselves with analyzing concepts, with exploring interrelationships among propositions, with posing and solving puzzles—all highly abstract. I have done relatively little of that. Life as lived has grabbed my attention: injustice, work songs, liturgy. Most of what I have written, though it's in the style of analytic philosophy, is a version of what philosophers call *phenomenology*.

And I have no interest in chiseling away at issues that have already undergone much chiseling. I am drawn, instead, to exploring alternative ways of thinking—alternative ways of thinking about justice, alternative ways of thinking about art, alternative ways of thinking about liberal democracy, alternative ways of thinking about being entitled to one's beliefs. I aim for a blend of vision and craftsmanship, imagination and tight dovetails!

Why have I continued thinking and writing long after my retirement? Because I love it. And because I regard the fit that I have been granted between my interests, my abilities, and the opportunities that have come my way as a call to make good use of that fit.

After completing *Justice: Rights and Wrongs* and *Justice in Love*, I turned to another writing project I had long wanted to get around to. In *Art in Action* (1980), after noting that philosophers of art in the modern period have focused almost all of their attention on absorbed aesthetic contemplation as a way of engaging works of the arts, and on the works that reward that mode of engagement, I went on to argue that we who are philosophers of art should expand the scope of our inquiries and attend to the many other ways in which human beings engage works of the arts, and to the works engaged in those other ways. This line of thought had been provoked by the art awakening I experienced in our living room that Saturday afternoon when I found myself listening to work songs on the University of Michigan public radio station. But I did not practice what I preached in *Art in Action*. I did not analyze ways of engaging works of the arts other than as objects of aesthetic contemplation. I had long wanted to do that.

Over the years I had come to realize that, to do so, I would have to expand the conceptual framework that I used in *Art in Action*. There I argued that, to take account of the many ways in which we engage works of the arts, we have to place artworks in the context of action rather than focusing on the works themselves in isolation from action. Hence the title of the book: *Art in Action*. Gradually it became clear to me, however, that to say no more than that was to invite too atomistic a way of thinking. Intrinsic to the arts are long-enduring social practices: social practices of creating or composing works, social practices of performing or presenting works, social practices of engaging works in the many ways we do engage them. Individual actions are embedded within the social practices. The social practices of art would have to be front and center if I was going to practice what I had preached in *Art in Action*.

It also became clear to me that I would have to employ the idea of the *meaning* of a work of the arts; or, more precisely, I would have to take account of the various kinds of meaning that works of the arts possess. There was a reason why I had not done that earlier. When I was spending my 1970–71 sabbatical in London, working on philosophy of art, I had it on my agenda to think about meaning in art. In the course of the year, I succeeded in getting an appointment with the great German art historian Ernst Gombrich in his study at the Warburg Institute in London. After some small talk, Gombrich asked me what I was working on. I mentioned some of the ideas I was exploring, including that of the meaning of artworks. His response was quick and blunt: "Stay away from meaning." As I recall, he addressed me as "young man": "*Young man*, stay away from meaning." He did not explain what he meant, and I did not ask. My guess was that he regarded the idea of meaning as too vague to be of any use. Since Gombrich was someone I revered, I stayed away from meaning for many years. Now I was finding the concept indispensable.

Not only would the conceptual framework of *Art in Action* have to be expanded by introducing the idea of the social practices of art and the idea of meaning in art, but *Art in Action* had also left unanswered an important and obvious question. In the book I asked why philosophers of art said such things as "Art requires leisure" and "Art lifts us above the stream of everyday life," when such comments are patently false for work songs and for many other works of the arts. The answer I proposed was that philosophers of art in the modern period have focused their attention on what I called our "institution of high art," where what they say comes close to being true. That answer invites this question: Why have philosophers of art focused their attention so exclusively on our institution of high art? I did not address that question. Some readers may have gotten the impression that I regarded philosophers of art as suffering from an inexplicable myopia.

Quite soon, I realized that the myopia was not inexplicable. Almost all philosophers of art in the modern period have embraced what I now call "the grand narrative of art in the modern world." The grand narrative notes that engaging artworks as objects of aesthetic contemplation became increasingly prominent in the modern period, and then argues that this development represented the arts coming into their own, rather than being in the service of princes and prelates, adding that when the arts come into their own in this way, they transcend the dynamics of capitalist society. If one thinks along these lines, one will naturally not pay attention to work songs and hymns. Doing so would be like studying the chrysalis when one can behold the butterfly.

My work was cut out for me. I would have to explicate the grand narrative, show that most philosophy of art in the modern period has indeed been in the thrall of that narrative, and explain why the narrative should be rejected. I would then have to develop the idea of the social practices of art and the idea of the meaning of works of the arts. And then, with that as my theoretical framework, I would be in a position to analyze some of the ways in which we engage works of the arts other than as objects of absorbed aesthetic contemplation.

I decided to discuss memorial art, art for veneration (of which the Byzantine icons would be my principal examples), social-protest art, work songs, and a recent development in the visual art world that I call "art-reflexive" art (art whose aim is to raise questions about art rather than to gratify aesthetic contemplation). The point of including the discussion of art-reflexive art was to establish that, whereas the grand narrative has nothing to say about such art, the social practice-cum-meaning framework that I was developing provides a conceptuality for analyzing it.

I was apprehensive about discussing work songs. My understanding of how such songs function is entirely from the outside. I have never sung such songs as an accompaniment to manual labor. But since it was work songs that provoked my long train of thought, I decided it would be cowardly not to take up the challenge of analyzing the social practices and meaning of work songs. The discussion turned out better than I expected. Some readers have told me that they regard the chapter on work songs as the best chapter in the book.[2]

Claire and I loved living in Charlottesville and being associated with the Institute for Advanced Studies in Cuture. The only significant negative was that we never found a church we could attach ourselves to. Of the new friends we made in Charlottesville, I must single out four for special mention: James and Honey Hunter, and Bev and Brian Wispelwey (the latter two both graduates of Calvin College). We had wonderful times with them and came to love them all dearly.

I have already introduced James, head of the Institute, which he founded about twenty years ago. He continues to give it direction and to solicit donations to keep it running. He sees it as a humble counterpart to the famous Frankfurt Institute, of which Theodor Adorno, Max Horkheimer, and Jürgen Habermas were the best-known members. His wife, Honey, writes fabulous children's stories. Bev Wispelwey is always busy with not-for-profit projects around the city. Her husband, Brian, is on the staff of the medical school of the University of Virginia, where he has the reputation of being one

2. As with *Justice: Rights and Wrongs* and *Justice in Love*, I owe the Institute for Advanced Studies in Culture a deep debt of gratitude for providing me with an ideal setting in which to write *Art Rethought: The Social Practices of Art* (Oxford University Press, 2015).

of its best teachers. For several years running he won their Teacher of the Year Award. The committee supervising the award decided that, in fairness to the other members of the faculty, he should be declared ineligible for a time. Immediately upon being returned to the list of eligible candidates, he again won the award.

After eight delightful years, we decided it was time to call it quits in Charlottesville. Not since I had begun teaching at the Free University of Amsterdam in the spring of 1986 had we lived year-round in our house in Grand Rapids. After I joined the Yale faculty in the fall of 1989, we would pack our SUV in Grand Rapids each September with the things we anticipated needing for the academic year, unpack it when we reached our destination, then in May do the same thing in reverse. We never guessed entirely right: always some of the things we needed were in the other house or apartment. Claire, especially, was getting weary of this nomadism. So in May 2013 we gave up our apartment in Charlottesville to live year-round in Grand Rapids.

One of the great joys of living year-round in Grand Rapids has been that we can now worship year-round at Church of the Servant. COS, as it is familiarly called, has flourished beyond any dreams Claire and I had when we joined with others in founding it. It has grown to the point where about five hundred people attend on Sunday mornings. Worship is vibrant, members are deeply committed to social justice, the congregation has enthusiastically embraced ministries that unexpectedly presented themselves, particularly a ministry to refugees and immigrants, and we have been blessed by the extraordinary preaching of Jack Roeda, pastor for thirty-three years (retired in 2016). Jack and his wife Carol have been our friends and supporters over these many years. The first funeral Jack conducted in COS was the funeral for our son Eric.

Another great joy of living year-round in Grand Rapids is that we now see a great deal more of our children and grandchildren who live here than we did previously. Those who live in Grand Rapids all have houses within a mile of us, in different directions: Amy, her husband Thomas ("T.J."), and their two children, Nick and Phoebe; Klaas, his wife Tracey, and their three children, Maria, Nina, and Kees; and Christopher. Robert and his wife, Mari, and their two children, Ian and India, now live in New Haven, Connecticut. Claire and I love them all, love them dearly. We rejoice over their successes, grieve over their accidents, their ills and disappointments, and worry about their futures. They take loving care of us.

Ours is, in many ways, an old-fashioned family. Those of us who live in Grand Rapids see each other often. Most Sundays we get together for coffee after church at our house, and usually my twin sister, Henrietta, who lives nearby, joins us. Anything whatsoever is up for discussion. For me, it's reminiscent of the after-church coffees in our house in Edgerton when I was growing up. We celebrate holidays together: Christmas, Easter, Thanksgiving, Fourth of July. I help out with driving grandchildren to school, to choir practice, to sports events. To celebrate our fiftieth wedding anniversary, Claire and I rented a house on the west coast of Ireland for a week and flew the entire family over—all the children and grandchildren. For our sixtieth wedding anniversary, we got everybody together for a week in a house that we rented on the coast of Maine. Everybody gets along with everybody.

To our great delight, the children and their spouses have all found worthwhile work that makes use of their talents, that gives them satisfaction, and that they can take pride in doing well. All of them have a deep moral core: they treat those with whom they deal justly, honorably, and considerately. Let me give a thumbnail sketch of them and of their children—nothing more than pointers to who they really are as persons.

Amy, the eldest, remains the steady one, unflappable. She is always turning up and signing onto worthwhile offbeat projects that keep her busy: writing articles about the neighborhood for a local newspaper, working as a freelance editor, grading student essays for a testing firm. She is extraordinarily gifted at working with her hands, especially working with fiber and fabric: knitting scarves and mittens, creating quilts and blankets out of recycled items of clothing. Her creations are imaginative and beautiful in design—and impeccably knit and sewn. She mentioned once that she thinks of her work with words as similar to her work with fiber: imagining patterns in combinations of words and imagining patterns in combinations of color and texture.

Her husband, T.J., is a renovation contractor who does impeccable work and does it quickly. He seldom has anyone working with him, because most of the assistants he has employed proved either not sufficiently skilled or not sufficiently fast to suit him. Better to do the work himself. There have been exceptions, most notably his son, Nick, whom T.J. reports as being the best assistant he has ever had. Renovation work requires imagination and outside-the-box skills in problem-solving. T.J. has those in abundance. Recently, someone who was watching him work remarked that he wished he were doing renovation work because it didn't require any thinking! T.J. was incensed—and rightly so. He's athletic, full of energy, always finding something that needs attention.

Their son, Nick, is winsome, gentle, laid back, not in a hurry. He's athletic, but, unlike his father, not competitive. Some years back, when he was a member of a hockey club, Nick invited me to come along to watch one of his games. I was amused to see that, even on the ice with a hockey stick in hand, he remained his noncompetitive self: "Here, if you want this puck so badly, take it." He had an unfortunate experience in a college on the West Coast in the first semester of his freshman year, and dropped out. He is now taking courses at Grand Rapids Community College, and is the supervisor of the cooking staff in a local restaurant. He's a hard and responsible worker, and is seriously considering going into business.

Phoebe, a young woman of few words, is shy and hates public attention. She's a gifted gymnast, and a hard worker at whatever task is before her. When school is in session, she is totally devoted to her school work. She loves to draw, and is exceptionally good at it. And she's a gifted instrumentalist, playing a number of different instruments, two of which she learned to play on her own.

No longer dreamy as he was when a child, Robert is intense, mercurial, sometimes volcanic. When confronted with some idiocy or injustice, a stream of verbally dazzling outrage pours forth. But not in public; in public he restrains himself. He has a doctoral degree in architectural history from Princeton, and is currently director of the Bennington Museum in Bennington, Vermont. When Claire and I visited him there a few years ago, a member of the museum's board took us aside and praised Robert's work to the skies. Far and away the finest director the museum has ever had, he said. Robert is wonderfully imaginative in the shows he organizes, and unfailingly considerate of his staff. He commutes on weekends to New Haven, where the family lives.

Mari, his wife, is a steady, calm, can-do person—the perfect complement to Robert's volatility. She is director for development at Choate School, a private prep school in Wallingford, a few miles outside New Haven. From what she says about her work, it's clear to us that she is very good at it. She has a gift for dealing patiently and effectively with problematic people in her department and in the school.

Ian is steady, always with a smile on his face, a quiet young man, though, to the surprise of the family, when there was a poetry-reciting contest in his class a few years ago, he won first prize. He's a fine cellist, and for several years he was on the rowing team at Choate, from which he graduated in May 2017. He is now enrolled in Northeastern University in Boston, where he intends to major in computer science. He's a whiz at computers.

India is beautiful, delicate, tender-hearted, and affectionate—as sweet a person as anyone I know. When the family moved from Portland to New Haven a few years ago, she was heartbroken over having to part with her friends. She is very good at the usual run of school subjects, but art is what she loves. And she is really good at it.

Klaas is the quiet one. He says he doesn't like people, but that's not really true. It's crowds he doesn't like. In small groups, he is at ease and often very funny. He is a vice president at Eerdmans Publishing Company in Grand Rapids and manages the production and art departments. He has also been responsible for the interior design and layout for all the books the company publishes. In my judgment (unbiased, of course!), there is no publisher in the entire world whose books are the equivalent of Eerdmans books in the consistently high aesthetic quality of their interior layout! Klaas is a hard worker, devoted to his work, unfailingly alert to whether those who work for him are being treated fairly and honorably. He is also a fine photographer and a great cook.

Tracey, his wife, is a dear: tender-hearted, open to the pain and joy of those around her, a friend of the forgotten. While continuing to do freelance work as a graphic art designer, she has in recent years been moving into clothing design. Her visual imagination and her tactile skill in bringing to reality what she imagines are extraordinary. She haunts secondhand stores, buys items at rock-bottom prices, and transforms them into beautiful and imaginative garments. Sows ears into silk purses. She has just recently taken a position as unit secretary in the orthopedic section of a nearby hospital. She loves it.

Their elder daughter, Maria, supremely gifted in many ways, has bouts of self-doubt. We laugh and groan at her proclivity for exotic accidents. Just within the past year: she was sitting on her bed, sewing, rolled over, and got an entire needle embedded in her flesh. She was using an awl to make holes in fabric, stumbled, and when she got up, the awl was sticking straight out of her. She was on an exercise bike, her clothes got entangled in the gears, and she fell over and severed her Achilles tendon.

A few years ago she accidentally took an overdose of Tylenol, resulting in incipient liver failure. The doctors in Grand Rapids said she needed a liver transplant and would have to be transported as rapidly as possible to the University of Michigan hospital in Ann Arbor for the procedure. She was flown at night to Ann Arbor in a helicopter. Claire and I rode with Klaas and Tracey on the two-hour trip to Ann Arbor by car. It was a night of sheer terror for me; I was overcome by the dread that Maria would either die or be a permanent invalid. Did I have residual memories of traveling through the night to Rochester when I was three years old to see my dying mother for the last time? I don't know. Maria has made a complete recovery, thanks be to God. She is taking courses at the local university, Grand Valley State University, with the aim of becoming a doctor. She is already a walking medical encyclopedia—and she's a superb photographer.

Nina is people-oriented: she collects friends as honey collects ants. She is athletic and was on the diving team at her high school. Like all our grandchildren, she's a gifted student, but she suffers from migraines and was often unable to attend classes, putting her academic progress in some jeopardy. To the great relief of all of us, however, she managed to finish her high-school work and to graduate with the rest of her class. She is now taking a year off between high school and college.

Kees, the youngest of our grandchildren, is like his father in that, if something has to be done, he does it without fuss. He dispatches his school homework speedily and without delay. Unlike his father, however, and like his sister Nina, he is people-oriented: classmates cluster around him. He's a whiz at science and math, and he loves mentally challenging games. He is a talented singer, and was a member of the highly rated Grand Rapids Choir of Men and Boys until his voice changed. He wants to be an astrophysicist. In February 2018, Kees was diagnosed as having stage 4 Hodgkin's lymphoma. The news hit me like a hard blow to the solar plexus. Was this bright, winsome, strapping 14-year-old, my dear grandson, to be felled, laid out cold before he had a chance to blossom, the Eric of the next generation? Could I endure another? Chemical treatment was begun immediately. At the end of June his doctors reported that there was now no sign of cancer anywhere in his body. God be praised!

Like his mother—and like Tracey—Christopher is tender-hearted and caring. People who know him often stop me to tell me how much they are taken by his quiet interest and empathy. After graduating from Calvin, he did graduate work for a few years in Latin American history at the University of Michigan. But he didn't like it: he found the academy too impersonal. So he left academic life and found a position taking care of brain-damaged adults at Hope Network in Grand Rapids. He was remarkably good at that—steady in patience and empathy. But after he had happily worked there for several years, the organization took a bureaucratic turn, and he felt that its leaders were becoming distracted from the needs of the clients and workers. So he resigned and enrolled in a program leading to a degree as a registered nurse. He now has a position as a nurse in one of the local clinics.

When I review what I have written in this section, what strikes me is that all of our children have unusual artistic gifts and sensibilities, as do most of their spouses and children. In the case of our children, they get that from both sides of their inheritance—Claire's and mine. Eric was not only a fine ceramist but also made a number of beautiful silkscreen prints. He and Robert both did graduate work in the history of architecture. T.J. is a superb woodworker. Amy and Tracey do beautiful work in fiber and fabric. Robert organizes imaginative shows at the Bennington Art Museum. Klaas designs many of the interiors of Eerdmans books. He, Christopher, and Maria are excellent photographers. Christopher, India, and Phoebe draw superbly. Kees and Phoebe are fine musicians. I could go on.

I worry about the future of our grandchildren. Mine has been a privileged life, the life of someone whose talents and interests happened to fit the opportunities that came his way during an extraordinary period in the history of the United States—extraordinary especially for white middle-class males like me in the field of higher education. All the positions I have held were offered to me; I have never applied for a teaching position.

That extraordinary period is ending. Higher education is undergoing drastic changes, especially in the humanities; departments across the country are shrinking, and jobs in philosophy are scarce. Our economy today is much more susceptible than it was in former years to what happens in other parts of the world. Our political culture is much more mean-spirited and contentious today than it was some years back; the habits and virtues essential to an ongoing liberal democracy are being eroded. Global warming is coming to our planet, and it's not at all clear that the nations of the world will act in concert to halt it. And then there is the dark side of social media: the erosion of face-to-face interactions. When we get together as a family, the grandchildren sometimes prefer doodling with their iPads to joining the conversation.

Completing *Art Rethought* cleared the decks for another writing project I had long wanted to get around to. The surge of interest in philosophy of religion that I mentioned earlier has focused almost entirely on religious belief, more specifically, on *theistic* belief. Philosophers have inquired into the conditions that must be met for religious beliefs to be justified; they have probed the consistency of theistic belief, and they have analyzed its content—omnipotence, omniscience, immutability, simplicity, and so on. Truly significant advances in understanding have been made in those areas.

But there's something strange about it. Whereas religious practice is prominent in all religions, someone who knew nothing about religion, other than what she gleaned from this recent philosophical literature, would conclude that religion consists almost entirely of believing things about God. Religion does include beliefs, of course. Yet for most adherents of most religions, religious *practice* is central in their lives, especially liturgy and ritual, rather than religious belief. I had long wanted to do what I could to address the myopia of my fellow philosophers of religion by writing a book of philosophical reflections on liturgy.

I had scarcely begun working on the project when another project, related but different, asked to be put on my agenda. Two theologians from Trinity Evangelical Divinity School, in Deerfield, Illinois, took me out for lunch and explained that, in honor of a much loved and recently departed colleague, Kenneth Kantzer, the school had established the Kantzer Lectures in Revealed Theology, intended as a counterpart to the Gifford Lectures in Natural Theology. They invited me to deliver the third set of lectures in this newly established series. I pointed out that I was a philosopher, not a theologian.

"Yes, we know that, but you do talk quite a bit about God."

"I suppose I do. How about a series of lectures on liturgy?"

"No, the lectures have to be about God."

I thought for a while, and then: "Okay, how about 'The God We Worship'?"

"Excellent!"

That's how my next book came about, *The God We Worship: An Exploration of Liturgical Theology* (Eerdmans, 2015), which is the text of the lectures I gave. I proposed the title without having any idea of what I wanted to say. For quite some time I was stymied; everything that came to mind seemed obvious, boring to call attention to it. Then it occurred to me that I had been dwelling on the understanding of God that is *explicit* in Christian liturgies. Why not identify the understanding of God that is *implicit* in liturgy, taken for granted rather than expressed, and talk about that? That was it!

It's obvious that a great deal of what people do when they participate in Christian liturgical enactments is address God: in praise, thanksgiving, confession, intercession, and so forth. It struck me one day—it now seems blindingly obvious—that in addressing God, the participants are taking for granted that God listens, or to speak more cautiously, that God *can and might well* listen. Nobody *declares* that God is a listener. That God is a listener is implicit in what they do. I decided to devote a few lectures to God as listener.

I did what I have done in similar situations: I searched the literature for what others had said on the subject of God as listener. To my surprise, I found no substantial discussion by any theologian or philosopher about God as listener. There was a great deal about God as speaker, nothing about God as listener. I was out on my own. The core of the book is three chapters on God as listener. I had the sense, when writing those chapters, that the topic has depths that I had not even begun to fathom.

After delivering the lectures and revising them for publication, I turned to what I had long wanted to do, namely, reflect philosophically on liturgy. If I were to have any success in addressing what seemed to me the myopia of my fellow philosophers of religion, I would have to demonstrate that liturgy poses issues that merit and reward the attention of philosophers. Working on the book convinced me that liturgical participation is, in fact, one of the most complex, baffling, and fascinating of all human activities. For example, a feature of Christian liturgies that had long fascinated and puzzled me was that, on the high holy days, the hymns sung are in the present tense: "Jesus Christ is born today." "Christ the Lord is risen today." What is going on? Everybody singing those hymns knows that Jesus was born some two thousand years ago and resurrected thirty or so years later. So why are the hymns in the present tense? This was just one of the many aspects of liturgy that I found fascinating and puzzling.

The few philosophers who have written about liturgy have focused most of their attention on the formative effects of liturgy. I decided to focus, instead, on *what is done* when we participate in liturgical enactments: I call it the "performative" dimension of liturgy. It's what is done that is formative. The performative dimension is basic, in that way, to the formative dimension. The title of the book is *Acting Liturgically: Philosophical Reflections on Religious Practice* (Oxford, 2018). Writing it gave me great pleasure; at many points I had the sense of exploring terrain that no one had previously entered.

When the manuscript was nearing completion, John Witvliet at Calvin, liturgical scholar without peer, organized a small group of liturgical scholars to discuss the chapters. Though they were all conversant with philosophy, none of them was a philosopher. I was gratified to learn that they found the discussion interesting and valuable. I had feared that liturgical scholars would find a philosophical address to topics in their field strange and off-putting.

The most moving teaching experience of my entire life occurred during the spring of 2016. The main campus of Calvin College and Calvin Seminary is the Knollcrest campus, located in southeastern Grand Rapids. A few years ago, the college and seminary together established a second campus, this one in Handlon State Prison for Men, located outside Ionia, Michigan, about twenty five miles east of Grand Rapids. The Handlon campus, like the Knollcrest campus, offers an accredited baccalaureate degree. Prisoners from around the state can apply for admission to the program, and twenty new students are accepted per year. The courses are taught by professors from the college and seminary and are, for the most part, the same as courses taught on the Knollcrest campus. I was moved when I learned that one of Eric's closest friends in college, John Rottman, now a professor at Calvin Seminary, was one of the initiators of the program.

Kevin Corcoran, a member of the philosophy department at Calvin, was teaching his Introduction to Philosophy course in Handlon

Prison during the spring of 2016. For some years he has included my book *Lament for a Son* in the syllabus for his course. As they were discussing *Lament* in the prison class, Kevin happened to mention that he knew me and that I lived in Grand Rapids. The men in the class brought up the idea of inviting me to visit their class. So Kevin invited me, and I accepted.

The director of the Calvin program, Todd Cioffi, drove me to the prison, explaining the program as we drove and remarking that, to avoid church-state problems, Calvin had paid for decorating and furnishing the room the prison assigned them. After much paper shuffling at the front desk, I was admitted into the prison, and Todd led me to the classroom. I was immediately struck by how ample it was and how beautifully furnished—far more beautifully furnished than any classroom I had known on the Knollcrest campus. There was a lot of wood: wood trim, and wooden desks and chairs that had been made, and beautifully finished, in the prison workshop. Off to one side was an alcove for the library, and it, too, was beautifully finished. The entire ensemble spoke of dignity. Here, in this room at least, these men were not being warehoused.

What happened next brought tears to my eyes. The twenty men in the class—later I learned that seventeen of them were in prison for life—all had copies of *Lament*, and they lined up for me to sign their copies. As I was signing their copies they would say, "We are so honored, professor, that you have come to visit our class." Never before had students told me that they were honored by my presence in their classroom! Sometimes, when I am introduced as speaker, the person introducing me declares pro forma that the group is honored to have me as its speaker that evening. I take that to mean something like, "It's a feather in our cap that Professor W. accepted our invitation to speak." These prisoners were not saying it was a feather in their cap that I had shown up. They—who were daily demeaned, forced to knuckle under, and ordered around—were saying that my presence honored them, declared that they were not worthless scum, declared that they possessed honor. At any rate, that was what I understood them to be saying. I do not tear up when someone introducing me declares that the group is "honored" by my acceptance of their invitation to speak. I did tear up when these men declared that they were honored that I had come to visit their class.

After Kevin introduced me, I said a few words about how I came to write the book, and then opened it up for discussion. I had never before discussed *Lament* in a class. Every now and then I hear about its being discussed in some college or seminary course, but I have never been asked to participate in those discussions, and I wouldn't want to. I imagine that, when the book is discussed in a regular college or seminary course, the teacher poses to the class questions like: "What is Wolterstorff's understanding of grief?" "Does that understanding seem correct to you?" "What is the author's theology in the book?" "Do you agree with that theology?" I would find it impossible to participate in such discussions.

That is not how the discussion went in Handlon Prison. The men in the class were themselves in grief—most of them not over the death of a child but over the ruin they had wreaked on their own lives and the lives of others. They were reading the book not so much as *my* expression of *my* grief but as an expression of *their* grief, similar to the way in which we use the words of the Psalms to pray our own prayers. They would turn to a passage, read it aloud, and explain how the words spoke for them. They were amazingly open, more open than students in any other college class I have ever taught. Some described the crime they had committed; several spoke of how they had destroyed their relationships with the people they loved. Their comments were articulate, emotionally intense, suffused by life experience, eloquent. They offered interpretations of my words that had never occurred to me. I was the student that day—they were the teachers.

I felt profoundly my common humanity with these men. Yes, I was a professor who had never spent a day of his life behind bars, and they were prisoners, mostly lifers. But we were in this together, reading the text, discussing the text, sharing our grief. I felt more connected with these "lifers" than I have ever felt connected with eighteen- to twenty-two-year-old college students.

At some point the feeling washed over me: What a terrible waste of life! Yes, these men have committed serious crimes and deserve to be punished. But isn't there some alternative to locking them up for life? Must human lives be wasted in this way?

When the class session was over, they lined up to shake my hand, and they again said how honored they were that I had come to visit their class. As the last few filed past, I said what I felt but had not, until then, been able to put into words: They had honored me.

Grace and Gratitude

It's been a long journey from my humble origins. But long though the journey has been, I have never, in my inner self, left those origins. Each time I return to my home village, Edgerton, to visit with aunts and uncles and cousins—sharing news about children and grandchildren, about what's going on in the village and the church, about the state of our health, about the deaths of relatives and friends, telling stories about how it used to be, laughing, crying—I am reminded that these are my people. Over the course of my journey, many others have become my people as well. But these remain my people.

I almost didn't make it out of early childhood. When I was three years old, I came down with pneumonia. Some years later, my father told me that it was touch and go whether I would live. To this day I have the vivid image of looking down at myself from about five feet above the bed, a small figure lying in my parents' bed. When I recently mentioned this experience to Claire, she remarked that it was an out-of-body experience. It was that, of course, but it had never occurred to me to think of it that way.

The image has been returning more frequently in recent years. Each time it does, the realization washes over me that the life recalled in these pages might not have been. And with that realization comes a deep sense of gratitude for "having been granted a spell in this world of wonders"[1] and for the joy I have experienced. There has also been grief, of course, especially grief over the death of our son Eric, and now, with increasing frequency, grief over the death of longtime friends, and grief over the recent death of my youngest sibling, Ivan (of congestive heart failure). And there have been failures and failed causes, the failed cause that pains me most being the continuing occupation of the Palestinians. But in its totality, it's been a wonderful life.

I was fortunate in the upbringing I received, fortunate also in

---

1. J. M. Coetzee, *Age of Iron* (New York: Random House, 1990), 55.

the opportunities that came my way, and fortunate that my talents, interests, and loves fitted those opportunities. Everything I have accomplished is the result of that fit. The upbringing, the talents, the interests, the loves, the opportunities—they were not of my making. They were given to me. I received them. So what I feel is gratitude, deep gratitude, for the course of my life.

My gratitude, though deep, is uneasy, for I realize that there is little joy in the lives of many. Life is hell for some. How can I sing while they weep? Should I not join them in their weeping rather than singing my song of gratitude amidst their weeping? It feels indecent, unseemly. But I have not asked the gratitude to come. It comes, unbidden. I have been graced.